Public Relations in Japan

Despite its rapid economic development, Japan lacks a large public relations industry and its role is viewed very differently from that of its Western counterparts. PR functions are handled predominantly in-house, and a degree in a PR field is not a hiring requirement for those agencies which do operate. Mainstream PR history focuses entirely on its organizational aspects, and there are no Japanese PR "gurus" defining the field.

Public Relations in Japan is the first in-depth scholarly discussion of the political, social, and economic conditions that affected the development of PR in Japan. Drawing on historical and empirical studies from multiple perspectives, it explores how and why public relations management and education in Japan is fundamentally informed by Japanese working practices. Central to this is the culture of lifetime employment, which has created a fundamentally generalist approach to PR practice that discourages a high degree of professionalization.

This unique in-depth account provides both academic and practical insights for all researchers and advanced students of public relations, public relations history, and Japan studies as well as being of great interest to professionals working for Japanese companies.

Tomoki Kunieda, PhD, is Assistant Professor of public relations in the Department of Journalism of Sophia University, Tokyo. His research focus is on the history of mass communication, journalism, and government public relations. He is a member of the JSCCS board of directors. He has a doctorate in journalism from Sophia University.

Koichi Yamamura, PhD, is a visiting Senior Researcher at Waseda University, Japan. He is also a management and communication consultant with extensive experience in corporate communication, crisis management, corporate control, and technology communication. He has published case studies on hostile takeover defense, post-crisis CSR activities, and government PR. He has also co-authored an article and a book chapter on the historic evolution of PR in Japan.

Junichiro Miyabe is Research Scholar at the Research Faculty of Media and Communication, Hokkaido University, Japan. He has over 30 years of research experience at Nomura Research Institute, Ltd. He joined Hokkaido University in 2000 as a visiting professor and became a professor of international public relations in 2009. He remained in this role until 2015. He has published papers on human resource management and the organizational structure of the PR department, among other topics.

Routledge New Directions in Public Relations and Communication Research
Edited by Kevin Moloney

Current academic thinking about public relations (PR) and related communication is a lively, expanding marketplace of ideas, and many scholars believe that it's time for its radical approach to be deepened. *Routledge New Directions in PR and Communication Research* is the forum of choice for this new thinking. Its key strength is its remit, publishing critical and challenging responses to continuities and fractures in contemporary PR thinking and practice and tracking its spread into new geographies and political economies. It questions its contested role in market-orientated, capitalist, liberal democracies around the world and examines its invasion of all media spaces, old, new, and as yet unenvisaged. We actively invite new contributions and offer academics a welcoming place for the publication of their analyses of a universal, persuasive mind-set that lives comfortably in old and new media around the world.

Books in this series will be of interest to academics and researchers involved in these expanding fields of study, as well as students undertaking advanced studies in this area.

Public Relations in Japan
Evolution of Communication Management in a Culture of Lifetime Employment
Edited by Tomoki Kunieda, Koichi Yamamura and Junichiro Miyabe

Corporate Social Responsibility, Public Relations and Community Development
Emerging perspectives from Southeast Asia
Marianne D. Sison and Zeny Sarabia-Panol

Social Media, Organizational Identity and Public Relations
The challenge of authenticity
Amy Thurlow

For more information about the series, please visit www.routledge.com/
Routledge-New-Directions-in-Public-Relations – Communication-Research/
book-series/RNDPRCR

Public Relations in Japan

Evolution of Communication
Management in a Culture
of Lifetime Employment

Edited by Tomoki Kunieda, Koichi Yamamura and Junichiro Miyabe

Routledge
Taylor & Francis Group

LONDON AND NEW YORK

First published 2019 by Routledge

2 Park Square, Milton Park, Abingdon, Oxfordshire OX14 4RN

52 Vanderbilt Avenue, New York, NY 10017

Routledge is an imprint of the Taylor & Francis Group, an informa business

First issued in paperback 2020

British Library Cataloguing-in-Publication Data
A catalogue record for this book is available from the British Library

Library of Congress Cataloging-in-Publication Data
A catalog record for this book has been requested

ISBN: 978-1-138-63476-3 (hbk)
ISBN: 978-0-367-66537-1 (pbk)

Typeset in Sabon
by Apex CoVantage, LLC

Contents

Tables

Figures

Contributors

Yusuke Ibuki is Associate Professor at Kyoto Sangyo University. He is an executive director of the Japan Society for Corporate Communication Studies (JSCCS) and Japan Academy of Advertising. He is also active in the Academy of Management and International Communication Association, among others. He has published many articles on organizational management in PR and advertising. The PR textbook that he has co-authored has received the Educational Contribution Award from the JSCCS.

Seiya Ikari is Professor Emeritus at Tokyo Keizai University (TKU). Prior to joining the TKU, he worked for the publishing company Diamond Co., Ltd., as the editor-in-chief of *Management Today* and chief publishing officer. Between 2003 and 2011, he served as vice chairman of the JSCCS. He has edited and authored many books, including *Introduction to Public Relations* and *A Hundred Years of Public Relations in Japan*.

Naoya Ito is Professor at Hokkaido University. His research area widely ranges from public relations and marketing to the impact of social media on consumer behavior. He has won the Research Encouragement Award from the JSCCS. Since the Great East Japan Earthquake in 2011, he has been focusing mainly on risk communication in relation with consumer perception of trust and risk.

Takashi Kenmochi is a former Public Relations Professor at Nagoya Bunri University and at Edogawa University. Before joining the academy, he was engaged in the publishing industry as an editor at the publishing department of the Sanno Institute of Management and at the Japan Institute for Social and Economic Affairs. He is one of the co-authors of the book *A Hundred Years of Public Relations in Japan*.

Koichi Kitami, PhD, is an associate professor at Tokyo City University. He was formerly a senior researcher at Corporate Communication Strategic Studies Institute of Dentsu Public Relations Inc. He has been engaged in various projects in corporate communication, marketing communication, and crisis management. He is a co-author of Public Relations: Theories and Practice, the book that received the Educational Contribution Award from JSCCS.

Tomoki Kunieda, PhD, is Assistant Professor of public relations in the Department of Journalism of Sophia University, Tokyo. His research focus is on the history of mass communication, journalism, and government public relations. He is a member of the JSCCS board of directors. He has a doctorate in journalism from Sophia University.

Junichiro Miyabe is Research Scholar at the Research Faculty of Media and Communication, Hokkaido University. He has over 30 years of research experience at Nomura Research Institute, Ltd. He joined Hokkaido University in 2000 as a visiting professor and became a professor of international public relations in 2009. He remained in this role until 2015. He has published papers on human resource management and the organizational structure of the PR department, among other topics.

Masamichi Shimizu is a visiting Professor at Tsukuba Gakuin University and a corporate communication consultant in Tokyo with extensive experience as both a practitioner and educator. His interests focus on management reform and corporate communication. He has edited and authored many books including *Corporate Culture and Public Relations*, and *PR Practical*. His book, *Environmental Communication*, received the 2010 Academic Contribution Award from JSCCS.

Koichi Yamamura, PhD, is a visiting Senior Researcher at Waseda University. He is also a management and communication consultant with extensive experience in corporate communication, crisis management, corporate control, and technology communication. He has published case studies on hostile takeover defense, post-crisis CSR activities, and government PR. He has also co-authored an article and a book chapter on the historic evolution of PR in Japan.

Acknowledgments

We would like to thank the series editor, Dr. Kevin Moloney, for encouraging us to produce this book after listening to our presentations on the history of public relations in Japan at the International History of Public Relations Conference at Bournemouth University in 2012 and 2013. His patience and trust in our effort has been invaluable.

We wish to dedicate this book to the late Professor Seiya Ikari, who guided us throughout the process, from the initial planning phase until he passed away in April 2018. He was also a contributor to this book. Professor Ikari helped build the foundation for public relations research in Japan. Starting his career as a business magazine editor, he was involved in the establishment of the Japan Institute for Social and Economic Affairs, a PR arm of the Japan Business Federation. In 1987, he founded and led the Institute for Modern PR. He was a public relations professor at Tokyo Keizai University from 1995 until he retired in 2004 as dean of the School of Communication. He was also a vice chairman of the Japan Society for Corporate Communication Studies from 2003 until 2011. We are grateful to see his very last work come out in this book and be able to present this volume to his beloved wife and children.

Introduction

The culture of lifetime employment and the history of Japanese PR

Tomoki Kunieda

This book is the first in-depth discussion of Japan's public relations history published in English. It is about a PR industry that did not see any apparent substantial growth despite the country's rapid economic expansion during the 20th century and more than 70 years under a liberal democratic political system. While the practice has been common among both the public and private sectors for a long period of time, Japan's public relations have often been described as underdeveloped or even "unrecognizable" (Kelly et al., 2002, p. 278). It may be seen as an exception to the hypothesis set forth by Tom Watson (2015) based on a study of more than 70 countries that "PR thrives in democratic environments in which there is a relatively open economy" (p. 15). Through historical and empirical studies from multiple perspectives, this book provides multi-layered discussions on how public relations in Japan became what it is today.

This book considers three major questions: How did Japanese public relations develop? What were the political, social, and economic conditions that supported or inhibited its development? Why didn't it develop a large public relations industry despite rapid economic development? Although the chapters included in this book are written independently with separate interests and looking into different aspects of Japan's public relations, together, they provide an extensive understanding of how it originated and developed in different parts of society and how it is practiced today, providing insights to these three questions.

One major argument the editors make in this book is for the existence of a recurring pattern found in the history that may be conceptualized as *generalist public relations*, which will be introduced later in this chapter and will be discussed further in the concluding remarks through an overarching analysis of different chapters.

In Japan, just as in other parts of the world, the concept of public relations has long been discussed as something of an American origin that was brought to the country after World War II. The popular historical narrative has been that Japan learned the term, concept, and practice of public relations from the United States during the post-war occupation years (1945–1952) as a part of its democratization program. While similar practices were known to have existed before the war, the newly introduced public relations was considered to be a more democratic and humane form of communication that was largely absent at the time. However, recent historical studies have revealed that pre-war practices had substantial influence on the post-war development of public relations. As historical studies for both pre-war and post-war periods accumulated, a richer history of the country has come to light.

In such a sense, this book is in line with the historical research in other countries that points out the existence of PR-like activities prior to the introduction of American public relations and argues that such activities influenced how the field has developed since. Following the works of L'Etang (2004) and others that questioned the US-centered narrative of PR development through historical studies, the National Perspectives on the Development of Public Relations, a book series edited by Tom Watson and published between 2014 and 2017, included histories of countries around the world, providing further evidence that the path of PR development is indeed diverse and complex. In the series, Watson (2015) pointed out several patterns of historical development that differ from the predecessors, like the four models of public relations (Grunig & Hunt, 1984) or the functional-integrative stratification model (Bentele, 2013). An increasing number of studies have opened up discussions on many levels, from micro-level histories of public relations in a country, a specific field, or an organization to macro-level histories that theorize and generalize developments on a global scale.

One of the issues surrounding historical studies is the language barrier. While historical studies have been conducted in different parts of the world, only a portion of the findings has been shared in English, as is evident from the rich number of foreign language references contained in Watson's book series. In Japan's case, especially since the establishment of the Japan Society for Corporate Communication Studies in 1995, studies on PR history have appeared in the form of academic papers, presentation proceedings, research reports, and books. In fact, a major historical research project involving 25 members of the society was organized in 2006, resulting in the publication of an academic report in 2008 by the PR History Research Group that provided a detailed account of how public relations developed in Japan. A book based on the report was published in 2011, co-authored by Seiya Ikari and others. While both the report and the book were in Japanese, the essence of the findings was presented in English at the International History of Public Relations Conference in 2012. The presenters published an article on the *Public Relations Review* (Yamamura et al., 2013) and also a chapter in the aforementioned book series edited by Tom Watson (Yamamura et al., 2014). This book builds upon the legacy of the research projects that began in 2006 in an attempt to present the more detailed and recent discussions of the history of public relations in Japan.

Characteristics of public relations in Japan

In terms of industrial growth, Japan saw a major development after the 1990s. According to a survey by the Public Relations Society of Japan (2013), of 166 PRSJ member firms and 36 non-member firms (with a 27.7% response rate), more than half of the firms responded as having started their businesses during or after the 1990s. PRSJ (2015) estimated Japan's overall PR market turnover, regardless of the company's core business, at 435.1 billion yen (around 3.9 billion US dollars @113) and PR industry turnover at 94.8 billion yen (around 838.9 million dollars @113) for the fiscal year 2014. While an accurate international comparison of PR industry size is difficult, the industry turnover for 2016 in the UK at 12.9 billion pounds (around 17.0 billion dollars @0.76) (PRCA, 2016) and the US in 2016 at 14 billion dollars (IBIS-World, 2017) indicates that the Japanese PR industry is somewhere between 5% and 25% of those of the UK and the US.

According to the PRSJ survey published in 2013, the services provided by the majority of the respondents are planning and implementation of publicity, online PR, PR consulting, implementation of press conferences, and media relations. Only a few provide services such as M&A communication, investor relations, and compliance-related communication. This survey implies that most PR firms engage in technical, tactical support and rarely in communication of their core management agenda. In-house departments and practitioners are in a similar situation, as they often lack professionalism and recognition from other departments.

Previous research published in English has mentioned similar aspects of public relations in Japan, such as the tendency for practitioners to focus on media relations, placing importance on cultivating friendships with journalists typified by the personal influence model (Cooper-Chen & Tanaka, 2008; Sriramesh & Takasaki, 1999; Watson & Sallot, 2001). While those studies do mention the increase in two-way communication practices, the existence of an influential mass media industry and the close, institutionalized media-source relationship symbolized by the press club system, commonly known as *kisha clubs*, have characterized the industry. The studies also mention that Japanese PR is strongly affected by the culture, which places importance on matters such as harmony, conformity, collectivism, high-context communication, and superior-subordinate relationships.

However, the influence of management style on public relations has been hinted at but not discussed. The seminal work of *Excellence in Public Relations and Communication Management* (Grunig, 1992) referred to William Ouchi's *Theory Z: How American Business Can Meet the Japanese Challenge* (1981) as an important study on organizational culture, where collaborative, participative organizational cultures are important for public relations to flourish. Through a survey, Watson and Sallot (2001) also mentioned that the management styles and public relations activities at Japanese companies are becoming comparable to those of the US, where there is a mix of top-down and collaborative management styles practicing "a combination of public relations models and styles that may well contain some elements of Excellence Theory" (p. 399). Although many foreign researchers took interest in discussing the Japanese management styles in the 1980s when Japanese companies increased their global presence, the discussions receded as Japan's bubble economy collapsed and the country entered an age of prolonged economic stagnation. The Japanese management styles may have lost their global influence, but they provide historical insights into how Japanese organizations communicate.

Japanese management styles and public relations history

While previous literature stressed the importance of culture and media relations in understanding Japanese public relations, the chapters in this book look at historical facts and survey data to reveal how, by whom, and why certain types of public relations have been practiced. In the process of organizing this book, the editors came to recognize a recurring pattern, which we call generalist PR.

In this book, the concept of generalist PR does not refer to PR practitioners who take on various roles of public relations but instead to a style of PR management that includes the following characteristics: in-house PR practitioners engage in not only public relations but also a variety of corporate functions; in-house practitioners only hold the role for several years until they are transferred to another role, often unrelated to public relations, which is a form of human resource management typically called job-rotation; PR functions are rarely outsourced; a degree in a PR-related field is not a hiring requirement for PR agencies; undergraduate and graduate schools rarely provide lectures on PR; mainstream PR history mentions no "father of PR" or "history of great (wo)men" but instead a history of how organizations practiced PR. Many of these characteristics can be explained through the organizational management style commonly seen in Japan over the past century.

The concept is derived from the studies included in this book but is closely related to what Ouchi (1981) listed as key characteristics of Japanese management: lifetime employment, slow evaluation and promotion, nonspecialized career paths, implicit control mechanisms, collective decision making, collective responsibility, and holistic concerns for people. Prior to Ouchi, Abegglen (1958) also pointed out lifetime employment, a seniority-based wage system, periodic hiring, in-company training, and an enterprise union (a system of one labor union for each enterprise) as features of Japanese corporations. While the value and effectiveness of such management styles or features to organizational success may be debatable, they are instrumental in understanding public relations in Japan. The title of this book, *Public Relations in Japan: Evolution of Communication Management in a Culture of Lifetime Employment*, indicates how the system of lifetime employment, among others, has dictated the development of both internal and external communication management.

This book is unique in the following ways. First, it provides narrowly focused historical and empirical research on Japanese public relations, most of which has not been discussed in English. Second, while most previous research published English on Japanese public relations was based on data collected through interviews and surveys, much of the research and many of the arguments in this book are based on rich historical resources. Third, it is the first academic book written in English, dedicated to the PR history of an Asian country. Finally, it brings forth a historically grounded concept of generalist PR as a major characteristic of public relations in Japan that is open to further discussion and international comparative studies.

This book will, therefore, be of interest to researchers, advanced students, and practitioners with an interest in public relations history, public relations management, and Japan studies. Also, the individual chapters may be of interest to researchers and practitioners involved in the specific fields, such as government communication, internal communication, human resource management, management, and public relations.

Chapter outline

Chapter 1 provides a brief overview of Japan's PR history in both public and private sectors since the Meiji Restoration in 1868 to the present day. Chapter 2 focuses on the 15-year period after WWII, on how the concept and practice of PR was introduced by the United States and how the diffusion of public relations receded after Japan regained its independence in 1952. Together, Chapters 1 and 2 introduce the overview of history and a detailed look into the most important period that set the course of public relations development in the country for the next 70 years.

Chapter 3 looks at the history of government public relations, focusing on the long-term development of the PR-related functions and departments in the Tokyo government from 1868 to present. Chapter 4 explores the history of internal communication through in-house magazines between the late 19th century and the 1970s. Chapters 3 and 4 provide a discussion on how a government organization's PR-related departments or a specific PR practice by companies developed over a long period of time, including the previously mentioned 15-year period.

Chapter 5 looks at the issue of Japan's underdeveloped PR industry by tracing the origin and development of the PR industry and PR professionals in relation to the advertising industry, which grew rapidly during the postwar years. Chapter 6 analyzes the educational and professional backgrounds of PR managers from the 1960s to 2015. Chapters 5 and 6 look at the history of PR practitioners in terms of in-house practitioners, PR departments, PR agency practitioners, and the types of services provided by PR agencies.

Chapter 7 looks at how corporate PR practitioners responded to two major disasters: the global financial crisis of 2008 and the Great East Japan Earthquake of 2011. Chapter 8 introduces a 2016 survey that revealed the characteristics of today's PR practices in different industries. Chapters 7 and 8 provide discussions on the recent situation of public relations in Japan, of its developments and challenges.

The concluding remarks by the editors will provide answers to the three questions presented early in this introductory chapter through cross-sectional analysis: How did Japanese public relations develop? What were the political, social, and economic conditions that supported or inhibited its development? Why didn't it develop a large public relations industry despite rapid economic development? It also discusses the concept of generalist public relations that is instrumental in understanding the characteristics of Japanese public relations. The appendix section includes a glossary of PR-related key terms and organizations that appear repeatedly in different chapters, a chronology of public relations in Japan, and a note on Japanese employment practices that is important in understanding the country's PR practices.

References

Abegglen, J. C. (1958). *The Japanese factory: Aspects of its social organization*. Glencoe, IL: Free Press.

Bentele, G. (2013). Public relations historiography: Perspectives of a functional-integrative stratification model. In Sriramesh, K., Zerfass, A., & Kim, J. (Eds.), *Public relations and communication management: Current trends and emerging topics* (pp. 244–259). Abingdon: Routledge.

Cooper-Chen, A., & Tanaka, M. (2008). Public relations in Japan: The cultural roots of kouhou. *Journal of Public Relations Research*, 20(1), 94–114.

Grunig, J. E., & Hunt, T. (1984). *Managing public relations*. New York, NY: Holt, Rinehart and Winston.

Grunig, J. E. (Ed.). (1992). *Excellence in public relations and communication management*. New York, NY: Lawrence Erlbaum Associates.

IBISWorld. (2017, July). Public relations firms in the US. Retrieved on October 24, 2017, from www.ibisworld.com/industry-trends/market-research-reports/professional-scientific-technical-services/professional-scientific-technical-services/public-relations-firms.html

Ikari, S., Ogawa, M., Kitano, K., Kenmochi, T., Morito, N., & Hamada, I. (2011). *Nihon no kouhou PR no 100 nen* [A hundred years of public relations in Japan]. Tokyo, Japan: Douyukan.

Kelly, W., Masumoto, T., & Gibson, D. (2002). Kisha kurabu and koho: Japanese media relations and public relations. *Public Relations Review*, 28(3), 265–281.

L'Etang, J. (2004). *Public relations in Britain: A history of professional practice in the twentieth century*. New York, NY: Routledge.

Ouchi, W. (1981). *Theory Z: How American business can meet the Japanese challenge*. Reading, MA: Basic Books.

PR History Research Group. (Ed.). (2008). *Nihon no kouhou PR shi kenkyu* [Japanese PR History Research]. Tokyo: Japan Society for Corporate Communication Studies.

Public Relations and Communications Association. (2016). *PRCA PR census 2016*. Retrieved from http://prmeasured.com/wp-content/uploads/2016/06/PRCA-PR-Census-2016.pdf

Public Relations Society of Japan. (2013, April). *2013 nen PR gyokai jittai chosa houkokusho* [2013 PR industry survey report]. Retrieved from www.prsj.or.jp/wp-content/uploads/2013/06/PR-company_report.2013.pdf

Public Relations Society of Japan. (2015, May). *2015 nen PR gyo jittai chosa* [2015 PR industry survey report]. Retrieved from http://prsj.or.jp/wp-content/uploads/2015/05/022ceb90138943a79aafb1fce7ff12ba.pdf

Sriramesh, K., & Takasaki, M. (1999). The impact of culture on Japanese public relations. *Journal of Communication Management*, 3(4), 337–352.

Watson, D. R., & Sallot, L. M. (2001). Public relations practice in Japan: An exploratory study. *Public Relations Review*, 27(4), 389–402.

Watson, T. (2015). What in the world is public relations? In Watson, T. (Ed.), *Perspectives on public relations historiography and historical theorization* (pp. 4–19). Basingstoke, Hampshire: Palgrave Macmillan.

Yamamura, K., Ikari, S., & Kenmochi, T. (2013). Historic evolution of public relations in Japan. *Public Relations Review*, 39(2), 147–155.

Yamamura, K., Ikari, S., & Kenmochi, T. (2014). Japan. In Watson, T. (Ed.), *Asian perspectives on the development of public relations: Other voices* (pp. 63–77). Basingstoke, Hampshire: Palgrave Macmillan.

1 History in brief

Koichi Yamamura, Seiya Ikari,
and Takashi Kenmochi

Until the early days of industrialization in Japan, there was a fairly high mobility of factory workers. Such mobility caused uncertainty and inconvenience to employers trying to retain a constant labor force. To counteract the mobility of workers, management policies gradually shifted toward keeping workers for a longer time. By the beginning of the 20th century, larger enterprises were starting to develop management policies such as various welfare benefits and company housing at nominal rent. The labor shortage after World War I further accelerated such trends. As a regular employment system, accepting a considerable number of new graduates fresh out of school every spring took root. People without prior working experience were thought to have high potential for nurturing loyalty toward the company (Nakane, 1970/1998).

The employment system was further strengthened by additional devices such as a seniority payment system and retirement payment. The development of the bureaucratic structure of business enterprises during the second and the third decades of the 20th century and the strong influence of the military system during World War II further strengthened the shift toward a lifetime employment system. The labor union activities during the post-World War II period further encouraged the familism-oriented management style, welfare services, and extra payments supplied by the company (Nakane, 1970/1998).

The familism in Japanese companies and their preference for new graduates who can be easily molded into the company's corporate culture is quite different from the purely contractual relationship between employer and employees that is based on the evaluation of professional skills. There are signs of changes to this labor practice in Japan to this day, such as the large-scale discharge of employees by large companies during economic downturns in the 1990s and 2000s and an increase in mid-career employment since the 1990s, but lifetime employment still influences various aspects of labor practice as the underlying philosophy of major Japanese organizations.

Public relations in the early days

Today in Japan, public relations is called *kouhou*. The word, in its original meaning, means to "widely notify," and it represents only a part of public relations' functions. The first appearance of the term can be traced back to the May 9, 1872, issue of the *Yokohama Mainichi Shimbun*, the oldest daily newspaper in Japan. The term was used to denote advertisement or announcement (Kitano, 2009).

Many newspapers were born during the late 19th century and the early 20th century, and in response, many press agencies that handle domestic news were born. Some of them were backed by the government, and one of their main tasks was to convey government-released documents to newspapers and government officials stationed in the regional offices (Yamamoto, 1981). These press agencies were the first organizations to systematically engage in the publicity business.

The first Japanese organization to set up a *kouhou* department was the South Manchurian Railroad (Mantetsu), although it was established overseas. The company was founded in 1906. Japan obtained the right to manage railroads in Manchuria (the northeastern part of today's China) as the result of its victory in the Russo-Japanese War. Mantetsu set up a *kouhou* department in 1923, and from the early 1920s, Mantetsu had an office in New York for the introduction of capital and technology as well as provision and collection of information (Ogawa, 2008). According to Cutlip, the railroad industry was among the first in the United States to use the term "public relations" (1995). Mantetsu had close contacts with the US railroad industry (Ishii, 1997), and it had opportunities to study public relations from the US railroad organizations (Yamamura et al., 2014).

One of the purposes of Mantetsu's public relations activities was to inform Japanese in the home country that Manchuria was a frontier land with enormous opportunities and to encourage them to emigrate. The other was to guide Japanese in Manchuria to live in harmony with local people. Mantetsu's publicity activities included inviting a group of journalists from the United States to Manchuria; inviting storytellers, painters, and opinion leaders from Japan to introduce Manchuria through their work; holding Manchuria Exhibitions at various locations in Japan; producing movies on Manchuria; and publishing magazines (Ogawa, 2008).

In 1932, Japan established a puppet regime, Manchukuo, in Manchuria, and Japanese undertook the administration. The Manchukuo government set up a *kouhou-sho*, a public relations department, to jointly engage in public relations activities with Mantetsu. The *kouhou-sho* published a research journal on propaganda and public relations, and Harold Lasswell's *Propaganda Technique in the World War* and Nazi propaganda minister Joseph Goebbels were listed in the journal as references (Matsumoto, 1938/1981).

Within Japan, in 1932, the Ministry of Foreign Affairs and the Ministry of Army jointly but informally set up an information committee. In 1937, the committee officially became the information division of the Cabinet Office, and the division controlled the collection and dissemination of information for both inside and outside of the country. By the time Japan entered World War II in 1941, there was a propaganda machine in place (Tobe, 2010).

As Japan's economy boomed during World War I, big corporations needed to retain experienced workers. They employed various employee relations tactics, including the seniority wage system and lifetime employment. These systems became the icons of Japanese-style employment practices. The largest textile company in Japan at the time, Kanebo, was hiring female workers in their early teens, and the company built schools for the workers and taught reading and writing, mathematics, and sewing. In 1903, it published an in-house magazine called *Kanebo no Kiteki* [The whistle of Kanebou]. The magazine's stated goal was to share information with everyone in the company from the president to female factory workers (Nihon PR Kondankai, 1980). Although it had been widely believed that *Kanebo no Kiteki* was the first in-house magazine in Japan (e.g., Ikari et al., 2011), a recent discovery of an older in-house magazine is introduced in chapter 4.

The concept underlying such employee relations was that a company was a community and employees were expected to devote themselves to the prosperity of the community. In return, companies treated their employees as family members (Hazama, 1996). This kind of company-employee relationship was ubiquitous in Japan until the 1970s; since the 1980s, as financial capitalism took over industrial capitalism, it started to gradually fade away (Dore, 2000).

Introduction of PR from the United States in the post-World War II era

Defeated, Japan unconditionally surrendered to the Allied Forces in August 1945. In an effort to democratize Japan, the Allied Forces urged the formation of labor unions, which led factory workers to eagerly engage in the union movement. Labor disputes boiled up in every corner of the country, and the labor-management relationship was the worst in the history of Japan. Two management organizations were established in the late 1940s to help revive the economy. One was Keizai Doyu Kai [Japan Association of Corporate Executives], and the other was Nihon Keieisha Renmei (JFEA) [Japan Federation of Employers' Association] (Ikari et al., 2011). Keizai Doyu Kai was an association of young executives in their 40s with a progressive mindset. They advocated the introduction of management councils that included labor unions as its members (Yamamura et al., 2014).

JFEA's mission was to plan and practice ways to bring about a healthy labor-management relationship. JFEA sent its first management delegation to the United States in 1951 to learn how to improve the labor-management relationship. During the visit, the members of the delegation learned the concept of public relations. However, as their concern was primarily the improvement of the labor-management relationship, their proposal upon returning from the United States was primarily the adoption of human-relationship-oriented labor-management practices, such as employee suggestion systems, publication of in-house magazines, and management training focusing on human relationship with their subordinates – a mere portion of the public relations concept (Nihon PR Kondankai, 1980).

Dentsu, the largest advertising agency group in Japan and the fifth largest in the world today, also played an important role in introducing the public relations concept to Japan. Founded in 1901, the company managed both wire services and advertising until it divested the wire service business under the war-time government policy in 1936. The company had branches in Manchuria before World War II and was engaged in radio advertising. At the time, radio advertising as commercial media did not exist in mainland Japan. Hideo Yoshida, who later became the president of Dentsu in1947, learned about public relations and began studying it (Ogura, 1976). In February 1946, Dentsu announced the six company policies that included the introduction and popularization of public relations as one (Kitano, 2014). Around 1955, as Japan entered the era of rapid economic growth, marketing was introduced from the United States as a mass sales promotion technique. Dentsu, as an advertising agency, spearheaded the efforts to popularize marketing in Japan. Books written by Vance Packard, *The Hidden Persuaders* (1957) and *The Waste Makers* (1960), were translated into Japanese and became best-sellers. Packard criticized marketing as playing with the deep psyche and the depletion of natural resources. He also noted that in the United States, public relations was conceived as one of the marketing techniques. Packard listed unhealthy marketing practices that tried to take advantage of consumer psyches, but some in the advertising industry in Japan tried to promote these practices to advocate the concept of marketing (Yamamoto, 1994).

The US-led General Headquarters of the Supreme Commander for the Allied Powers (GHQ) was another path for public relations to make an entry into Japan. GHQ and its branches began providing suggestions to Japan's national and local governments, starting from 1947, to install public relations offices. Each ministry and local government tried to understand GHQ's intention and what public relations was. One by one, they established the public relations offices (Nihon PR Kondankai, 1980). Various names in Japanese were assigned to these offices as translation of public relations; eventually, they converged into a Japanese word *kouhou*. As the Japanese government did not have the mindset and systems to seek input from citizens, *kouhou* offices disseminated information from the administration or, at best, surveyed public opinion (Yamamura et al., 2014).

The assignment of *kouhou* as the translation of public relations caused many Japanese to misconceive public relations even to this day. The word *public relations* was also used, in particular, among marketing people. As foreign words are difficult for Japanese to pronounce they are often abbreviated. PR, or its sound representation in Japanese, became a common term in the context of marketing, however, often meaning *self-promotion*. Whether it was called *kouhou* or PR, certain aspects of public relations such as two-way communication, mutual understanding and trust, were lost in translation.

(Yamamura et al., 2014, p. 67)

In November 1949, GHQ authorized Ms. Day to engage in public relations activities (*Nihon Keizai Shimbun* as cited in Morito, 2008). The agency, Georgia Day and Associates, was the first public relations agency on record (Morito, 2008). Only nine PR firms were known to have existed in the 1940s and 1950s. Among them were Falcon Advertising and PR founded in 1952 by an American Rose Falkenstein; Japan PR, founded in 1958 by a second-generation Japanese American; and Hill and Knowlton, which opened its office in Tokyo in 1958. It is unclear how long Georgia Day and Associates existed, but it did appear in Dentsu PR's internal newsletter in 1968 (Morito, 2008).

1960s: public relations as a marketing function

The 1960s saw Japan's economy burst into full bloom. The rise of consumerism was foreseen in 1959 when the phrases "consumption is a virtue" and "consumers are the kings" became buzzphrases. Increasing demand for television sets, refrigerators, and washing machines drove Japan's economy in the early 1960s. In the late 1960s, color television sets, automobiles, and air conditioners took over this position. Consumers began to feel they were in the middle class, as they could afford these durable consumer goods. It was in 1968 that Japan's GNP became the second largest in the free world, paving the way for the country to be one of the leading economic powers of the world.

Alongside the economy, mass media also grew. Newspapers increased the number of pages. Many weekly magazines were launched. Publicity caught attention as a marketing tool, and newspapers, radio, and weekly magazines became vehicles of publicity. It was in this decade that full-scale public relations agencies were born. In 1961, Dentsu established the Dentsu PR Center (currently Dentsu Public Relations). In a decade-to-decade comparison, the largest number of PR firms were born in the 1960s. This trend spilled into the next decade until 1973 when the oil crisis changed the business environment (Morito, 2008).

In the 1950s, public relations activities were handled by the general affairs department, but in the 1960s, many corporations set up public relations departments as an independent function (Kenmochi, 2008). One newspaper reporter said that "mass media welcomed corporate publicity activities as it helped them increase the volume of articles" as his recollection of the 1960s (Morito, 2010).

Public relations industry organizations, both in the public and private sectors, were established in the 1960s. In the private sector, four public relations firms that were engaged in international PR formed the Japan PR

Society in 1964. Later in 1975, domestic-focused agencies formed the PR Work Japan Society. These two organizations merged in 1980 to form the Public Relations Society of Japan, which is still active today. In the public sector, the Japan Public Relations Association was formed in 1963 to assemble and support the public relations departments of the national and local governments (Yamamura et al., 2014).

1970s: criticism of corporations and the establishment of the kouhou departments

In the 1970s, Japan was polluted with by-products of mass production. It was a consequence of unparalleled rapid economic growth. Sensational headlines such as "Drop Dead GNP" decorated newspapers as they accused big corporations of lacking social responsibility. Corporations faced severe social criticism for their role in the destruction of human lives and peaceful living.

Pollution was not the only thing that corporations were criticized for. The oil-shock-related price hikes, dual pricing, land price speculation, drug-induced diseases, and harmful food products all led to severe criticism of corporations. They were viewed as not fulfilling their social responsibilities. It became a common understanding that there was a need to monitor corporate activities and protest against corporations that had not fulfilled their social responsibilities. Consumer activism in Japan gained momentum to an unprecedented level (Kenmochi, 2008). The consumerism movement in Japan was also influenced by the overseas movements. From time to time, newspapers and TV reported the consumer movements and the anti-war movements in the United States and the students' demonstrations in France. The Japanese followed suit with a slight time lag. The rise of consumerism in Japan can be interpreted as a sign that the citizen, as a layer of the society, was being formed in Japan (Yamamura et al., 2014).

People became highly aware of social issues surrounding them. Suddenly the public became important to corporations. The number of corporations setting up sections responsible for dealing with consumers grew substantially in the 1970s. Many companies set up specific sections under the umbrella of public relations to handle complaints and inquiries from consumers. Mass media rushed to companies that caused environmental pollution. These companies were suddenly busy handling media inquiries. In the 1970s, the importance of public affairs was recognized, and certain corporations set up departments and sections focused on dealing with the communities and environmental issues (Ikari et al., 2011). There were certain executives who thought that corporations would need to bear increased social responsibility. For most corporate executives, however, their priority was helping the economy continue to grow and dealing with the liberalization of capital and the internationalization of businesses. These issues were deemed more important than attending to social responsibilities (Nihon no top, 1970).

From the early 1970s, business organizations, such as the Japan Federation of Employers' Associations, Japan Committee for Economic Development, and Japan Federation of Economic Organizations (JFEO), made recommendations that corporations fulfill their social responsibilities. Concerned about the rising criticism of corporations, JFEO established the Japan Institute for Economic and Social Affairs (JISEA) as a public relations function to facilitate communication between the business community and society (Yamamura et al., 2014).

1980s: the enhancement of public relations departments

From the natural-resource-dependent heavy and chemical industries, Japan's economy began shifting to energy-efficient knowledge-based industries in the 1980s. Japan's reputation rose, but at the same time, the economic conflicts with other countries increased: with the United States, in areas such as automobiles, semi-conductors, communications, agriculture, and finance and with Europe, in automobiles and household electric appliances. In the United States, "Japan Inc.," which symbolized the cohesiveness of Japanese business society, became the focus of criticism. The economic conflict expanded to a cultural conflict, resulting in "Japan bashing." In the domestic market, consumers began choosing products based on their personal preference rather than simply following the mass trend and started to demand cultural flavor in products and advertisements (Fukuhara, 1999). In response, corporations tried to enhance their corporate image and added cultural flavor to their management strategies (Kenmochi, 2008). With the expansion of business domains and changes in consumer behavior, corporations were no longer able to exist in society without rethinking their corporate identity and adopting the concept of corporate citizenship flavored by corporate philanthropy.

With the changes in the corporate culture and employee mindset, internal communication became even more important. Corporations also recognized that external communication activities were critical for improving the awareness of their identity. The corporate identity business boomed, though for the most part, it was about company name change and the development of new logos. *Kouhou* led the corporate identity activities. Against this backdrop, the *kouhou* sections gained ground in many corporations. In 1980, 34% of the companies had independent *kouhou* sections. In 1992, the figure had grown to 72% (Japan Institute for Social and Economic Affairs, 1981, 1993).

In the 1980s, Japanese corporations that expanded their businesses abroad had to develop businesses while coping with the heightened Japan bashing. In particular, corporations expanding their business into Europe and the United States engaged in corporate philanthropic activities and proactively made donations to universities and research institutions. In the United States and England, donations worth more than US $1 million were often made by Japanese corporations (Japan Institute for Social and Economic Affairs, 1982 April, 1984 December, 1987 January, 1989 May).

The price of stock and land soared from the late 1980s. It was the coming of the bubble economy. Many corporations made direct overseas investments to acquire buildings, golf courses, hotels, and even film companies. The acquisition of the Rockefeller Center, an American icon, by a Japanese company led to a huge backlash. Such cultural insensitivity contradicted with and offset the effects of the social contribution activities of Japanese corporations abroad (Yamamura et al., 2014).

1990s: from crisis management PR to CSR PR

Japan's bubble economy collapsed in 1991, ushering in the so-called lost decade, the period of long stagnation of its economy. During this period, there were frequent occurrences of various corporate scandals. *Kouhou* sections managed crisis situations at the forefront and were exposed to probes by media. Scandals, such as improper lending and stockbrokers' compensations for preferred clients' losses, revealed the interdependence among politicians, bureaucrats, and business circles in political and business interests. Trust in corporations reached rock bottom as corporate scandals became the focus of social concern.

The Association for Corporate Support of the Arts (ACSA), which aimed to support corporate philanthropic activities, was established in 1990 when the wave of revelations of corporate scandals began. The 1% Club, a social contribution arm of JFEO that advocated spending 1% of the annual profit for social contribution activities, was also born in the same year. *Kouhou* was busy dealing with both corporate misdeeds and good deeds.

The conservative Liberal Democrat Party, which had controlled the government since 1955, gradually lost its power during this period. Coupled with growing distrust in corporations, the business circle was concerned about the sustainability of the social systems. They feared that the social distrust might spread to companies that had nothing to do with corporate greed and misdeeds. In an attempt to facilitate a conversation between corporations and society, JFEO and JISEA jointly held a forum in 1991 with a wide range of participants, including journalists, labor union members, educators, researchers, and housewives who expressed harsh views on corporate ethics and behavior (Kenmochi, 2008). Later in the year, reflecting the discussions in the forum, JFEO drew up the Charter of Corporate Behavior. The JFEO's charter has been constantly reviewed and became the social responsibility standard for Japanese corporations. In an effort to promote abidance with laws and regulations, with the lack of an appropriate term for translation, the English word "compliance" was used without translation. *Compliance* became the key concept to help prevent crises, and JFEO's Charter of Corporate Behavior incorporated the concept (Nippon Keidanren, 2009).

Many of the Japanese corporations began creating corporate behavior charters of their own from the late 1990s. Many of these charters incorporated measures such as the creation of watchdog committees and employee training programs to ensure observance of the charter. Furthermore, certain corporations set up schemes to protect whistleblowers. Internal communications activities concerning compliance issues became one of the roles of *Kouhou* departments.

Because of the emergence of the Internet, the rise of investor relations, and the need for environmental communications, the field of *kouhou* further expanded beyond media relations, crisis management, and corporate social responsibility. With the advancement of information technology, the Intranet became the main internal relations tool, although in-house publications remained as the key internal communication tool. Investor relations became more important because of changes in corporate fundraising schemes and the introduction of the concept of shareholder value. Many of the important issues in investor relations, such as management change and merger and acquisition, overlapped with the issues handled by *kouhou*, and some corporations moved the investor relations function from the accounting or the finance department to the *kouhou* department. The development of information technology also led to the emergence of consultancies that focused on online PR (Omori, 2008).

The 1992 Earth Summit in Rio de Janeiro shed light on sustainable development. In the 1970s, corporations handled the environmental issues reactively, but in the 1990s, Japanese corporations tackled environmental issues as part of their management strategy, leading to the development of environmentally friendly products and services. Many corporations published environmental reports or sustainability reports, and in many cases, corporate *kouhou* departments supported production of these reports. Environmental reports were often incorporated into CSR reports as one pillar of corporate social responsibility activities. Since the beginning of this millennium, CSR has become a common business term in Japan, and the promotion of CSR management is one of the key functions of *kouhou* today (Yamamura et al., 2014).

2000s and beyond

The Great East Japan Earthquake on March 11, 2011, revealed both positive and negative aspects of the Japanese people. It revealed the problems in communicative behaviors often observed in Japan, particularly among large organizations. One was the manipulation of outbound information by withholding, partially releasing, and distorting. The other was the efforts to manipulate public opinion by lining up influential pundits, overtly and covertly, to speak on behalf of the powerful organizations. Shuichi Kato (2000), a literature scholar, pointed out conformity as one of the key attributes of the Japanese people. It has almost become a national characteristic to follow the majority without expressing disagreement. However, not everything revealed was negative. Many corporations mobilized their employees for victim support and rebuilding communities and made company-wide donations as CSR initiatives.

The Japan Society for Corporate Communication Studies was established in 1995 to support research on public relations. As of 2017, the society has 631 individual members, including educators, researchers, students, and practitioners with an interest in research. The size of the public relations industry remained small. A 2013 industry survey by the Public Relations Society of Japan (2013) identified 202 PR firms, excluding advertising agencies and sales promotion companies that also engage in public relations. The average employee count of those that responded to the survey was 57, and 53% of those were female. Although it has been more than 50 years since Sophia University in Tokyo offered public relations courses in 1951, public relations education is still not well-established. Today, many universities offer one or more courses in public relations, but only a handful of universities have a public relations department or offer multiple courses in public relations. One notable move in recent years is the establishment of the Graduate School of Information and Communication, an independent graduate school with its primary focus on public relations and media studies. The school was founded in April 2017 and offers night courses, mainly for public relations practitioners who lack formal PR education. In corporations, most of the public relations managers come from other sections within the company (Miyabe, 2011), and it implies that public relations in corporations is not yet a well-established profession. The types of public relations activities that are the most often practiced by corporate public relations departments are media relations, followed by internal public relations and external information gathering (Japan Institute for Social and Economic Affairs, 2012). In 2007, the Public Relations Society of Japan started a professional accreditation scheme. In 2016, the aggregate number of qualified "PR Planners" surpassed 2000. Currently, it is the only PR-related accreditation in Japan.

Duality of public relations

We have briefly reviewed the path public relations (*kouhou*) in Japan has gone through to this day. Before World War II, public relations was not widely practiced. Where public relations was practiced, it mostly assumed the propaganda role to show the world that a small country in Asia had successfully joined the major forces of the world. After the war ended, public relations was introduced to Japan from the United States through various organizations. In corporations in particular, in response to the changes in societal and business environments, public relations went through dynamic change and gradually came to assume the core management role. In the 1950s, when labor and management confronted each other, public relations was a buffer between them. In the 1960s, it was an important part of the marketing strategy. In the 1970s, when pollution and defective products were critical issues for society, it ushered in the concept of corporate social responsibility while acting as an interface between organizations and society. In the 1980s, it supported the transformation of corporate identity to cope with changes in society. In the 1990s, with globalization and rising interest in environmental issues as its backdrop, public relations adjusted itself to drastic changes in communication strategy resulting from the emergence of the Internet and advancement in IT. From the late 1990s through the 2000s, waves of financial globalization and corporate scandals have forced corporations to take social responsibility issues seriously.

Through the cyclical changes in the key theme in corporate public relations in Japan, two aspects of public relations emerged. One aspect of public relations moves human emotions by manipulating information through mass media, and the other appeals to human rationale through continuous dialogue (Ikari, 2003). Yamamura et al. (2014) noted,

> In the days of economic up-swing, the advertising spending increases to stimulate consumers, the focus of public relations shifts to marketing communication, and there is an inclination toward spin through manipulation of information to further expand business activities. After a while, criticisms against corporations emerge and people come to think that corporations should prioritize public interests and observe the ethical standards. The business environment suddenly changes and public relations departments have to change the focus of their activities, guiding internal departments to comply with rules and regulations, and communicate externally that the company is compliant and ethical. When the days of harsh business environment prolong, the economic activities lose vibrancy and people start to long for the re-energization of businesses. While corporations respond to the environment, mass media sense and respond to the public sentiment by proactively reporting "bright news" that support economic revitalization. This cyclical phenomenon seems to appear in the history of public relations activities in Japan.
>
> (p. 74)

References

Cutlip, S. M. (1995). *Public relations history: From the 17th to the 20th century: The antecedents*. Hillsdale, NJ: Lawrence Erlbaum Associates.

Dore, R. (2000). *Stock market capitalism: Welfare capitalism -Japan and Germany versus the Anglo-Saxons*. New York, NY: Oxford University Press.

Fukuhara, Y. (1999). *Bunka shihon no keiei* [Management with Cultural Capital]. Tokyo: Diamond.

Hazama, H. (1996). *Keizai taikoku wo tsukuriageta shiso* [The Philosophy that Built a Major Economy]. Tokyo: Bunshindo.

Ikari, S. (2003). Gendai Nihon no kouhou [Public relations in modern Japan]. In Tsuganezawa, T., & Sato, T. (Eds.), *Kouhou, koukoku, puropaganda* [Public Relations, Advertising, and Propaganda]. Tokyo: Minerva Shobou.

Ikari, S., Ogawa, M., Kitano, K., Kenmochi, T., Morito, N., & Hamada, I. (2011). *Nihon no kouhou PR no 100 nen* [A hundred years of public relations in Japan]. Tokyo, Japan: Douyukan.

Ishii, K. (1997). *Nihon no sangyo kakumei -Nisshin, Nichiro senso kara kanngaeru* [Industrial Revolution in Japan – Think Through the Sino-Japanese War and the Russo-Japanese War]. Tokyo: Asahi Shimbunsha.

Japan Institute for Social and Economic Affairs. (1981). *Dai 1kai kigyou no kouhou katsudou ni kansuru ishiki jittai chousa* [The First Survey Report on the Attitude and Status of Corporate Public Relations Activities]. Tokyo: Japan Institute for Social and Economic Affairs.

Japan Institute for Social and Economic Affairs. (1982, April). *Keizai kouhou* [Economic Affairs Public Relations]. Tokyo: Japan Institute for Social and Economic Affairs.

Japan Institute for Social and Economic Affairs. (1984, December). *Keizai kouhou* [Economic Affairs Public Relations]. Tokyo: Japan Institute for Social and Economic Affairs.

Japan Institute for Social and Economic Affairs. (1987, January). *Keizai kouhou* [Economic Affairs Public Relations]. Tokyo: Japan Institute for Social and Economic Affairs.

Japan Institute for Social and Economic Affairs. (1989, May). *Keizai kouhou* [Economic Affairs Public Relations]. Tokyo: Japan Institute for Social and Economic Affairs.

Japan Institute for Social and Economic Affairs. (1993). *Dai 5 kai kigyou no kouhou katsudou ni kansuru ishiki jittai chousa* [The Fifth Survey Report on the Attitude and Status of Corporate Public Relations Activities]. Tokyo: Japan Institute for Social and Economic Affairs.

Japan Institute for Social and Economic Affairs. (2012). *Dai 11 kai kigyo no kouhou katsudo ni kansuru ishiki jittai chousa hokokusho* [The 11th Survey Report on the Attitude and Current Status of Corporate Public Relations Activities]. Tokyo: Japan Institute for Social and Economic Affairs.

Kato, S. (2000). *Watashi ni totte no 20 seiki* [The 20th Century for Me]. Tokyo: Iwanami Shoten.

Kenmochi, T. (2008). Sengo kigyou kouhou shi [History of post war corporate public relations]. In PR History Research Group. (Ed.), *Nihon no kouhou PR shi kenkyu* [Japanese PR History Research] (pp. 125–200). Tokyo: Japan Society for Corporate Communication Studies.

Kitano, K. (2009). Wagakuni ni okeru yougo to shite no PR kouhou no gogen to hakyu katei ni tuite [The origin and the spreading process of PR/kouhou as a term in Japan]. *Corporate Communication Studies*, 13, 15–33.

Kitano, K. (2014). Sengo Nippon ni PR wo honkaku donyu shita otoko Tanaka Kanjiro (1) [Kanjiro Tanaka, the man who introduced PR in post-war Japan (1)], *Dentsu ho*. Retrieved on June 5, 2017, from http://dentsu-ho.com/articles/686

Matsumoto, T. (1938/1981). Mantetsu to kouhou gyoumu [South Manchurian Railroad and public relations activities]. *Senbu Geppou*, 3(10). Manchukuo/Tokyo: Fuji Shuppan.

Miyabe, J. (2011). An attempt on quantitative profiling of PR practitioners in Japanese companies: Applicability of "revealed preference" approach. In *Proceedings of the 14th International Public Relations Research Conference*, Miami, IPRRC.

Morito, N. (2008). PR gyoukai zenhan shi [The first half of the history of PR firms]. In PR History Research Group. (Ed.), *Nihon no kouhou PR shi kenkyu* [Japanese PR History Research] (pp. 248–297). Tokyo: Japan Society for Corporate Communication Studies.

Morito, N. (2010). An interview with Norio Morito/Interviewer: Takashi Kenmochi. May 20, 2010.

Nakane, C. (1970/1998). *Japanese Society*. Berkeley, CA: University of California Press.

Nihon no top no ishiki chousa [Survey of top management in Japan]. (1970, January). *Nikkei Business* (pp. 22–28). Tokyo: Nikkei BP.

Nihon PR Kondankai. (1980). *Waga kuni PR katsudo no ayumi* [Footsteps of Public Relations Activities in our Country]. Tokyo: Nihon Keieisha Renmei Kouhou-bu.

Nippon Keidanren. (2009). *Kigyo koudou kenshou* [Charter of Corporate Behavior]. Tokyo: Nippon Keidanren.

Ogawa, M. (2008). Kouhou ha senzen ni hajimaru [Public relations began before the war]. In PR History Research Group. (Ed.), *Nihon no kouhou PR shi kenkyu* [Japanese PR History Research] (pp. 12–30). Tokyo: Japan Society for Corporate Communication Studies.

Ogura, S. (1976). *PR wo kangaeru* [Think About PR]. Tokyo: Dentsu PR.

Omori, Y. (2008). PR gyoukai 50 nen no rekishi [The 50 years history of PR industries: its hypothetical review]. In PR History Research Group. (Ed.), *Nihon no kouhou PR shi kenkyu* [Japanese PR History Research] (pp. 303–313). Tokyo: Japan Society for Corporate Communication Studies.

Packard, V. (1957). *The hidden persuaders*. New York, NY: McKay.

Packard, V. (1960). *The waste makers*. Brooklyn, NY: Ig Publishing.

Public Relations Society of Japan. (2013, April). *2013 nen PR gyokai jittai chosa houkokusho* [2013 PR industry survey report]. Retrieved from www.prsj.or.jp/wp-content/uploads/2013/06/PR-company_report.2013.pdf

Tobe, R. (2010). *Gaimu sho kakushin ha* [Reformists in the Ministry of Foreign Affairs]. Tokyo: Chuo Koron Sha.

Yamamoto, F. (1981). Meiji jidai koki [Late Meiji era]. In Yamamoto, F. (Ed.), *Nihon mass communication shi* [History of Mass Communication in Japan]. Tokyo: Tokai University Press.

Yamamoto, N. (1994). *Watashi no iwanami monogatari* [My story on Iwanami Shoten publisher]. Tokyo: Bungei Shunju.

Yamamura, K., Ikari, S., & Kenmochi, T. (2014). Japan. In Watson, T. (Ed.), *Asian perspectives on the development of public relations* (pp. 63–77). London: Palgrave Macmillan.

2 The democratization of Japan and the introduction of American PR

Koichi Yamamura

Background

Most researchers agree that modern public relations activities were introduced to Japan after World War II (e.g., Inoue, 2009; Yamaura et al., 2013). However, in public administration, activities for public notification of laws and regulations can be traced back to the 8th century; the notice board called *Kosatsu* has been utilized from about 1,000 years ago, and in the process of modernization in the late 19th century, the national government's own media, titled *Dajokan Nisshi* [State Grand Council Daily], was used to inform people of laws and regulations as well as personnel appointments (Kunieda, 2013). In the corporate realm, it is known that house journals as internal communication tools already existed in 1904 (Ikari et al., 2011), and the first corporation to install a public relations section was, although an overseas Japanese corporation, the South Manchurian Railway in the 1920s (Kenmochi, 2013). However, the public relations activities of the South Manchurian Railway focused on publicity activities as a state-owned company and intelligence activities as a supporting function of the intelligence agency. Even though various publicity techniques were employed, their activities remained the most primitive of the Grunig's four models of public relations, the press agentry model. In Japan, until the end of the World War II, there was no consciousness of "accurate and truthful information" in public relations activities, much less two-way communication.

Then, why didn't modern public relations activities take root in pre-1945 Japan? According to Ikari, the prerequisite for the birth of public relations is the emergence of a popular newspaper that guides the formation of and helps spread public opinion. However, the Japanese government began suppressing speech in 1875 by imposing regulations on press contents. From then until 1945, when World War II ended, there was no freedom of the press in Japan. This also means that public relations could not exist in Japan. Only propaganda could exist (Ikari et al., 2011). Yamamura et al. presented their perception that public relations began as a persuasive technique to gain popular support amid a power struggle. Japan's modernization took in Western technologies but not the spirit of democracy. The Meiji

Restoration in the late 19th century was not a popular movement of the suppressed; rather, it was achieved as lower-class samurais persuaded feudal lords. Consequently, the major component of modernization, the destruction of the class system and the family system, did not take place (Yamamura et al., 2013). As a result, the introduction of modern public relations had to wait for the time to be ripe, when the US-led Allied Forces occupied Japan after World War II.

This chapter tries to look at the introduction of US-style public relations in Japan during the post-World War II period in four areas, namely, local government, the advertising industry, the securities industry, and labor management.

Overview

After World War II, during the occupation of Japan by the US-led Allied Forces, US-style public relations was introduced to Japan (Hinoue, 1952; Ikari et al., 2011). It has been commonly accepted that it was first introduced as a part of the occupation policies (e.g., Hinoue, 1952; Inoue, 2009). However, Nihon Denpo Tsushinsha[1] (hereafter called Dentsu) was the first to mention public relations in an official statement. In February 1946, six months after World War II ended, the company issued six "interim operating policies." The second policy was to "introduce and popularize public relations that broaden the scope of vision and the planning of advertising" (Kitano, 2014a). Following Dentsu, local governments, the securities brokerage industry, and economic organizations introduced public relations.

At the time, the concept of public relations was a completely new idea in Japan. A public relations textbook published in 1951 provides a clue as to how public relations was viewed by Japanese people. The introduction of the textbook was written by the Information Policy Planning Unit, Civil Information and Education Section of the General Headquarters of the Supreme Commander for the Allied Powers, the US-led de facto government of the post-World War II period in Japan. The following statement in the textbook illustrates how the General Headquarters of the Supreme Commander for the Allied Powers (GHQ)[2] viewed the situation surrounding public relations in Japan.

> Modern public relations professionals combine the roles of educator, salesperson, and show manager, and their duty is to convey publicity to citizens by effectively utilizing various means. To think that until 1945, the majority voice within the Japanese government was that publicity was something to control, not to inform, this is a totally new idea for Japan. In other words, for Japan until then, publicity was not something to provide, rather, their policy was to censor publicity. As a result, the overall attitude was rather passive, not active.
>
> (General Headquarters of the Supreme Commander
> for the Allied Powers Civil Information and
> Education Section, 1951, pp. 1–2)

For local governments in Japan that had traditionally been authoritative, public relations that aimed to materialize democracy through two-way communication was a totally foreign concept (Ide, 1967). Government organizations in Japan had long followed the framework that information needed to be controlled. Because of this, it was very difficult to implement public relations activities (Nihon Koho Kyokai, 1951).

As we have seen, the introduction of public relations was not an easy endeavor. However, it gradually gained a foothold in government and businesses as various efforts were made. In 1949, from July until October, GHQ held a series of 13 PR seminars for over 100 PR practitioners in the central government and ad agencies (Nihon Koho Kyokai, 1951). In the private sector, the leading economic daily newspaper Nihon Keizai Shimbun and the Tokyo Chamber of Commerce jointly held a three-day PR seminar (Kotani, 1951). In 1951, three textbooks, *Koho no genri to jissai* [Principle and practice of public relations], *PR no riron to jissai* [Theory and practice of PR], and *Public relations kowa* [Public relations lectures] were published. In the same year, the national broadcasting station NHK covered PR in its program, and newspapers and magazines often covered PR (Kotani, 1951). The term PR had a wide recognition by then.

Introduction of public relations in government

After World War II, in 1947, GHQ suggested that the national and local governments actively promote public relations, focusing mainly on the provision of information materials to the press. This was for the execution of their occupation policy and a part of the policy for the democratization of Japan (Administrative History Compilation Room of Saitama Prefecture, 1987). By July 1949, every single prefecture of Japan had a section dedicated to public relations (National Governors Association, 1959). The fact that every single prefecture followed GHQ's "suggestion" within two years tells us that in those days, GHQ's suggestions were almost synonymous with orders. Government public relations in the post-World War II period began as a part of the occupation policy. On September 10, 1945, GHQ issued a *Press Code for Japan* and guaranteed freedom of the press with a restriction not to criticize the Allied Forces (Yamamoto, 2013).

As stated earlier, in Japan, government public relations in a broad sense, focusing mainly on publicity, has more than a 1,000 years of history. Since the abolishment of the feudal domain and the establishment of prefectures in 1871 as part of political reforms of the Meiji Restoration that continued until around 1930, publicity activities in local governments were carried out by departments such as the document and secretarial department. In the Tokyo metropolitan government, the document department publicity section was set up in 1934 (Kunieda, 2013). The views on how government public relations in the pre-World War II period differed from that of the post-World War II period vary from one author to another, partly because the definition of the word *kouhou* (public relations) is vague (Kunieda,

2013). At least the kind of government public relations activities that envision the provision of correct information and two-way communication did not begin until during the occupation by the Allied Forces.

Take Saitama prefecture, which is adjacent to Tokyo, for example. They established a policy research section in August 1946 and began public relations work as part of their assignment. This was in response to GHQ's instructions to enhance public relations activities with the main focus on providing information materials to the press. From the prefecture's outbound documents, they chose materials suitable for publicity and provided them to newspapers and other media (Administrative History Compilation Room of Saitama Prefecture, 1987). Around June 1947, the local military government unit of GHQ responsible for Saitama prefecture issued a suggestion, and in response, the Saitama prefectural government established a press room and began full-fledged public relations activities (Administrative History Compilation Room of Saitama Prefecture). It is not clear how GHQ gave orders to the national and local governments in the early days of the occupation, but many books report that between the spring and fall of 1947 each regional unit of the military government issued suggestions for the establishment of a public relations office to each prefectural government (e.g., Administrative History Compilation Room of Saitama Prefecture, 1987; Nihon Koho Kyokai, 1979). Although it took the form of *suggestions*, it is fair to regard this as an absolute order in Japan in those days when GHQ engaged in indirect rule through the Japanese government. One of the reasons behind the establishment of the public relations offices was the first unified nationwide local elections in April 1947. Until then, prefectural governors were appointed by the Minister of the Interior; city mayors were also appointed by the Minister of the Interior upon the recommendation of the city council, and town and village chiefs were elected by the town and village assemblies and appointed upon approval of the prefectural governors. They all became subject to election (Ministry of Internal Affairs and Communications, n. d.). Governors, mayors, and town and village chiefs were now responsible for the welfare of the residents representing citizens. Therefore, there arose a need to inform citizens of their policies while incorporating citizens' opinions. It was for such reasons that by July 1949, every single prefectural government had a section responsible for handling public relations (National Governors Association, 1959), and many cities, towns, and prefectures set up public relations departments (Nihon Koho Kyokai, 1979).

The new constitution was enacted in June 1947, and public relations activities in the central government also gained momentum. In order to carry out comprehensive public relations activities, the government considered establishing an independent public relations agency under the Cabinet Office; however, in the end, it was decided that the planning section of the Cabinet Office would be responsible for communication and coordination among the public relations sections of each ministry. Starting in May 1949, "the meeting of ministry public relations department chiefs" was held, and in October of the same year, in order to promote coordination of public relations between national and local governments, the Local Administration Office of the Cabinet Office organized "a national conference of department chiefs in charge of public relations" (Public Relations Office of the Prime Minister's Secretariat Office, 1990). During this period, GHQ not only supported the establishment of public relations organizations among local administrations but also actively promoted the philosophy of public relations and implementation of public relations activities. In July 1947, GHQ's East Japan Military Government Office organized a study session for the prefectural government's press department chiefs in East Japan and emphasized the importance of press and public relations. It also provided direction toward the active implementation of public relations activities (Administrative History Compilation Room of Saitama Prefecture, 1987). Such regional public relations department chief meetings have become the foundation for the national meetings as mentioned earlier.

The medium for public relations in public administration in those days was public relations magazines, wall newspapers, posters, and pamphlets. Using these media, upon request from GHQ, commentary on democracy and commentary on and promotion of democratization policies were disseminated. In 1951, local administrations started utilizing radio broadcasting as a public relations medium and then soundtracks and movies (Nihon Koho Kyokai, 1979). In the central government, the majority of public relations media were publications, but movies, optical lanterns, traveling exhibitions, radio broadcasts, and lecture presentations were also used. The National Personnel Authority, the Ministry of Education, the Ministry of Welfare, and the Ministry of Agriculture and Forestry had a section dedicated to government public relations through broadcasting.

The introduction of public relations as a marketing tool

As introduced earlier, one of the six company policies that Dentsu announced in 1946 was "the introduction and popularization of public relations" (Dentsu PR Center 20 Year History Compilation Committee, 1981; Ikari et al., 2011; Kitano, 2014a). However, the entire passage reads "the introduction and popularization of public relations (PR) that broadens the framework and the design of advertising" (Kitano, 2014a), and it shows that PR was perceived as advertising's supporting function. This perception, along with the power that Dentsu could exercise on the industry, had a great influence on the positioning of public relations in Japan.

It is not clear as to how Dentsu management learned about public relations back then. A former Dentsu employee and retired Teikyo University professor Kunihiko Kitano (2014c) presumes that the Dentsu management learned about public relations from Shintaro Fukushima, who was stationed in New York in 1937 as the first press attaché of Japan's Ministry of Foreign

Affairs and later in 1966 became the president of Kyodo News, a wire service company that holds a large share of Dentsu. In his article for a Dentsu publication, Fukushima stated that he learned the phrase "public relations council" but could not find an adequate Japanese translation and reported it to the Ministry of Foreign Affairs as it sounded in English (Dentsu ho vol. 1139, 1981, as cited in Kitano, 2014b). In 1947, Dentsu president Hideo Yoshida ordered external affairs manager Kanjiro Tanaka to translate the books and documents Yoshida had obtained from GHQ and the foreign wire service companies. In addition, Yoshida upgraded the external affairs section to the foreign affairs division and started activities such as lectures and book writing to promote public relations (Dentsu PR Center 20 Year History Compilation Committee, 1981). Two of the books Tanaka used as public relations textbooks have now been identified. One is the public relations feature in the July 30, 1948, edition of *Printers' Ink*, an advertising industry journal, and *Blueprint for Public Relations* by Dwight Hills Plackard and Clifton Blackmon, published by McGraw Hill in 1947, which Tanaka borrowed from the deputy director of the GHQ Government Section (Kitano, 2014c). Tanaka and the members of the Dentsu workshop translated the *Blueprint for Public Relations* (Kitano, 2014d).

In July 1949, Dentsu and the Japan Advertising Association jointly held the first advertising training session. As one of the speakers, Tanaka gave a lecture titled "On Public Relations" (Kitano, 2014d). During this period, Dentsu published a series of PR pamphlets. Tanaka's lecture at the first advertising training session was published as the first of the PR pamphlet series, and the summary translation of *Blueprint for Public Relations* was published as the second of the series. Other titles include "Planning and medium of PR – PR is the most profitable investment" and "PR advertising, PR has advanced advertising by one step." A supplement to the series entitled "Cases of public relations – PR is the philosophy of management" summarized public relations cases in the US.

Dentsu engaged in public relations as its own business. In 1948, Dentsu placed the first PR advertisement for the Ministry of Finance that promoted payment of taxes, followed by an advertisement for a campaign against illegal tobacco transactions. In 1949, Koho Renraku Kyoukai [Public Relations Liaison Association] was established to promote the government PR movement, and in 1951, Dentsu set up a PR department (Dentsu PR Center 20 Year History Compilation Committee, 1981). Shibuya (1991) gave three reasons why Dentsu was eager to promote public relations. The first was to improve the image of advertising, which was not trusted and had a negative image, by casting the image of public relations such as, science, modernity, and sincerity. The second was that by placing public relations at the core of management, advertising agencies could approach top management. The third was to enlarge Dentsu's own businesses. Public relations advertisements increased their businesses, and other media such as posters, pamphlets, billboards, and exhibits all helped increase the agencies' work.

Dentsu was not alone in the business circle promoting public relations. In July 1952, a book titled *Sales and Public Relations* was published. The book stated that in the June 1948 issue of the Department Store Association newsletter, a translation of a *Wall Street Journal* article said that the study of public relations was actively carried out for merchants to appeal to consumers. The book also mentioned a lecture entitled "PR and Sales Spirit," given at a lecture session held in October 1949 by the Japan Management Association, an organization that aimed to promote research and consulting on management (Tsuchiya et al., 1952). Also, in 1952, a book titled *Atarashii kokoku to PR* [New advertising and PR] was published, and in it, Yoneyama stated that there had been enough introduction and discussions as to what PR was, and it seemed rather silly to try to throw an argument about PR to those who handled advertising (Yoneyama, 1952). The advertising section chief of the Mitsukoshi Department Store, Mr. Okada, also wrote a chapter in the same book, entitled "Service News Reporting and PR News Reporting" (Okada, 1952).

As we have seen, public relations seems to have found its place as a supporting function for advertising and marketing; however, there were already critical views on the state of public relations in those days. Kisaku Ikeda, in his book published in 1954 titled *Introduction to PR*, under the subtitle "Merits and demerits of advertising agencies who introduced PR," presented his view that although advertising agencies deserved credit for promoting and popularizing PR, they had overemphasized PR's role as an auxiliary means for corporate money-making, and PR had gained an image that was closely tied to advertising. Without changing this image, PR could not function properly (Ikeda, 1954). In a round table discussion published in a business journal in 1967, the head of public relations of the liquor company Suntory said the following:

> When PR was introduced to Japan after WWII, it was a little confused with advertising. It was Dentsu who imported the word PR to Japan, but when Dentsu did so, they brought it in a way that could support their own policy. In other words, PR does not generate advertising fees and advertising agencies cannot make money by doing PR alone. If PR is introduced the way it should be, as it developed in America, it would not be good for advertising agencies. PR was intentionally mixed with sales promotions and introduced in such a way.
>
> (Kore ga gendai PR senryaku da, 1967, p. 81)

Dentsu itself seems to endorse this view. In the 1956 edition of *Dentsu AD Annual*, it touches briefly on public relations.

> What brought the new wave to the post-World War II advertising industry was the public relations movement. From the advertising point of view, we did have something similar to public relations since before

the war, but following the examples of U.S. advertising industry that utilized this method in every medium to enhance its influence over the public, Dentsu has stood on the forefront advocating public relations.

(Dentsu, 1956, pp. 44–45)

This issue still remains surrounding the term "public relations." Because of a lack of consensus about the Japanese translation, the mixed use of the Japanese translation and the English expression and its sound representation, and the vagueness of its meaning still remains (Kitano, 2008). The boundaries among public relations, advertising, and propaganda still remain vague. The way Dentsu handled public relations could be one of the factors that hindered its healthy growth in Japan.

Introduction of public relations in the securities industry

The securities industry also actively studied public relations (Kitazawa, 1951). This was in response to the dissolution of Zaibatsu (a family-run conglomerate) by GHQ as part of the non-militarization and democratization of the Japanese economy (Fukunaga, 2014). The holding companies of Zaibatsu were dissolved, and massive amounts of operating company stock were going to be publicly offered. The smooth absorption of these stocks became a critical issue for the democratization of the economy. In order to support the sales of stock, the securities industry, in collaboration with the Ministry of Finance, initiated a "securities democratization movement" and implemented various measures including open lecture sessions, investment roundtables, investment counseling offices, securities fairs, and the production of promotional movies (Daiwa Securities, 2003).

At Nomura Securities, the leading securities house in Japan, in May 1949, the publicity team in the planning department was upgraded to a publicity division. In December of the same year, the division absorbed other divisions and was upgraded to a publicity department (Nomura Securities, 1951). Nomura Securities recognized public relations as "a means to raise trust in the company, by the public both inside and outside the company," and they published books and held circuit lecture sessions to promote stock ownership (Nomura Securities). In a newspaper advertisement, Nomura Securities announced that they would hold a series of seminars on public relations for corporate management, with the tag-line "PR is the fourth pillar of management," to be held in major cities in various regions of the country (Tsuchiya et al., 1952). At Daiwa Securities, the second largest securities house, the publicity department was established in August 1948, shifting work from the planning department and further intensifying its public relations activities (Daiwa Securities, 2003). Around that time, the management of Daiwa Securities stated as one of its management strategies, "By utilizing various measures such as advertising, print materials, various customer services, and public relations that is catching public attention these days, incite public awareness of our company." In response to this strategy, with a tag-line "publicity is the best investment," the publicity department obtained increased funding and aggressively engaged in public relations activities (Daiwa Securities, 1963). In September 1951, with the launch of commercial radio broadcasting, Daiwa Securities began its radio advertisements, and in April 1953, the moving investment consulting office service began. The investment consulting office was set up in a van and offered live stock price information to customers by equipping the van with a radio receiver. The company also set up an investment consulting office in its headquarters and provided customer services, such as study sessions on economic issues and current affairs, speaker sessions, and site tours to investment destination companies. The company also organized a wives investment club and published the weekly *Daiwa News* in March 1952. One proof of the success of these activities was the percentage of individual shareholders of listed companies. In 1950, the percentage of individual shareholders of listed companies rose to 69% (Daiwa Securities, 2003).

In October 1950, the Japan Securities Investment Association published a monthly magazine entitled *Public Relations*. The comments on its publication, in its inaugural issue, state that the magazine was published under the firm belief that through practicing public relations, the residue of feudalism would be wiped out, leading to the promotion of democracy, and the virtues of a capitalistic economy would be further sophisticated and be more efficient. To that end, the association published the magazine as it wished to contribute to the popularization of public relations. The editor's note at the end pointed out that there was no uniform translation of the term "public relations," and many Japanese words were still used (Nihon Shoken Toshi Kyokai [Japan Security Investment Association], 1950 October). In the same issue, an executive director of the Japan Securities Investment Association and former president of Nomura Securities, Seizo Iida wrote an essay entitled "the characteristics of Japanese style PR" and stated that the reason why the need for public relations in Japan was not recognized as much as in the US was because companies were poisoned by the long years of a controlled economy and did not possess adequate consciousness regarding autonomy and responsibility that any company should intrinsically possess. He also mentioned that, unless companies rationalized themselves and their operation, and placed themselves in a glass box, it would be difficult to develop public relations into its true form (Iida, 1950 October). Out of 15 articles in the inaugural issue, four included in the title words such as "PR" or "community relations," and two other articles discussed PR practice in the US and investor relations (Nihon Shoken Toshi Kyokai [Japan Security Investment Association], 1950 October). In the second issue published in November 1950, there were three articles that included PR in the title (Nihon Shoken Toshi Kyokai [Japan Securities Investment Association]). In the December 1952 issue, the third year of its publication, there were two articles with the word PR in the title; however, four articles were about interviewing and another was on sales promotions. These were PR-related topics in a broad sense (Nihon Shoken Toshi Kyokai [Japan Securities Investment Association]). However, out of 87 key articles published in 12 issues in 1958, none of the articles were about public relations (Nihon Shoken Toshi Kyokai, 1959 January). The magazine changed its title from *Public Relations* to *Sogo Keiei* [Comprehensive Management] with the March 1959 issue. A remark to its subscribers explains the reason for the change.

> Building a democratic society, and sophistication and streamlining of capitalistic economy as two aims, this magazine PR (sic) was born in October 1950 when the country was still suffering from the wounds of the defeat of the war, to nurture PR spirit and encourage PR practice as the most effective means to achieve above mentioned aims. Ten years have passed since then and as studies of PR spirit progressed, we thought that we needed to grasp and study management issues comprehensively. When the first phase of promoting PR spirit seemed to be over, since April 1953 issue, we added a subtitle "general magazine for management" and shifted the editorial focus to studies and clarification of various management issues to support rationalization and modernization of comprehensive management [. . .]
>
> (PR Henshubu [PR Editorial Office], 1959 February, p. 104)

When the securities industry learned the skills of public relations as a sales support tool, there was no need to further understand, study, research, or promote public relations. Nor did they recognize the need for public relations professionals.

Introduction of public relations as a labor-management tool

In Japan during World War II, because of severe suppression, labor unions hardly ever functioned (Ikari et al., 2011); however, GHQ encouraged the formation of labor unions and the labor union law was enacted in December 1945. Labor unions were given the right to collective bargaining, and all public servants, with the exception of policemen, firefighters, and prison officers, were given the right to strike (Fukunaga, 2014). Labor unions became strong, and many strikes occurred. With the outbreak of the Korean War, Nihon Keieisha Renmei (Japan Federation of Employers' Association: JFEA) was established in 1948 as an organization for management to collectively tackle labor issues. During the labor dispute at a film company Toho, the labor union's tactics became extremely radical, and US Army tanks were deployed in August 1947. This was a turning point for GHQ's policy toward labor issues, and the birth of JFEA was a counterblow to the union movement by Japan's business circles (Ikari et al., 2011).

For the management of large businesses in the days immediately after World War II, re-constructing businesses amid increasingly fierce labor unrest was the most urgent agenda. They could not afford to care about business administration or labor-management issues. It was a state of chaos. It was around 1947 that human relations as a labor-management concept was introduced to Japan (Mizutani, 1957). In 1951, GHQ organized a labor status study mission, and JFEA members visited the US. One of the members of the mission wrote in a book that they visited the Tennessee Valley Authority, which was actively engaging in public relations activities at the time, to listen to a lecture on public relations. Throughout the trip, they were repeatedly told about human relations and public relations (Kato, 1957). Thus, with the support of GHQ, they studied public relations, but as JFEA was struggling to improve the labor-management relationship, their adoption of public relations focused only on a part of the entire public relations arena, namely, in-house newsletters, an employee suggestion system, and management tactics such as complaint settlements and managers' handling of junior staff. Of these, in-house newsletters were given the most weight as an employee public relations measure (Ikari et al., 2011). Magazines for human relations staff also covered public relations concepts. The May 1953 issue of *Rosei jiho* [Labor relations times] had an article entitled "Kaisha kojo ni okeru roumu gaikyo no sakusei jirei-jugyoin PR taisaku toshite no kiso shiryo" [Example of labor conditions report at a company and factory: basic information as a public relations measure]. In the article, the author first acknowledged the importance of in-house newsletters as an employee relations tool and then introduced the labor conditions report as an important communication tool that informs employees and brings about cooperation between management and labor (Kaish kojo ni okeru roumu gaikyo no sakusei jirei-jugyoin PR taisaku toshite no kiso shiryo [Example of labor conditions report at company and factory-basic information as public relations measure], 1953). Another human relations magazine, *Roumu Kenkyu* [Labor Studies] had a multiple article section entitled "Several Chapters on Important Points for Employee PR." The first article entitled "Arayuru chance wo ikaso" [Let's utilize every single opportunity] claims that, although some people think that PR means in-house newsletters, it is only one public relations opportunity. It is important to think about the timing and time sequence of every public relations opportunity, such as newsletters, bulletin boards, small group meetings, and so on (Kubota, 1954). Other articles in the section were entitled, "On Employee Public Relations Organization" (Nagashima, 1954); "Verbal Employee Public Relations" (Horikawa, 1954); "Employee Public Relations Through Audio Visual Materials" (Ohta, 1954); and "Let's Develop Workplace Photos" (Yonosuke, 1954). At the end of the section, a small article entitled "Recent Trends in Corporate Communication Planning" was included and introduced the result of a survey cited from the *Encyclopedia Americana* 1954 edition.

Decline of the momentum for the introduction of public relations

When something new is introduced, there will come a time when the initial momentum diminishes. The more rapid the rise, the harsher the fall. Whether that something takes root depends on its ability to get over the stagnation. Public relations in Japan was no exception.

As we have seen, the public relations activities of local governments seemed to have steadily expanded, but it was not built on solid ground. In April 1952, the San Francisco Peace Treaty was signed between Japan and the Allied nations, bringing an end to the indirect rule by GHQ. In the fall of that year, a "review of occupation policies" began in various fields. Government public relations, as it was a new concept introduced by GHQ, was regarded as if it was the "occupation policy's war baby," and it lost steam (Nihon Koho Kyokai, 1979). At the end of 1949 in 46 prefectures, there were 29 independent public relations sections and 17 sections that were combined with other functions such as documents, planning, secretariat, culture, and research. However, in 1953, in a reversal, there were only 17 independent sections, less than those combined with other functions. This was a period when each prefecture was simplifying and streamlining its organization to cope with financial difficulties, but public relations was one of the functions that was most heavily affected (Hinoue, 1963, as cited in Nihon Koho Kyokai, 1979). Ide (1967) noted,

> Public relations aims to realize democracy in public administration by securing channel for two-way passage between the public administrator and the citizens. It was a totally alien concept for the tradition of local administrations of Japan that had been defined in an authoritative manner. The fact that, in the first phase of the introduction of public relations, people had a hard time trying to grasp the concept and select a Japanese word for translation – even the Japanese word *kouhou* that seems to have been established as the translation still does not seem to be an adequate translation of "public relations" – vividly show the fact that the reality that corresponds to the concept of public relations was missing in the public administration in Japan. Based on such historical conditions, it may be possible to say that the introduction of public relations was made possible only with foreign pressure as a direct and foremost factor; however, if we see it from the reverse side, it exactly means that there was a possibility of repercussions when the foreign pressure disappeared. Public relations' setback after the signing of the peace treaty, the period of re-organization of the post-World War II system, was exactly the manifestation of that.
>
> (p. 83)

What is worth noting is that, during this period, there was no identifiable report of layoffs in local government public relations departments. Nor was there a report of public relations practitioners moving to corporations or public relations firms. Although anecdotal, this could be one of the pieces of evidence of "generalist-turned-PR practitioners" who managed public relations. This will be discussed in more detail in Chapter six.

At about the same time, there was also a setback of public relations in the private sector. The active period in the dawn of public relations ended at the end of 1952. In 1953, Dentsu's newsletter, *Dentsu ho*, and monthly magazine, *Public Relations*, both seem to have lost enthusiasm for public relations, and the number of articles on public relations decreased drastically. The media's disengagement from public relations was a reflection of the stagnation of public relations practice. There was growth in the establishment of public relations departments in corporations, but public relations as a business did not prosper as expected (Shibuya, 1991). It was also because of the poor use of public relations. Some companies spent money on beautiful-looking annual reports or placed public relations advertisements in newspapers and thought that they were doing good public relations. They simply incorporated tactical aspects of public relations and ignored the most important aspects – self-reflection and correction (Dentsu, 1956). According to Ikari et al. (2011), it was because the philosophical aspect of public relations took a lead, but there was no grounding in Japanese society or corporations to accommodate the skills and methodologies that back up such a philosophy. They also pointed out that during the time when the Japanese economy was recovering from the wounds of the war, there was a shortage of paper, and newspapers didn't have enough space to write articles based on public-relations-generated information. Also, the mass media, reporters of general newspapers in particular, were cautious of playing into the hands of big corporations. It was because they believed, reflecting upon their own experience during the war when they could not criticize the system, that they should be critical of power (Ikari et al., 2011). It was not until the days of rapid economic growth that the media environment changed with commercial radio broadcasting, television broadcasting, and the publication of weekly magazines.

As we have seen in this chapter, the government and private sectors of Japan introduced public relations after World War II in a rather hurried manner. For local governments, GHQ's "suggestions" were synonymous with "rigid orders." For the securities industry, smooth sales of stocks were crucial as GHQ forcing the dissolution of conglomerates meant a massive outflow of company stocks. For members of JFEA, keeping labor disputes under control was critical to their survival, as GHQ's initial stance helped accelerate the labor movement that had long been suppressed by the Japanese government until the end of World War II. Dentsu seemed to be the only player in the "Japan's post World War II encounter with American PR" arena that was strategic and proactive. However, Dentsu's close relationship with the media, its relatively dominant power in the industry, and Japan's drastic economic growth, resulting in positioning PR under marketing, seemed to have cast a shadow on how the public viewed PR in Japan. The hurried adoption of public relations that lacked full understanding may be the reason why public relations had to be set back when GHQ withdrew from Japan and rapid economic growth wiped away some of the worries corporate management had at that time.

Notes

1 Founded in 1901 as two separate companies, one providing advertising services and the other wire services, the company merged in 1906. Later in 1936, the company spun out its wire service division. The company is now named Dentsu, the Japanese abbreviation of its old name, and currently, it is an advertising agency, the largest in Japan and the fifth largest in the world.
2 GHQ was not merely an acronym. Since the days of the post-World War II occupation, Japanese people, even when speaking in Japanese, referred to the General Headquarter of the Supreme Commander for the Allied Powers as GHQ.

References

Administrative History Compilation Room of Saitama Prefecture. (1987). *Administrative history of Saitama prefecture, Volume 3*. Urawa: Saitama Prefecture.

Daiwa Securities. (1963). *60 years history of Daiwa Securities*. Tokyo: Daiwa Securities.

Daiwa Securities. (2003). *100 years history of Daiwa Securities*. Tokyo: Daiwa Securities.

Dentsu, Inc. (1956). *Dentsu koukoku nenkan* [Dentsu AD Annual]. Tokyo: Dentsu PR.

Dentsu PR Center 20 Years History Compilation Committee. (1981). Chikyu teki shiya deno hiyaku wo [Leap forward with global perspective]. In Committee, D. P. (Ed.), *20 years history of Dentsu PR* (pp. 4–5). Tokyo: Dentsu PR.

Fukunaga, F. (2014). *Nihon senryo shi 1945–1952* [History of the Occupation of Japan 1945–1952]. Tokyo: Chuo Koron Sha.

General Headquarters of the Supreme Commander for the Allied Powers, Civil Information and Education Section. (1951). *Kouhou no riron to jissai* [Theory and Practice of Public Relations]. Tokyo: General Headquarters Supreme Commander for the Allied Powers.

Hinoue, R. (1952). *Jichitai koho no riron to gijutsu* [Theory and Techniques of Local Government PR]. Tokyo: Sekaishoin.

Hinoue, R. (1963). *Kouhou no moten to shoten: taiken 15 ne no kenkyu kiroku* [Blind Spot and Focus of Public Relations: Record of 15 Years Research]. Tokyo: Daiichi Hoki Shuppan.

Horikawa, N. (1954). Koto ni yoru jugyoin PR [Verbal employee public relations]. *Roumu Kenkyu* [Labor Studies], 7(9), 26–28.

Ide, Y. (1967). *Gyosei koho ron* [Government public relations]. Tokyo: Keiso Shobo.

Iida, S. (1950 October). Nihon gata PR no seikaku [Characteristics of Japanese style PR]. *Public Relations*, 1(1), 16–17.

Ikari, S., Ogawa, M., Kitano, K., Kenmochi, T., Morito, N., & Hamada, I. (2011). *Nihon no kouhou PR no 100 nen* [A hundred years of public relations in Japan]. Tokyo, Japan: Douyukan.

Ikeda, K. (1954). *PR nyumon* [Introduction to PR]. Tokyo: San-Ichi Publishing.

Inoue, T. (2009). An overview of public relations in Japan A self-correction concept. In Krishnamurathy, S., & Vercic, D. (Eds.), *The global public relations handbook: Theory, research, and practice* (pp. 68–85). New York, NY: Routledge.

Kaish, M. (1953). Kojo ni okeru roumu gaikyo no sakusei jirei-jugyoin PR taisaku toshite no kiso shiryo [Example of labor conditions report at company and factory-basic information as public relations measure]. *Rosei Jiho*, 22.

Kato, R. (1957). Waga sha no shanaiho wo chushin to shita jugyoin PR [Employee PR of our company centering around in-house newsletter]. In Renmei, N. K. (Ed.), *Human Relations*. Tokyo: Nihon Keieisha Renmei Koho bu.

Kenmochi, T. (2013, July). Mantetsu no koho katsudo [Public relations activities of South Manchurian Railway]. *Keizai Koho*, 16–17.

Kitano, K. (2008, March). "Koho, koho, PR" no gogen ni kansuru ichi kousatsu [An examination on word origin of "koho, koho, and PR". *Teikyo Journal of Sociology*, 21.

Kitano, K. (2014a). Sengo Nippon ni PR wo honkaku donyu shita otoko Tanaka Kanjiro (1) [Kanjiro Tanaka, the man who introduced PR in post-war Japan (1)], *Dentsu ho*. Retrieved on June 5, 2017, from http://dentsu-ho.com/articles/686

Kitano, K. (2014b). Sengo Nihon ni PR wo honkaku donyu shita otoko Tanaka Kanjiro (3) [Kanjiro Tanaka the man who introduced PR in full scale to Japan (3)], *Dentsu ho*. Retrieved on June 5, 2017, from https://dentsu-ho.com/articles/765

Kitano, K. (2014c). Sengo Nihon ni PR wo honkaku donyu shita otoko Tanaka Kanjiro (4) [Kanjiro Tanaka, the man who introduced PR in full scale to Japan (4)], *Dentsu ho*. Retrieved on June 10, 2017, from https://dentsu-ho.com/articles/796

Kitano, K. (2014d). Sengo Nihon ni PR wo honkaku donyu shita otoko Tanaka Kanjiro (5) [Kanjiro Tanaka, the man who introduced PR in full scale to Japan (5), *Dentsu ho*. Retrieved on June 10, 2017, from https://dentsu-ho.com/articles/836

Kitazawa, S. (1951). *Public Relations Kowa* [Lectures on Public Relations]. Tokyo: Diamond.

Kore ga gendai PR senryaku da [This is modern PR strategy]. (1967, September). *Sougou Janarizumu Kenkyu* [Journalism Quarterly Review], 4(9), 81–89.

Kotani, S. (1951). *PR no riron to jissai* [Theory and Practice of PR]. Tokyo: Nihon Denpo Tsushinsha.

Kubota, N. (1954). Arayuru chance wo ikaso [Let's utilize every single opportunity]. *Roumu Kenkyu* [Labor Studies], 22–24.

Kunieda, T. (2013). Tokyo no kouhou zenshi [Prehistory of Tokyo's public relations]. *Corporate Communication Studies*, 17, 28–41.

Ministry of Internal Affairs and Communications. (n. d.). *Chiho jichi seido no rekishi* [History of local administration system]. Retrieved on June 5, 2017, from www.souomu.go.jp/main_sosiki/jichi_gyousei/bunken/history.html

Mizutani, M. (1957). Waga kuni ningen kankei kanri no genjo to mondai ten [Current status and issues of human relations management in our country]. In Organizations, N. K. (Ed.), *Human Relations*. Tokyo: Nihon Keieisha Renmei Kouhou bu.

Nagashima, R. (1954). Jugyoin PR no soshiki ni tsuite [On employee public relations organization]. *Roumu Kenkyu* [Labor Studies], 7(9), 24–25.

National Governors Association. (1959). *Todofuken kouhou 10 nen* [10 Years of Prefectural Government Public Relations]. Tokyo: National Governors Association.

Nihon Koho Kyokai. (1951). *Koho no genri to jissai* [Theory and Practice of Public Relations]. Tokyo: Nihon Denpo Tsushinsha.

Nihon Koho Kyokai. (1979). *Nihon Koho Kyokai 15 nen shi* [15 Years History of Japan PR Association]. Tokyo: Nihon Koho Kyokai.

Nihon Shoken Toshi Kyokai [Japan Securities Investment Association]. (1950, November). *Public Relations*, 1(2).

Nihon Shoken Toshi Kyokai [Japan Securities Investment Association]. (1950, October). Hakkan no kotoba [Words upon new publication]. *Public Relations*, 1(1), 1.

Nihon Shoken Toshi Kyokai [Japan Securities Investment Association]. (1952, December). *Public Relations*, 3(12).

Nihon Shoken Toshi Kyokai [Japan Securities Investment Association]. (1959 January). PR dai 9 kan shuyo mokuji [PR volume 9 key articles]. *Public Relations*, 10(1), 83.

Nomura Securities. (1951). *Nomura Shoken 25 nen shi* [25 Years History of Nomura Securities]. Tokyo: Nomura Securities.

Ohta, H. (1954). Shichokaku ni yoru jugyoin PR [Employee public relations through audio visual materials]. *Roumu Kenkyu* [Labor Studies], 7(9), 28–30.

Okada, S. (1952). Hanbai houdou oyobi PR houdou [Service reporting and PR reporting]. In Yoneyama, K. (Ed.), *Atarashii kokoku to PR* [New Advertisement and PR]. Tokyo : Kinseido.

PR Henshubu [PR Editorial Office]. (1959, February). Shimei henko no goaisatsu [Greetings upon changing the name of magazine]. *Public Relations*, 10(2), 104.

Public Relations Office of the Prime Minister's Secretariat Office. (1990). *Seifu Kouhou 30 nen no ayumi* [30 Years Progress of Central Government Public Relations]. Tokyo: Public Relations Office of the Prime Minister's Secretariat Office.

Shibuya, S. (1991). *Taishu sosa no keifu* [Genealogy of Mass Manipulation]. Tokyo: Keiso Shobo.

Tsuchiya, Y., Uekuri, F., & Manda, K. (1952). *Hanbai to paburikku rire-syonnzu* [Sales and Public Relations]. Tokyo: Nihon Keizaisha.

Yamamoto, T. (2013). *GHQ no kenetsu chouhou senden kousaku* [GHQ's Censorship, Intelligence, and Propaganda Activities]. Tokyo: Iwanami Shoten.

Yamamura, K., Ikari, S., & Kenmochi, T. (2013). Historic evolution of public relations in Japan. *Public Relations Review*, 39(2), 147–155.

Yoneyama, K. (1952). Koukoku tantosha-PR-shohi taishu [Person in charge of advertising, PR, and consumers], In Keio Advertisement Society (Ed.), *Atarashii Kokoku to PR* [New Advertising and PR] (p. 1). Tokyo: Kinseido.

Yonosuke, N. (1954). Shokuba shashin wo sodate you [Let's develop workplace photo]. *Roumu Kenkyu* [Labor Studies], 7(9), 31–33.

3 Public relations by a local government

150 years of Tokyo's PR

Tomoki Kunieda

Introduction

Even though governments are, by definition, more public in nature than private organizations, the history of government public relations has received relatively little scholarly attention. While there is a rich accumulation of historical studies in political communication and propaganda, there are fewer studies in public administration's PR concerning law-based missions and programs (Lee, 2014).

PR has long been discussed as a communication practice that was invented and developed by the American private sector and exported to other countries after World War II. Today, however, an increasing amount of historical literature points out PR-like practice by governments prior to American influence. For example, after analyzing PR histories in more than 70 countries, Watson (2015) mentioned that the general pattern of PR development begins with the government. Through extensive review of literature concerning PR prior to the 19th century, Lamme and Russell (2010) concluded that PR cases in the business sector appeared well after those in the religious, educational, nonprofit, reform, political, and government sectors. Historical cases of government PR have come to be mentioned more frequently, but there is a paucity of analytical research into how and why government PR developed over time.

Through a historical study of the local government of Tokyo, this chapter aims to fill the gap in PR history research. Tokyo's 150 years of history reveals how and why PR functions and PR-related departments emerged and developed over time, particularly through the years of modernization, militarization, democratization, and economic growth. While Tokyo may be an unusual prefecture that today has a population and an economy larger than some countries, as the center of the country's politics, economy, and culture, it has been regarded as a model for many other local governments within the country.

Literature review

While there are limited attempts at theorization in the field of government PR, Lee (2014) elaborated on the findings of Lamme and Russell (2010) that listed profit, recruitment, legitimacy, agitation, and advocacy as five generic themes or motivations found in PR history's literature, mentioning that recruitment, legitimacy, and advocacy are the motivations of government PR. Lee excluded profit and agitation, as the government is not for profit and does not agitate its citizen to, for example, rally against other organizations or groups.

In terms of PR's development, Lee (2014) also pointed out that even though the methods of implementation and execution change over time, the purposes are relatively fixed. Lamme and Russell (2010) listed centuries-old cases that utilize various forms of communication tactics that can be seen today.

> The concept of public relations' *development* over time is therefore relevant primarily to the scale at which tactics were employed and to the gradual development of the rules of engagement. . . . It was not progressive; in fact much about the public relations functions was found to remain fairly consistent over time.
>
> (Lamme & Russell, 2010, pp. 354–355, emphasis added according to the original text)

Taking their claim into account, PR history that follows the four models of PR (Grunig & Hunt, 1984) can be regarded as developing progressively as the model provides certain scales, such as directions of communication, truthfulness, and scientific methods to evaluate progress. Since Lamme and Russell's findings and the four models provide a general meta-level understanding of PR development, they fall short in explaining or predicting what happens to PR development in specific fields, such as the government sector. Instead of attempting to reveal the general PR development trend in multiple sectors of society, this chapter focuses on a single local government to present a detailed account of how and why PR functions and departments emerged and developed.

The political context of Tokyo makes its PR history a case of a local government that experienced 80 years of limited democracy between 1868 and 1947 and then 70 years of liberal democracy from 1947 to the present. A recent study on the effect of dictatorship on the development of PR revealed that contrary to the idea that PR is a by-product of a pluralist political system or a democratic dividend, PR has existed in a non-democratic setting:

> [P]ublic relations practices not only survived experiences of dictatorship and strong political control . . . but it was formed during dictatorships . . . and thrived subsequently. There is little doubt that public relations, and all forms of communication, prosper in "democratic environments in which there is a relatively open economy" (Watson, 2015) but these practices are sustainable in some disadvantageous political situations where democratic activity is very controlled.
>
> (Rodríguez-Salcedo & Watson, 2017, p. 380)

Rodríguez-Salcedo and Watson (2017) compared 13 countries with a specific political system and looked at the development of PR in different sectors. As political systems are closely related to the legal basis for which government PR is practiced, a closer look into the relationship between the political system and government PR reveals further details about PR development in specific sectors of society.

Methods

This chapter utilizes the historical method in uncovering the transition of PR-related departments and their functions since the establishment of the Tokyo government in 1868. The Tokyo Metropolitan Archives (1996, n.d.), the official record of all organizational change in the government of Tokyo from 1868 to the present, was used to sort out the year-to-year changes in PR-related departments. Various primary and secondary sources, such as Tokyo's official records, political history literature, newspaper articles, and others were used to reveal how and why those transitions occurred and the functions practiced by the departments.

A study of PR-related departments and their functions reveals how a certain set of PR functions came to be regarded as valuable enough to be institutionalized, to have a department of their own rather than be handled by staff in other departments. This chapter utilizes functionalist logic since specific PR functions were introduced to solve certain challenges, but more emphasis is placed on institutional logic because once a department is established, it develops routines and patterns to face challenges that are adjusted when new challenges surface or the situation changes (Vos, 2011).

The following sections introduce six periods of PR history and describe how PR-related departments and functions emerged and transitioned over time. It also discusses their implications for the idea of development in government PR and the relationship between political structure and PR. It is important to note that the naming of departments that appear in this chapter is based on a common, three-layered Japanese governmental hierarchical structure with *offices* or *bureaus* at the top, right under governors or mayors, followed by *departments* at the second and *sections* at the bottom layer. For the sake of clarity, names of the departments are capitalized and the word *public relations* is only used in the names of departments that use the word *kouhou*, the Japanese translation of the word public relations, in their name.

Age of modernization (1868–1900s)

In 1868, a 265-year-old feudal political system called the Tokugawa shogunate ended and the new Meiji government was established. The prefectural government of Tokyo was established in September of the same year.

During the earlier years, institutionalized communication between Tokyo, or *Edo* as it was called, and its local citizens was limited. Relatively well-documented PR practice during these years was the process of distributing official notifications, especially legislation carried out by the Correspond-ence Section. The name of the department occasionally changed to what could be translated as Record-Keeping or the Secretarial Section, which were mostly situated under the Department of General Affairs. The Cor-respondence Section and its neighboring departments were responsible for functions such as drafting and distributing legislation and notifications and gathering statistical data. While similar functions had been practiced well before the 19th century, the new government faced a major challenge of modernization led by the national government, rapidly changing the coun-try's political, economic and social system.

Through the early years of political instability, the national government promoted modernization on many fronts, which were to be notified and realized by the local government. Initially, Tokyo utilized a traditional notice board system known as *kosatsu* and personal networks in order to deliver legislative information and other notifications as they had done under the previous regime. However, as modernization involved major and dynamic changes on political, economic, and social fronts, important notifications, including changes to civil or criminal laws that affected many, had to be widely distributed promptly and accurately.

To handle the problem, Tokyo began circulating printed notifications in 1872. By 1876, Tokyo had introduced a public notification system where the land was segmented, each with a group of influential figures who were responsible for introducing and explaining legislation to 50 households. In the same year, it began posting notifications in the *Tokyo Nichi Nichi Shim-bun*, the daily newspaper published in Tokyo since 1872, only a year after the very first daily Japanese newspaper appeared.

While freedom of speech was not guaranteed, the national government supported the development of newspapers partly because they were useful in distributing information to and educating the public. In 1880, as news-papers increased their circulation, Tokyo began to publish public journal entries periodically in both the *Tokyo Nichi Nichi Shimbun* and the *Yomi-uri Shimbun*, two of the most influential newspapers at the time. As many newspaper companies emerged in the 1880s and '90s, Tokyo posted their notifications in different newspapers.

In 1889, the government of Tokyo organized 15 of its major wards into Tokyo City, led by the government-appointed city mayor, who worked under the governor of Tokyo Prefecture. Two years later, the prefecture began providing its legislative notifications as a supplement to the public journal *Kanpou*, issued by the national government. From 1897 to 1916, the city issued its own public journal, which included not only legislative information but also various reports and advertisements as supplements to some of the newspapers.

During the late 1800s, both the prefecture and the city attempted to con-tinue improving the way they delivered legislative news and other informa-tion to the public in order to introduce a new system of governance and maintain public order. Tokyo modernized its communication methods by institutionalizing the traditional, ambiguous notification system into a faster and more accurate system, publishing public journals that employed simpler language for better understanding by the public. Also, unlike today when governments can publish their own journals either in print or online and deliver them directly to almost every household, in the late 1800s, Tokyo had to rely on newspapers to both publish and distribute journals in the form of articles, advertisements, and supplements.

Age of urbanization (1900s–1920s)

Toward the end of the 19th century, a rapidly increasing population and urbanization became new issues for Tokyo. Tokyo's official records of population can be traced back to 1872, when it was around 860,000. Once it reached one million in 1878, it grew by a million every twenty years, reaching three million by 1919. From the 1920s, the population grew even faster, reaching 5.4 million by 1930 and 7.3 million by 1942. Accordingly, the number of city officials more than tripled between 1900 and 1912, from 600 to 2,000. The number continued to rise, and by 1924, it had grown to 7,000, eventually reaching 15,000 by 1942 (Tokyo Metropolitan Government, 2008).

As its infrastructures became outdated or incapable of handling the growing population, urban development projects were planned and executed but faced internal conflict within the legislative branch and external conflict with the local residents affected by the projects. While the only observable change in organizational structure happened in Tokyo City, when the Correspondence Section was raised to a department in 1920, the executive branch faced countless challenges during the years in which it implemented various new methods of communication.

Some of the challenges included the strong legislative body, the Council of Tokyo City, whose members were composed of often corrupt political and economic elites who slowed the decision-making and the execution processes. Local residents sometimes rioted against construction projects because they were often left out of the planning process, which affected their lives. There was distrust among the people inside and outside of the government.

Yoshiro Sakatani, the fourth mayor of the city (1912–1915) is known for his attempt to gain public support for an urban development project. In 1914, the Tokyo Taisho Exposition was held from March to July. Mayor Sakatani gave orders to build the Tokyo pavilion to present the city's programs and future projects to the public. The goal was to gain public understanding of and cooperation with the city's activities through eye-catching presentations. According to the Tokyo Metropolitan Government (2004), more than 2.5 million people visited the pavilion during the five-month event. Back then, it was rare for local governments to participate in such an event.

In addition to the pavilion, Mayor Sakatani published a booklet with an overview of the city's projects, making extensive use of visual aids, such as photos, tables, and graphs. The idea of the booklet was expanded by another mayor of the city, Shinpei Goto (1920–1923), who began publishing it on a yearly basis in 1922 to promote disclosure and public discussion. With minor changes to the title and content, its publication has been continued since, with the exception of the years between 1942 and 1946.

The government's approach to gaining public support changed in the 1920s. In 1918, the Rice Riot, an uprising by the people against rising rice prices, occurred around the country. The price of rice went up as the national government sent troops to Siberia. The government responded to the riots by force and a gag law that led to major public resentment and eventually the dismissal of the cabinet. The following cabinet actively introduced social policies and urban development projects in order to establish stable urban governance.

While the City Planning Act of 1919 limited the rights of local residents to facilitate the implementation development projects, one of the ways Tokyo dealt with the public resentment was by organizing a research group composed of influential figures. The group worked on awareness campaigns that claimed individual rights must be sacrificed for the greater good. Mayor Goto was a former member of such a research group. In the year he became the mayor, he invited more than 100 intellectuals to hear and draft a pamphlet containing examples of public dissatisfaction toward city promotion projects. The pamphlet contained a questionnaire sent to 65,000 citizens with voting rights, receiving 6,111 responses. It contained a wide range of public demands that included information and communication matters, such as the disclosure of council minutes, greater coverage of the city's activities by the newspapers, and more representation of public demand by the city councils and officials. Although it was a collective voice of the elite population with means, it was one of the early cases where the head of a local government used the voice of the public to improve and realize public policies that faced resentment from multiple fronts.

The Great Kanto Earthquake of September 1, 1923, prompted the city to issue various new publications to share information with the local residents. The effect of the M7.9 earthquake, which killed around 140,000 people, was so severe most of the city's functions were directed toward reconstruction efforts. Although Goto had left the mayor's office in April of that year, he became the Minister of Home Affairs of the national government the day after the earthquake, eventually drafting the so-called "800-million-yen reconstruction plan," which he discussed with the general public through newspapers.

When the city first published its public journal in 1916 in the form of a magazine published and sold twice a week, it included official announcements, legislative announcements, and reports. In 1928, in order to raise awareness of the city's events and projects among a wider range of its population, the journal was redesigned. Specifically, it now had a photograph on the cover followed by academic reports, official announcements, personnel changes reports, city project overviews, current events, local news, statistics, comments from the local residents, and advertisements. During the first three decades of the 20th century, there were no significant changes made in departments that handled PR-related affairs, but the volume and manner of communication between the government and the local residents increased and diversified.

Age of militarization and efficiency (1930s–1945)

Major changes in Tokyo's PR-related departments and their practices were seen during the years of militarization and war. When the Japanese Imperial Army invaded Manchuria, the northeastern part of China, in 1931 and created the puppet state Manchukuo, there were such confusion and misinformation within the Japanese government and the military that they recognized the need for information coordination among different sectors of the government (Kushner, 2006). As the national government attempted to mobilize the entire nation through propaganda, communication systems in the local levels were restructured for greater efficiency, giving rise to a departmental structure and institutionalized PR system that resembled that of post-war Japan.

In Tokyo, changes began with the establishment of an Official Announcement Sector and a City Information Sector under the Correspondence Department in 1934. The two sectors were established soon after the expansion of the city area in 1932 to include 20 more wards within the prefecture. This was the first time that a single department was devoted to PR functions in the city or the prefectural office.

In the months following the outbreak of the Second Sino-Japan War in July 1937, the city enlarged the cover-page photo of its public journal and placed news concerning the city before legislative announcements, making the journal even more reader-friendly. The journal's guideline for editors included the following seven policies (Tokyo Metropolitan Government, 1995, p. 5).

1   The journal must encourage cooperation between the city and its citizens, be an agency for civic education, and be an agency shared by its citizens.
2   Its language must be plain and simple.
3   What citizens must be informed of should be reported regardless of its importance.
4   Articles must be accurate without speculations.
5   Interesting articles and commentaries are to be posted.
6   It welcomes contributions by ordinary citizens.
7   Information that may be of use to the citizens should be included with charts or organized as a brochure.

The city apparently began accepting requests or complaints from the citizens to improve bureaucratic efficiency. In July 1937, the first edition of the monthly report on office function improvements was issued. It was distributed to each department within the city government and included a list of issues that must be improved along with citizen's voices that were published in newspapers. In a sense, the revised public journal and the monthly report served as a point of two-way communication. These movements were influenced by the cabinet decision to improve administrative affairs not only through the efforts of individual agencies but also through the cooperation of the citizens.

Internal communication was also improved with information officers appointed to each department. From September 1937, daily activities of the city were recorded and published twice a day, in the morning and afternoon, for better coordination within the office.

In 1938, the Imperial Diet passed the National Mobilization Act. Almost every aspect of the society was now mobilized for wartime needs. Local governments were required to reduce expenditures and improve efficiency even further. The city's various publications for local residents were consolidated into a single comprehensive weekly journal called the *Shisei Shuho* (Weekly Report on the City Government). Several thousand to 15,000 copies were published every Saturday. It also included a column where contributions from citizens were posted. The column disappeared in August 1940, but during the year and four months of its publication, it posted articles including those requesting improvements of compartmentalized administration.

Emergence of the information department

The *Shisei Shuhou* was modeled after the *Shuho* (Weekly Report), a weekly journal issued by the national government beginning in 1936. By the 1930s, information strategy had become a major issue at the national level, and *Shuho* was issued in October 1936 by the Cabinet Intelligence Committee. The committee was established to coordinate information policies among different departments and perform wartime propaganda. The *Shuho* and several other journals were used as a form of propaganda, published not only to inform and subjugate but also to relieve people from wartime difficulties and to motivate the home front. In the beginning, the *Shuho* contained professional discussions about legislations and current events. However, as the war expanded, the journal gradually shifted toward posting articles that related to everyday lives.

In 1939, the Information Department was established under the city's General Affairs Bureau. The major functions of this department included gathering, organizing, coordinating, and presenting information related to the city and drafting and distributing materials or hosting events to gain public support. It was also responsible for managing newspaper and radio reports. The city's news was broadcasted on the radio almost every day in a program that started at 5:30 p.m.

In 1941, the Information Department's budget was cut significantly, decreasing the number and volume of publications. In the *Shisei Shuho* published on January 17, 1942, the editor's note mentioned that the journal had changed from being a method of gaining people's understanding to "a printed bullet, a marching horn and an army at the front line of national propaganda."

Reconstruction of neighbor associations as communication channels

While public journals like the *Shisei Shuho* and the Information Department developed during this period as new forms of government PR and its management system, the traditional, personal network-based flow of information was also institutionalized. While neighborhood associations had existed unofficially for centuries to provide mutual support and share responsibilities, from 1939, the associations were embedded into the government structure and membership became mandatory. The associations circulated government announcements. Tokyo issued announcements that were originally meant to promote activities within the associations and to raise public awareness of city-related matters, but it gradually shifted toward issues that were closer to everyday lives, such as food rations, food conservation methods, disaster prevention, and support for those who had lost their relatives in the war.

For the sake of administrative efficiency, in 1943, the city government of Tokyo was dismantled, and the city's governing functions were delegated to the prefectural government. Since 1889, when the city system was established, the city had been responsible for direct communication with its residents. From 1943, the prefecture became responsible for controlling and executing communication to the greater number of residents spread across a wider range of areas.

Age of democratization and the birth of the PR department (1945–1960s)

The years of occupation by the Supreme Commander of Allied Powers between 1945 and 1952 were arguably the most important years for Japanese PR history, as that is when the democratic, American concept and practice of public relations was introduced and institutionalized in local governments around the country.

One of the fundamental changes that set the course for post-war public relations occurred in 1947 when the new Constitution of Japan was enforced. Unlike the Constitution of the Empire of Japan (1889–1947), which gave the emperor sovereign power over the country, the new constitution gave sovereign power to the people (Article 1). Likewise, government officers who were meant to serve the emperor under the previous constitution became servants of the people (Article 15).

The Local Autonomy Act enforced in 1947 also laid out the legal grounds of institutionalizing citizen-centered PR. It gave the local residents over the age of 18 the right to elect their own local governor and councilors (Article 17 and 18). By giving the governors more power over the office, the act created a trend where the elected governors realized their campaign promises by restructuring the organization soon after taking office. The first election in Tokyo under the new legal system was thus held in 1947. The winner was Seiichiro Yasui, a government official who had assumed various positions in the government around Japan and Korea, including the position as the government-appointed governor of Tokyo between July 1946 and March 1947.

The period between the end of WWII and the 1950s is characterized by constant changes in the names and functions of PR departments. By the end of WWII, the Press Division existed under the Document Department. The Press Division was renamed the News Report Division in 1946 and then the Public Relations Division (*Kouhou ka*) in 1948. In 1949, there was a major organizational restructuring where the Public Relations Department and the Public Hearing Division were established under the Office of the Governor. In 1956, this department was raised to the PR Liaison Bureau, reaching the highest level of office hierarchy under the governor. While there have been changes in names and responsibilities, bureau-level departments focusing on PR functions existed from 1956 to 2001 and department-level departments dedicated to disseminating information and gathering people's voices have continued to exist since 1949 to this day.

The establishment of PR departments and their new functions was prompted by the need for reconstruction. Over a hundred air raids by the US military between 1944 and 1945 destroyed a wide range of areas, including the Tokyo government's office building. The death toll rose above 100,000, and many evacuated Tokyo, dropping its population from 7.3 to 3.5 million between 1943 and 1945. The recovery from the wartime devastation was delayed by major typhoons that hit Tokyo three years in a row from 1947. A series of urban problems, including public health crises, surfaced as people poured back into Tokyo. Between 300,000 and 800,000 people returned every year after the war ended, and the population went back from 3.5 to 7.3 million by 1953.

While the post-war reconstruction was still on its way, the economy began to grow rapidly beginning with wartime demands from the Korean War between 1950 and 1955. While people's standard of living improved, factories caused large-scale pollution. Reconstruction efforts and economic developments led to corruption in the government. Once post-war reconstruction settled down, people began to criticize the government for its corruption and lack of environmental protection policies.

In terms of PR practice, very few publications were circulated in the 1940s because of the restrictions on the consumption of paper, but by 1950, Tokyo began publishing and distributing news and announcements to its local residents. One example is 1.2 million copies of the public journal called

Tokyoto kara no oshirase (Notifications from Tokyo Metropolitan Government) meant to be distributed to all households. Its function was similar to the public journal published by Tokyo since 1916: to disclose information, enlighten the public, and gain support for the government's projects. However, it was published under an entirely new premise of a democratic government with national sovereignty. The publication was renamed several times but has continued its publication, and as of 2017, the circulation of its print version is 3.7 million.

Among the PR practices seen during this period, the Public Hearing Division participated in public events and provided consultation services in and out of government offices to understand people's situations, concerns, and opinions. The first public opinion poll was held in 1952 with the goal of understanding people's living conditions and assessing the government's performance. In 1955, a phone line was established in response to the growing need for consultations by government officials. Unlike publications for the residents, such practices were rare during the pre-war period.

Age of two-way communication (1960s–1970s)

During the 20-year period of the 1960s and 1970s, PR departments grew in number and diversified their functions in response to various accusations against the government. Governor Ryutaro Azuma (1959–1967), known for realizing the Tokyo Olympic Games of 1964, was constantly under criticism and introduced multiple PR-related reforms. The succeeding governor, Ryokichi Minobe (1967–1979), won three elections with promises to tackle corruption and promote dialogue with the people, actively establishing new departments and expanding PR functions.

Under Governor Azuma, while Tokyo prepared for the 1964 Olympic Games with a new bureau dedicated to hosting the event, it began facing major political scandals from around 1960. The governor and Tokyo Metropolitan Assembly members were even accused of election fraud in 1963, eventually leading to the arrest of several assembly members in 1965. Through a series of corruption cases around post-war reconstruction and Olympics-related projects, the party in power, the Liberal Democratic Party (LDP), gradually lost public support. The winner of the gubernatorial election in 1967 was Ryokichi Minobe, backed by the Japan Communist Party and Socialist Party.

During Governor Azuma's term in office, departments such as the Office for Inquiries, the Office for Complaints, and the Information Office for City Policy were established. Various PR activities were institutionalized during his term, such as the City Policy Monitor, where 500 residents were selected to monitor the city's progress and provide feedback. The City Policy Monitor and other programs were considered to be the governor's attempts to restore trust in the government.

Governor Minobe's term saw the greatest increase in the number of PR departments and PR activities. From the beginning of his term, Minobe held a series of town meetings with the residents, where he spoke with the people directly. During his term, Tokyo's publications increased in volume and frequency, public opinion polls increased from once a year to four to six times a year, more communication routes were established between the governor and government officials, and, most important, Tokyo became a major focus of media attention. As a popular media figure, Minobe succeeded in gathering media attention through his eye-catching policies.

As for the department structure, in 1969, the bureau-level Public Relations Office had three departments (Public Relations Department, Dissemination Department, Citizen Inquiries Department) with 11 subdivisions, compared to eight in 1965. In 1971, media relations and resident relations functions were divided. The PR Bureau now had two departments (the Public Relations Department and the Dissemination Department), and the Citizen's Bureau had five departments (the Research Department, the Hearing Department, the General Inquiries Department, the Specialized Inquiries Department, and the Proposal Reception Department). The growth in the number of PR-related departments led to a greater chance of communication between the government and the people.

Governor Azuma and Minobe's terms coincided with a national trend toward solving political, social, and environmental issues. For example, the national government faced massive public demonstrations in 1960 concerning security agreements with the US. In order to counteract the resentment of the public, the central government established the Cabinet PR Department (Uchino, 2004). The national government's slow reaction to serious health issues caused by industrial pollution also stirred widespread criticisms, resulting in stricter environmental regulations from the 1970s. In general, such reactions to criticisms were welcomed. However, through the increased spending on welfare and the stagnant economy caused by the oil crisis in 1973, Minobe gradually lost public support.

Age of consolidation (1980s–)

The expansion of PR-related departments and functions during the 1960s and 70s may be seen as a progressive movement toward greater democracy through active, multi-level communication among different levels of the government and its people. However, from the 1980s, the number of departments slowly decreased as election agendas moved toward economic recovery from the two oil crises in the 1970s. By 2007, the number of PR-related departments decreased to four (Media Section, Public Relations Section, Information Disclosure Section, and Citizens' Voice Section) compared to 11 in 1969. The number and names of the departments has not changed as of December 2017 despite the fact that there have been four governors since 2007.

The agenda of the 1979 gubernatorial election was figuring out how to tackle Tokyo's stagnant economy. Shunichi Suzuki, the deputy governor from 1959 to 1967 under Governor Azuma, backed by the Liberal Democratic Party, won with a catch phrase, "Tokyo's Trustee in Bankruptcy," with a promise to solve Tokyo's deficit problem. During his four terms (1979–1995), he decreased expenditures by cutting the number of city officials by nearly 18,000 (about 10%) and boosted the economy by implementing a series of public construction programs. Although Tokyo seemed to have solved the deficit problem for a few years, the collapse of the bubble economy in 1992 hit Tokyo heavily.

Under Governor Suzuki, the policy-making process was led by professionals, namely the private advisory organ. His close relationship with the Metropolitan Assembly involved backdoor negotiations, making the process even less clear to the public. Unlike with the previous governor, the citizens and city officials were not considered to be an integral part of policy formation. When he passed the Tokyo metropolitan ordinance for information disclosure in 1984 to realize a more open, democratic governance, the ordinance received criticism for having too many loopholes, such as not allowing the disclosure of minutes for advisory organ meetings (Tsukada, 2002). The information disclosure ordinance was amended in 1999, but its content and the manner of enforcement has remained a heated topic since.

The two succeeding governors, Yukio Aoshima (1995–1999) and Shinichiro Ishihara (1999–2012), were eager to make use of the press, partially because they were famous TV figures by the time they ran for the governor's position and because they constantly fought against the Metropolitan Assembly. Governor Ishihara was especially famous for his performances and controversial comments, which gained a lot of media attention. He accepted media interviews more often than previous governors did. For example, a newspaper reported that he had at least 217 interviews during his first two years compared to 126 by the previous governor (Ishihara ryu no hodo senryaku, 2001). While the local residents elected Governor Ishihara four times for his leadership skills, the media has often been critical of him because of his questionable performances in economic policies.

Since the 1980s, one-directional distribution of information continued to grow and diversify. Governor Suzuki increased the number of TV and radio programs that dealt with Tokyo's policies and announcements. A new broadcasting station called Tokyo MX was established in 1995 and began broadcasting programs that included live broadcasting of press conferences by the governor and the Metropolitan Assembly. Also, as the number of foreign residents grew, publications in English increased.

In contrast, Governor Minobe's attempts to have the local residents and government officers involved in the decision-making process have decreased since the 1980s. Governor Suzuki did follow Minobe by keeping the town meeting practice in place, but he limited the number and type of participants in the meetings to avoid confrontation. As his decisions were primarily based on discussions with the advisory organs and negotiations with the Metropolitan Assembly members, the town hall meetings lost their impact.

Discussion

"Development" of government public relations

This chapter looked at the history of PR-related departments in the government of Tokyo and their functions through six different periods. In terms of PR development, in general, the scale and diversity of PR have constantly evolved while the political structure before and after WWII defined the course of development.

Tokyo's history can be seen as a development in terms of scale and diversity of practice and department. Lamme and Russell's (2010) claim that PR developed in terms of the scale at which the tactics were employed may be evident in Tokyo's case – at least from the 1870s, as various media were strategically used to gain public support for specific purposes and, in some cases, public voices were collected to assess the situation and promote policy or administrative change. However, while PR practice, particularly the effective dissemination of announcements among the local residents, has been its concern since the establishment of the government itself, the establishment of a department dedicated to its function in 1934 signaled a new age of institutionalization. The establishment of the department was in part due to a growing demand for publishing public journals with reader-friendly layouts and content. As the name of the department changed several times toward the end of the war, its responsibilities expanded, incorporating the increasing number of media types, such as music, radio, and movies, in its activities while continuing to deal with newspapers and publishers.

After losing WWII, Japan went through a major political change where the Tokyo government was responsible for democratizing its structure and its communication practice with its citizens, which involved teaching the citizens about the value of democracy. Under the new democratic system, Tokyo adopted new PR practices, such as public opinion polls and active consultations to hear people's voices and provide support. The practice and departmental structure continued to expand until the 1970s. After the 1980s, the scale of practice expanded as radio and television programs increased and as the age of the Internet arrived, opening whole new routes of communication.

However, the number of departments decreased and the dialogic relationship between the government and its citizens receded. A symbolic case may be the ordinance for information disclosure that has been in effect since 1984. Although the government is expected to communicate extensively with the public and is legally required to disclose a wide range of information upon request, Tokyo's decision-making process has often been criticized for its lack of transparency. In such respects, the scale and diversity seem to have decreased.

Political system and PR

As Watson (2015) implied, PR in Tokyo did develop rapidly after the country was democratized. While it may be said that the years of militarization between the 1930s and the end of WWII prompted PR development, post-war developments were far more extensive. While pre-war PR didn't develop until the country was under the state of war, post-war PR increased in both scale and diversity throughout the years of peace.

In terms of the political system, irreversible changes set by the new Constitution of Japan and the Local Autonomy Act of 1947 are apparent in the history of Tokyo. The first department dedicated to gathering people's voices appeared in 1949 and has existed ever since. The method of collecting people's voices has diversified since then; it was often provided in close coordination with the consultation services that attempted to offer guidance or resolutions to individual inquiries. The number of such departments had grown by the 1960s, until they began decreasing toward the end of the millennium. The reason for the expansion of such functions was originally for democratization and recovery from the wartime devastation. However, by the 1960s and 1970s, it became a political agenda that was promoted by the governors, often reactively in the early years and later more proactively, to tackle criticisms against the government for its corruption and to gain public support. From the 1980s, as economic recovery became Tokyo's agenda, PR functions, especially the democratic practices concerning discussions between the governor or government officers and the local residents, ceased to be a focus of political attention.

The gradual decline of interest in the democratic form of discussion between the government and its people seems to have occurred for two reasons. One is the fact that the people's standard of living improved through the rapid economic growth that lasted for nearly four decades from the 1950s, and the other is environmental reform since the 1970s. As the standard of living improved, people became less dependent on the local government and seem to have lost interest in it. Another factor for the decrease may be the fact that the governors after the 1980s gradually decreased the channels of communication that gave people the sense that they can, in fact, affect the course of the government. While it is still possible to submit proposals, suggestions, and complaints to the government and the assembly members, promotion of public participation and discussion has ceased to be a topic of major interest. Tokyo's case suggests that while the democratic political system may promote the development of government public relations, the path of development is strongly affected by the political, economic, and social situation that may set progress back on some fronts.

Although this chapter only looked at the case of Tokyo, further research into the PR history of other governments will enable a generalization of how and why government public relations develops over time. While Rodríguez-Salcedo and Watson (2017) analyzed the effect of dictatorships, the path of development in democratizing societies, such as Tokyo after WWII, will also reveal the relationship between democracy and institutionalized communication. As trust toward the government is declining in many parts of the world, such research is expected to contribute not only to the understanding of the history of public relations but also to the policy discussions over how government should communicate with the public in order to create a better, more democratic society.

References

Grunig, J. E., & Hunt, T. (1984). *Managing public relations*. New York, NY: Holt, Rinehart and Winston.

Ishihara ryu no hodo senryaku [Ishihara-style media strategy]. (2001, April 24). *Asahi Shimbun*.

Kushner, B. (2006). *The thought war: Japanese imperial propaganda*. Honolulu, HI: University of Hawaii Press.

Lamme, M. O., & Russell, K. M. (2010). Removing the spin: Toward a new theory of public relations history. *Journalism and Communication Monographs*, 11(4), 280–362.

Lee, M. (2014). Government is different: A history of public relations in American public administration. In St. John III, B., Lamme, M. O., & L'Etang, J. (Eds.), *Pathways to public relations: Histories of practice and profession* (pp. 108–127). London: Routledge.

Rodríguez-Salcedo, N., & Watson, T. (2017). The development of public relations in dictatorships -Southern and Eastern European perspectives from 1945 to 1990. *Public Relations Review*, 43(2), 375–381.

Tokyo Metropolitan Archives. (1996). *Tokyoto shokusei enkaku* [History of Office Organization in the Tokyo Metropolitan Government]. Tokyo: Tokyo Metropolitan Government.

Tokyo Metropolitan Archives. (n.d.). *Tokyoto shokusei enkaku* [History of Office Organization in the Tokyo Metropolitan Government]. Retrieved on January 10, 2018, from www.soumu.metro.tokyo.jp/01soumu/archives/0702enkaku.htm#t

Tokyo Metropolitan Government. (1995). *Toshi kiyo 36 senjika "Tocho" no koho katsudou* [Annals of the History of Tokyo 36 Wartime PR by the "Tokyo Government Office"]. Tokyo: Tokyo Metropolitan Government.

Tokyo Metropolitan Government. (2004). *Toshi shiryo syusei dai 4 kan bocho suru Tokyo shi* [Collection of Tokyo Metropolitan Government Archives Vol.4 Tokyo City Expands]. Tokyo: Tokyo Metropolitan Government.

Tokyo Metropolitan Government. (2008). *Toshi kiyo 40 zoku refarensu no Yashiro – Edo Tokyo Rekishi Mondou Sono 2* [Annals of the History of Tokyo 40, Office of Reference Part 2 -Q&A on Edo Tokyo History]. Tokyo: Tokyo Metropolitan Government.

Tsukada, H. (2002). *Tokyoto no shozo: Rekidai chiji ha nani wo nokoshitaka* [Portraits of Tokyo Metropolitan Government: What the Governors left behind]. Tokyo: Tosei Shinposha.

Uchino, M. (2004). *Showa no seifu koho: Sourifu Koho Shitsu tanjo* [Government PR During Showa Period: Birth of Cabinet PR Office]. Tokyo: Sankosha.

Vos, T. (2011). Explaining the origins of public relations: Logics of historical explanation. *Journal of Public Relations Research*, 23(2), 119–140.

Watson, T. (2015). What in the world is public relations? In Watson, T. (Ed.), *Perspectives on public relations historiography and historical theorization* (pp. 4–19). Basingstoke, Hampshire: Palgrave Macmillan.

4 The history of internal communications in Japanese companies

Masamichi Shimizu

Introduction

Today, nearly all listed large companies in Japan have tools of internal communication, such as corporate intranet or in-house magazines (Japan Institute for Social and Economic Affairs, 2015). However, despite its importance, the history of internal communication has rarely been discussed compared to that of external communication. In Japan, the historical literature on corporate public relations often mentions an in-house magazine published in 1903 by a leading cotton spinning company as the earliest known case of internal communication and refers to the 1950s as the time when such magazines spread among Japanese companies but does not discuss the history between the two or their relationship to today's practice. As all companies must communicate with their employees in one way or another and as Japan has experienced modernization and economic growth since the late 1800s, there seems to be a long history of internal communication practices that has not been documented or studied.

To understand the history of internal communication, this chapter focuses on in-house magazines. While in-house magazines are but one of many practices in internal communication, the fact that they have been regarded as one of the earliest examples of corporate public relations in Japan and the fact that they are currently being published by many companies imply that in-house magazines may be able to provide substantial insight into the history of internal communication.

The Japan Federation of Employers' Associations (JFEA) defined in-house magazines as publications issued indefinitely that report accurately, promptly, and comprehensively on various topics, such as management policy, issues inside and outside of the organization, and employees' voices, targeted toward employees in general, along with their family members, to improve communication within the organization and realize smooth management (JFEA, 1964b, p. 7).

JFEA's definition implies that in order to understand how in-house magazines originated and developed, one must understand their relationship with management, especially concerning human resources. By uncovering the history of in-house magazines between the early years of the 1890s and the peak of their publication in the 1970s, this chapter will discuss how early in-house magazines were conceived, how they grew and diversified, and how their editorial policy involved management concepts similar to those adopted from the United States after World War II.

For the historical research, the author referred to various in-house magazines and company histories for primary sources. The Shibusawa Shashi Database (SSD), a major database of company history that was made available in 2014, was used to search for in-house magazines and other internal communication practices. The SSD contains the table of contents, appendix, chronology, and index information of around 1,500 history publications by companies related to Eiichi Shibusawa (1840–1931), sometimes called the "father of Japanese capitalism," who is credited for introducing Western capitalism to Japan following the Meiji Restoration in 1868. While there are estimated to be around 15,000 company history publications in Japan, SSD is considered to be the most comprehensive company history database to date.

As L'Etang (2008) mentioned, "organizations often do not retain archives that would be useful to PR historians" (325). The problem is that as company histories are edited and published by the companies, they may not include records for in-house magazines or other types of internal communication, and they may downplay or even exclude inconvenient facts, such as labor-management confrontations that directly or indirectly led to changes in internal communication. Even with such limitations, company histories provide a starting point for further research into the understudied field of internal communication history.

On a side note, while there are many names for such publications, including house organs, house magazines, house journals, employee magazines, and employee newsletters, for the sake of simplicity, this chapter will use the term in-house magazines to refer to the group of publications defined by the JFEA.

The most comprehensive study of post-war in-house magazines in Japan was published in 1972 by the In-House Magazine Center of JFEA. JFEA (1972) described the development of internal communication beginning with the prehistory of in-house magazines before WWII, followed by the early period (1945–54), the development period (1955–64), and the enhancement period (1965–74). Ikeda (1970) and Ikari et al. (2015) have summarized the history of internal communication since the publication of the first in-house magazine in 1903, briefly describing the origin and the development of in-house magazines before WWII. What happened before or during WWII is often regarded as a prehistory that has little to do with the post-war development of in-house magazines. However, the fact that there was a substantial number of in-house magazines published before WWII and companies began publishing them soon after the war indicates a connection between the two periods.

In the following sections, the development of in-house magazines is described in chronological order.

The spread and diversity of pre-WWII in-house magazines

While there were in-house magazines before WWII, the pervasiveness of the publication practice remains a question. For example, according to Ikari et al. (2015), the in-house magazines were published before the war by only a small number of companies that focused on familial friendship and harmony within the company, and the history of the full-fledged publication of in-house magazines began in the 1950s (p. 27). However, Hazama (1964) noted that headquarters and branch offices of major companies published their own office reports and in-house magazines even before WWII, pointing out examples like the spinning companies Kanegafuchi and Nisshinbo, which published four and five different in-house magazines respectively. Leading companies had in-house magazines not only in their headquarters but also in individual factories. Hazama (1964) also noted that 20–30% of leading companies in the mining industry published such magazines, including the *Kyou-ai* (Mutual Affection) by the company Mitsui Kushikino and the *Kuro daia* (Black Diamond) by Mitsui Miike.

Hazama's examples show that the publication of in-house magazines was not a rare practice and that they were published along with company or factory reports. By researching the published histories of 302 companies that were established between the 19th and 20th centuries, the author found 105 companies that had records of publishing some kind of internal communication media before 1945. Considering the fact that the SSD does not contain all the published company histories, it is possible to assume that there were more companies that published in-house magazines.

Interestingly, the company histories use different words to describe in-house magazines, including *shaho* (company reports), *jumpo* (ten-day reports), *shoho* (office reports), *shonaiho* (in-office reports), *jiho* (timely reports), *gyoho* (practice reports), *giho* (technology reports), and *gijyutu kikanshi* (technology house organ). In general, shaho and shumpo focused on management information while jiho reported news on market and industry trends and giho reported technology-related news. These examples show the wide diversity of in-house magazines published before WWII.

By searching for a wide range of names for in-house magazines in SSD, it was possible to locate those that were published from the late 19th century. The following are three of the leading companies that published in-house magazines from such an early stage.

Nippon Life Insurance Company

According to Nippon Life Insurance Company (1963), in 1892, the company launched an in-house magazine called *Naniwa no Otozure* (Sound of

Naniwa). An interview with the company's PR department revealed that the magazine contained business reports and other information meant to foster friendship among the employees. The company also published *Shaho* (Company Report) in 1902, on the completion of the construction of their Osaka headquarters. Furthermore, Nippon Life Insurance Company created an editorial function in the general affairs division and assigned a company report officer to each department. The company report included official notices, letters of appointment, recruitment reports, various statistics, business regulations, miscellaneous articles, editorials, theories, and foreign insurance situations. The duodecimo-sized company report was published monthly with 40–50 pages. It was also sold to the public for 0.07–0.1 yen, which in today's value is roughly between 13 and 19 USD.

Itoh Thread and Yarn Store

As the sewing industry developed during the late 1800s, Chubei Itoh, the president of Itoh Thread and Yarn Store (currently the Itochu Corporation), recognized the need to export cotton products that were in overproduction and established a wholesale company. Itoh placed importance on communicating with the employees, having monthly and half-year meetings to present management-related information and gather employees' opinions. He famously advocated the "profit sharing among three parties," where the company pledged to invest its profit in the company business, customer service, and society; incorporated Western bookkeeping systems; and published a monthly magazine called *Jitsugyo* (the Business) in 1898, which became a leading magazine in the textile industry.

In terms of internal communication, Itochu also published *Honbu Jumpo* (Headquarters' Ten-Day Report) three times a month from 1909. The goal of the publication was to connect headquarters with branches in and out of the country, delivering information concerning the employees, orders from the headquarters, rules and instructions, business situations of each branch, reports from fact-finding tours and opinions on business (Usami, 2013).

Kanegafuchi Spinning

One of the most well-known case of early internal communication activities among Japanese companies was the in-house magazine published in 1903 by the leading cotton spinning company Kanegafuchi Spinning, targeted toward factory workers. Both JFEA (1972) and Ikari et al. (2015) describe the magazine as the beginning of modern corporate public relations in Japan.

Following the Meiji Restoration in 1868, the new government of Japan worked on transplanting and fostering modern industries, striving to nurture new industries through the development of industrial infrastructure and the establishment of government-owned factories. Among many rising

industries, the spinning industry achieved the most remarkable development. In the decade from 1887 to 1897, the number of workers in the spinning industry increased by 19 times (Arisawa & Yamaguchi, 1967). The
spinning industry hired many wives and daughters of the samurai who had
become unemployed as a result of the Meiji Restoration as well as many
poor farmers' children from rural areas to their labor force and "treated
them like slaves" (Hirschmeier & Yui, 1977, pp. 170–172). The competitive hiring environment also led to widespread labor piracy and refusal of
employee resignation.

In light of the harsh working environment, Sanji Muto, a manager of
a local factory who eventually became the president of Kanegafuchi Spinning, promoted a more humane working environment, which led to the
establishment of 39 employee welfare plans in five and a half years from
1902 to 1907. He was also dedicated to hiring skilled workers with higher
wages compared with his counterparts in other companies. Muto's attempts
improved company production and led to its growth (Hazama, 1964). By
1907, Kanegafuchi Spinning had approximately 12,000 employees, including skilled workers in 10 factories (Business History Society of Japan, 2004).

Publication of the first in-house magazines was part of Muto's improvement
plans. The magazine was created along the lines of *The N.C.R.*, the in-house
magazine of the National Cash Register, which had attracted his attention
when he was studying in the United States (JFEA, 1972). The magazine's goal
was not only to retain but also to recruit a labor force. In the first edition of
the magazine, Muto posted a statement about his labor-management policy,
including lifetime employment to tackle the labor shortage problem, and
about his editorial policy to report what had happened across the company
and communicate management's intentions to the workers.

Kanegafuchi's first in-house magazine was published twice a month from
June 1903. Originally, it was titled *Hyogo no Kiteki* (Hyogo's Steam Whistle) but was re-named a month later from the third edition as *Kanebo no
Kiteki* (Kanebo's Steam Whistle). A year later, Kanegafuchi also began publishing a new magazine for female employees called *Joshi no Tomo* (Friends
of Women).

The editors of the in-house magazine operated within the sales department. Interestingly, the magazine was not only distributed to the workers
in the company but was also sent to the local city office where the company
recruited workers. It was not only a tool for internal communication but
also for recruitment.

Pre-WWII management and in-house magazines

Kanegafuchi Spinning was but one of many companies that grew rapidly
during the late 19th century to the early 20th century. Expansion of the
business necessitated the improvement of production management. For
example, *The Principle of Scientific Management*, published in 1911 by

Frederick Taylor, was translated and published in Japanese by 1913. The book became popular among leading companies. Such efforts to improve management by large companies gradually led to the institutionalization of labor-management conference in the 1920s, where some companies went further and institutionalized the publication of in-house magazines as a tool for promoting communication between the management and labor.

According to Hirschmeier and Yui (1977), the lifetime employment system in Japan was established around the 1920s. In addition to lifetime employment, modern large-scale manufacturers, such as the heavy and chemical, spinning, paper, glass, cement, flour, and sugar industries, also adopted a similar training system and seniority-based wage system. These measures were aimed at fostering a sense of loyalty and solidarity, as well as retaining the supply of skilled workers.

Some large companies provided a variety of educational and cultural programs, including cooking, flower arrangement, and cultural education; supported the establishment of organizations such as those for employee savings schemes and for mutual aid; and incorporated a wide range of welfare policies, such as foundation anniversaries, company parties, employee travels, athletics meetings, cultural activities, and sports clubs. In-house magazines were published in order to mediate the implementation of these policies.

Post-war labor management and human relations theory

Although there was a considerable number of in-house magazines published before WWII, as the war progressed, many of such publications were discontinued either because of shrinking company activities or restrictions on the consumption of paper. The post-war revival of in-house magazines was slow during the late 1940s but gained speed after the 1950s. As a series of policies, including the 1949 monetary contraction policy, called the Dodge Line, were implemented to recover and stabilize the Japanese economy, companies were exposed to American management theories and practices, such as public relations and human relations, that provided the grounds for the post-war development of internal communication.

The concept of human relations, introduced as a way to humanize the working environment, was integrated with traditional Japanese familistic business management, eventually becoming popular among Japanese companies (Ueda, 1974, p. 154). In fact, according to Mizutani (1957), human relations theory was introduced and promoted between 1947 and 1951, was gradually implemented by leading companies, and became widely practiced after 1955.

Company managers became interested in human relations theories, as they had to confront the labor movement that was spreading rapidly after the war. Labor movements tried to change labor relations that were based on pre-war familial relationships and to promote the modernization of management, which expanded the rights of the workers.

In-house magazines that used to focus on familial relationships were inspired by the human relations theory that was meant to foster friendship among employees from informal aspects. In reality, however, the new in-house magazines were sometimes used as a sort of "paper bullet," a propaganda paper to counteract the labor movement (Ikeda, 1970).

Early cases of post-war in-house magazines

Although the ideas of publishing company reports for the purpose of informing employees about management policies and business situations and for improving communication and employee fellowship were often mentioned by previous literature as having been based on human relations theories introduced from the United States, some companies resumed their publication with similar goals even before the introduction of such new concepts. For example, the Matsushita Electric Industrial (currently the Panasonic Corporation) began publishing the in-house newspaper twice a month from May 1, 1946. The following five publication policies were spelled out in the first edition (translation by the author).

1   Inform all members about management policies.
2   Advocate fairness in management, disclose the situation, and inform all members.
3   Promote constructive contribution by all employees, reflect employees' collective opinion on management to realize management by all.
4   Disclose management-related research and report on company's situation.
5   Promote education, entertainment, physical exercise, and hobbies.

These policies indicate that while Japan was still under the Allied occupation and labor movements were becoming increasingly influential, some leading managers were already actively seeking to share information and promote welfare among the employees.

Matsushita Electric Industrial, founded in 1918, established an employee organization called *Hoichi-kai* (One-Step Society) in 1920 to promote employee welfare and familial relationships. A variety of employee events, including picnics and athletics meetings, were held. In 1927, the company launched a newsletter for the Hoichi-kai and later in 1934 published the internal newspaper *Matsushita Denki Shonai Shimbun* (Matsushita Electronics Internal Newspaper) to share the company's goals, purposes, and management information. Later, a monthly report was published for distributors not just to provide information for promotional tools but to gather demands and opinions from them (PHP, 1999). These pre-war practices laid the groundwork for the company's quick revival of post-war in-house magazines.

As the restrictions on paper usage were alleviated, more companies resumed their publications. In September 1949, the electric company Kanto

Haiden (currently the Tokyo Electric Power Company) separated sections such as sub-committee news and letters from employees from their traditional in-house magazine to be included in another independent magazine called the *Kanpai Bunka* (Kanto Haiden Culture). *Kanpai Bunka* was a magazine created by employees and their families. While the company report was published by the document management department, *Kanpai Bunka* was published by the culture section in the welfare department, as it was meant to benefit employee welfare (Ikeda, 1970).

Establishment of the PR Study Group

While companies set such positive editorial policies for in-house magazines, they were sometimes considered to be anti-union and drew strong protests from labor unions. In May 1952, JFEA launched the PR Study Group, which examined the ideal methods and editorial production technologies of in-house magazines and gathered publication officers from about fifty companies. In doing so, the JFEA attempted to shift the in-house magazine from anti-union media to a publication with four objectives: (1) establish a cooperative system based on communication and understanding, (2) improve employee capabilities, (3) foster friendship among employees, and (4) improve employee morale (Ueda, 1974, pp. 158–159).

Despite such efforts, it is widely believed that the purpose of in-house magazines at the time was to promote business by improving labor-management efficiency. According to a survey of in-house magazines between 1951 and 1954 that asked the goals of publication, "company business" was the most popular choice (88%), "products and technologies" was second (50%), and "workplace relations" was third (23%) (JFEA, 1972, p. 55).

According to the Shibaura Institute of Technology Management Science Research Group (1965), by 1952, 73% of the companies with employees numbering more than 1,000 and 52% of those with less than 1,000 published in-house magazines. In-house magazines had become an important part of publication by human resource departments.

A survey by the JFEA in 1953 revealed that the main policies of human relations management involved employee public relations, opinion and attitude surveys, human resource consultation, and complaint management. For internal communication, 86% of the respondents used in-house magazines, 67% used notice boards, 25% used employee notebooks, and 20% used pamphlets (JFEA, 1972, p. 53). The survey also revealed that companies at the time continued their pre-war familial management styles with various employee welfare systems that even targeted their family members.

In particular, promotional activities in internal communications by JFEA were becoming more noticeable by 1957. While PR study groups were established in local organizations of JFEA and in-house magazine promotion groups were formed in each industry, Kisaku Ikeda established an organization including journalists and launched the first All-Japan In-House Magazine

Competition in 1957. Twenty-nine companies applied for the first competition, and the long-established department store Daimaru won the first prize. Ikari et al. (2015) pointed out that the trigger of the in-house publication boom from the late 1950s was the aforementioned national competition of 1957 and that significant contributions were made by famous editors-in-chief of leading media, including the business magazine *Diamond Weekly*. The spread of publication practices to a variety of businesses attracted attention from the media, and articles such as "The Third Journalism: In-House Magazines" were published (Ikari et al., 2015, p. 125).

Table 4.1 shows that by 1958, there were diverse institutionalized methods for internal communication. In fact, there were 556 in-house magazines launched in the five years between 1956 and 1960, followed by 1,063 magazines between 1961 and 1965.

Five years later, JFEA tried to classify these diverse communication activities by the objectives, the nature of communication, and the interactive nature among individual methods (Table 4.2).

A factual survey was conducted at that time considering problems similar to today's internal communications issues. In the research report *Actual Condition of Internal Communications* (JFEA, 1959), Hiroki Imazato, president of NSK Limited and the chairman of JFEA's PR group, wrote that he recognized that the actual implementations of internal communication activities are diverse and that the format and contents must be improved, which requires a deep understanding and proactive support by executives along with the appropriate organizational structure and budget.

In the same report, Professor Tsuneo Ouchi of Rikkyo University wrote that internal communication should be considered from both technical and human-related aspects, and the first thing to do is to create a place where people can feel free to communicate. The second thing to do is to streamline document administration and service affairs, and the third is to study the means of communication.

With Ohuchi's recommendation, the 1964 edition of the report modified the classification for in-house magazines. In the new classification,

Table 4.1 JFEA internal communication survey items: February 1958

Print	In-house magazines, employee notebooks, wall newspapers, fliers, leaflets included in pay envelopes, posters, letters, pamphlets, calendars, household account books, etc.
Audio visual	Announcements on blackboards, displays, wireless/recorded broadcasts, movies, slides, picture-story show, etc.
Gathering	Morning meeting, briefing, lectures, get-together meetings with family members, etc.
Event	Memorial services, awards ceremonies, safety campaigns, new lifestyle campaigns, sports and cultural events, etc.
Other	House visit

Source: Data compiled from JFEA (1959, pp. 18–19). Translated by the author.

Table 4.2 Communication media within a company

		Personal communication	Collective communication	Mass communication
Purposeful communication	Operational and administrative	instructions/ command/ settlement (T), awards and punishments (T), reports/ advice/ suggestions (B)	notifications (T), trainings/ education/ conferences/ adjustments (H), suggestion systems (B)	regulations/ company notifications (T), bulletin boards/internal broadcasts (T), in-house magazines (TB)
	Human resource management	interviews (TB), morale surveys (TB), counseling (TB)	proposal system (B)	in-house magazines (TB)
Spontaneous communication		chatting/ greetings (H), complaints (B)	rumors (H)	in-house magazines (TB)
Other		Communication by labor union		

T = top down, B = bottom up, TB = top-down and bottom-up, H = horizontal communication

Source: Data compiled from JFEA (1964b, p. 6). Translated by the author.

magazines were classified on the vertical axis from personal to collective to mass communication and on the horizontal axis from purposeful, operational and administrative practices and human resource management to spontaneous communication and other. Each practice was classified according to the direction of communication, from top-down to bottom-up and horizontal, where people share information among themselves.

JFEA did different research in 1958, where it surveyed not only publication and audio-visual materials but also a wider range of communication practices, including morning gatherings, training sessions, lectures, events, ceremonies, sporting events, cultural events, and employee field trips.

JFEA's decision to broaden the scope of internal communication may be seen as a pioneering understanding of internal communications. Five years later, JFEA classified internal communication according to media type. Some of the media tools included in the classification, from today's perspective, may be considered as being beyond the field of internal communication.

JFEA established the in-house magazine organization called the JFEA In-House Magazine Center in November 1962 as an alternative to the PR Study Group. The center held a national convention to promote the dissemination of their concept; published monthly data collection, theory, and practice books; and held seminars for producing and editing in-house magazines.

Between 1966 and 1969, the number of new magazine launches remained at 908. The publication boom of in-house magazines during the 1950s and 1960s changed its course through the economic crisis and the resulting slow economic growth triggered by the two oil crises during the 1970s. Many companies reduced their budgets and staff for in-house magazines and combined various PR-related departments in order to restructure PR functions.

Paths of development since the 1970s

The first oil crisis of 1973 ended the rapid economic growth that had continued since the 1950s, and many companies had to focus on cost-cutting measures. As the budgets for internal communications and in-house magazines were cut, practitioners began to shift toward new communication technologies. This brought about a movement to replace the conventional printed company reports and in-house magazines with new media. Since then, there has been continuous interest in new media, such as video in the 1970s, computer communication in the 1980s, and the Internet since the 1990s. In the 1970s and 1980s, company internal communications, which were temporarily focused on the deployment of company identity in response to the diversification of company management, showed a tendency toward media diversity rather than content diversity.

For example, the famous department store Isetan launched *Shaho Isetan* (Company Report Isetan) in 1957 and separated it into three publications in 1989 to promote reform through improving employee awareness. The three were a traditional company report *TVi*, a bi-monthly house magazine, and the semi-monthly report *i Press* for managers. This increased the efficiency of dissemination by refining the targets of PR methods.

Recruit Holdings Co., Ltd., founded in 1963, published about a hundred types of department news and branch office news through the in-house magazine *Kamome* (Seagull) and distributed video news. This created vertical, horizontal, and diagonal internal communication in the company. The company also held a competition once a year for the small in-house magazines published by individual departments to promote the creation of new employee relationships.

Conclusion

This chapter discussed the history of internal communication by looking at the development of in-house magazines from the 1890s to 1980s. The main findings can be summarized in four points.

First, although previous research on the history of internal communication in Japan has categorized the period before WWII as prehistory, as discussed in this chapter, the fact that in-house magazines were published for managerial purposes, such as improving business notifications and promoting management education and friendship among the employees, even before WWII, implies that in order to fully understand the development, spread, and changes of internal communication, it is necessary to uncover historical practices and analyze them from managerial perspectives from the 1890s.

Second, the reflection of new employee relationships, redefined from human relations theory, to the in-house magazines after WWII and the incorporation of journalistic interview methods and layout technology from the mass media industry in the 1960s reflected the growing needs of employees in the age of rapid economic growth, leading to the spread of in-house magazines. The development of in-house magazines was in no small part due to the JFEA and other organizations that provided training and promoted the practice. One major characteristic of in-house magazines in Japan is that they are written and published by employees who acquire journalistic skills after they are assigned to the role, unlike in countries like the US, where former journalists are often hired as professionals to be the editor of such magazines.

Third, in-house magazines developed and spread rapidly during the 1950s and 1960s but slowed down during the 1970s because of the oil crisis, when companies began using audiovisual media, such as television and video for internal communication. The diversification of internal communication media has continued since, and today, print, audiovisual, and online media are used to deliver a wide range of content.

Finally, the collapse of the bubble economy in the 1990s, which had far greater impact on the economy compared to the oil crisis of the 1970s, led to further cutbacks in in-house magazine publications. Surveys and publications on in-house magazines have decreased since, leading to a lack of understanding about how internal communication adapted to the age of the Internet and how today's complex and diversified world of internal communication may be evaluated.

Today's companies are active in complex and diverse environments. Human resources that make up the company also have diverse backgrounds and ways to work as well. In order to achieve strategic goals under such conditions, companies are developing various internal communications. The internal communication represented by the in-house magazine, which is discussed in this chapter, has come to possess many different aspects in recent years. In response to this situation, various departments, such as corporate planning, human resources, corporate social responsibility, and general affairs, are conducting internal communications in relation to the responsibility of each department. It is no longer an era when internal communication is sufficiently implemented only by the public relations department.

It is under such a reality that historical studies on internal communication are expected to not only track the development of individual practices but to grasp the transition of internal communication policies as part of management, draw out prospects for the future, and contribute to the development of management strategies.

References

Arisawa, H., & Yamaguchi, K. (Eds.). (1967). *Nihon sangyo 100 nenshi* [100-Year History of Industries in Japan]. Tokyo: Nikkei BP.

Business History Society of Japan. (2004). *Nihon keizaishi no kiso chishiki* [Fundamentals of Japanese Management History]. Tokyo: Yuhikaku.

Hazama, H. (1964). *Nihon romu kanrishi kenkyu* [The History of Labor Management in Japan]. Tokyo: Diamond.

Hirschmeier, J., & Yui, T. (1977). *Nihon no keiei hatten: kindaika to kigyo keiei* [Development of Management in Japan: Modernization and Corporate Management]. Tokyo: Toyo Keizai Shimpo.

Ikari, S., Ogawa, M., Kitano, K., Kenmochi, T., Morito, N., & Hamada, I. (2015). *Zouhoban Nihon no kouhou PR no 100 nen* [A hundred years of public relations in Japan, augmented edition]. Tokyo, Japan: Douyukan.

Ikeda, K. (1970). *Botomu appu shanaiho nyumon* [Introduction to Bottom-up In-House Magazine]. Tokyo: Institute of Industrial Labor Research.

Japan Federation of Employers' Associations. (Ed.). (1959). *Shanai kommunication no jissai* [Actual Conditions of Internal Communication]. Tokyo: Japan Federation of Employers' Associations.

Japan Federation of Employers' Associations. (1964a). *Oubei no shanaiho jijyo: daiikkai chosadann houkokusyo* [In-House Magazines in the US and Europe: First study Mission Report]. Tokyo: Japan Federation of Employers' Associations.

Japan Federation of Employers' Associations. (1964b). *Shanaiho: riron to jissen* [In-House Magazine: Theory and Practice]. Tokyo: Japan Federation of Employers' Associations.

Japan Federation of Employers' Associations. (1972). *Nihon no shanaiho no ayumi* [History of In-House Magazines in Japan]. Tokyo: Japan Federation of Employers' Associations.

Japan Institute for Social and Economic Affairs. (2015). *Dai 12 kai kigyo no kouhou katudo ni kansuru ishiki jittai cyosa houkokusyo* [12th Survey Report on the Mindset Toward Corporate PR Practice]. Tokyo: Japan Institute for Social and Economic Affairs.

L'Etang, J. (2008). Writing PR history: Issues, methods and politics. *Journal of Communication Management*, 12, 319–335.

Mizutani, M. (1957). Wagakuni no ningen kankei kanri no genjo to mondaiten [Current status and issues of Japan's human relationship management]. In *Japan Employers' Associations Federation, Huuman Rireshonzu* [Human Relations]. Tokyo: Japan Employers' Associations Federation.

Nippon Life Insurance Company. (1963). *Nippon Seimei 70 nenshi* [70-Year History of Nippon Life Insurance Company]. Tokyo: Nippon Life Insurance Company.

PHP Institute. (1999). *Kiiwado de yomu Matsushita Konosuke handobukku* [Reading Konosuke Matsushita Handbook Through Keywords]. Tokyo: PHP Institute.

Shibaura Institute of Technology Management Science Research Group. (1965). *Gendai kigyo keiei to shanaiho* [Contemporary Corporate Management and In-House Magazines]. Tokyo: Ochanomizu Shobo.

Ueda, T. (1974). *Kigyonai komunication* [Corporate Internal Communication]. Tokyo: Nikkei BP.

Usami, H. (2013). Ito "Honbu Jumpo" ni tuite [On Ito's "Headquarter ten-day report"]. *Bulletin of Archival Museum, Faculty of Economics, Shiga University*, 46, 49–58.

5 (Under-) development of the PR industry and profession

Yusuke Ibuki

Research question: why is the PR industry in Japan underdeveloped?

The purpose of this chapter is to explore how and why the public relations industry and its profession in Japan developed (or did not develop) in the way they did. The country became the second largest economic power in the world in 1968, surpassing the then West Germany, and Japan kept its status until 2010 (Chuugoku GDP, 2011). Still today, it is the third largest economy in the world. As a country under democracy and capitalism, public relations activities took hold in Japan after World War II and have continued to develop since then. However, research papers that give an accurate picture of the situation of public relations in Japan in non-Japanese languages are very few, if not nonexistent. Therefore, even if it is true that "Japan's PR industry remains under-developed compared to that of the United States," as stated by Cooper-Chen and Tanaka (2007, p. 94), it is difficult for people outside of Japan to understand why the industry is underdeveloped or why public relations activities can be conducted despite the lack of a mature PR industry. There are two reasons for this. One is the language barrier. Many Japanese researchers in the social sciences publish their work mainly in Japanese. Public relations is no exception. The other reason is that research on the historical development of public relations in Japan has only begun recently. The Japan Society for Corporate Communication Studies, the major organization for PR research in Japan, was established in 1995. It ran a research project on the history of public relations in Japan in 2006, and the results of the research project were reported in 2008 (PR History Research Group, 2008) and later published as a book in 2011 (Ikari et al., 2011, 2015).

With this as a backdrop, we will try to clarify in this chapter the factors for the (under-) development of the public relations industry and its professions in Japan, with reference to Ikari et al. (2015) and other research papers written in Japanese. In anticipation of the conclusion, the reason the public relations industry and its professions are underdeveloped is because of (1) the big power of advertising companies and (2) the lack of a professionalization trend in society as a whole. In this chapter, the PR industry is defined as an industry comprising companies that provide public relations support services as their main business. Advertising agencies and companies that provide public relations support services as a peripheral part of their businesses are not included in the PR industry.

The role of Dentsu in introducing PR to Japan

The prototype of public relations in Japan was born in the Meiji Era when popular newspapers appeared and mass communication was established (Ikari et al., 2015). The first public relations department at Japanese companies was born in 1923 to the South Manchurian Railroad (Ikari, 1998; Mantetsukai, 2007), but a full-fledged introduction of public relations took place after World War II.

After the defeat of World War II, public relations was introduced to Japan through four routes (Ikari, 1998; Ikari et al., 2015). Among them, the "Dentsu route" is the focus of this chapter. Dentsu is now the largest advertising company in Japan and the fifth largest group of advertising companies in the world (AdAge, 2017). Dentsu (then Nippon Denpo Tsushin Sha [Japan Telegraph and News Agency Corporation]), the largest advertising company in Japan at the time, announced "Interim Operating Policies" consisting of six items in February 1946, shortly after the defeat (Dentsu, 1968). The first policy was the "implementation and promotion of commercial broadcasting and any and every project and preparation necessary for that end." And the second policy was the "introduction and popularization of public relations (PR) that broadens the framework and design of advertising and promotion."

Regarding the first policy, the first radio broadcasting in Japan had already started in 1925 by Nippon Hoso Kyokai [Japan Broadcasting Corporation] (hereafter NHK); however, NHK was a public broadcasting station and was operating with subscription fees[1] without carrying commercial advertisements. In Japan-controlled Manchuria, commercial broadcasting had been in place since before the end of World War II, and Dentsu was engaged in advertising sales at its Manchurian branch (Ikari et al., 2015). After Japan lost the war, Hideo Yoshida, the senior executive director of Dentsu, who, at the time, practically managed the business and later became the president in 1947, gathered people from the business field and applied for the establishment of "The broadcasting private limited company" in December 1945, but it was rejected by the General Headquarters of the Supreme Commander for the Allied Powers (hereafter GHQ) because of the prematurity of the socio-economic conditions (Kitano, 2008). Dentsu had experience marketing radio broadcasting in Manchuria and had anticipated that the era of television would come in the near future. It was necessary for Dentsu to materialize commercial broadcasting in order to expand their advertising business. That was concretely shown as their first policy.

The first commercial radio broadcasts began in 1951, the first television broadcasts by NHK began in February 1953, and the commercial television broadcasts began in August 1953. Dentsu deeply committed itself to the establishment of commercial broadcasting stations, which would ensure their prosperity as an advertising company.

Regarding the second policy, the introduction and popularization of PR, it is not clear why Yoshida emphasized (or could emphasize) public relations at that time. Ikari et al. (2015, p. 65, translated by the author) suspects that "Yoshida, who saw the way advertising companies existed before WWII as questionable, may have wanted to place the concept of public relations at the center of the advertising philosophy of the future." Regardless of his motive, in 1946, Yoshida included the introduction of public relations in the action policy and placed it as the second among six policies. It implied the importance Yoshida placed on public relations. Later, Dentsu supported the implementation of the "Public Relations Workshop" sponsored by the Civil Information and Educational Section of GHQ. During an "Advertising Workshop" sponsored by Dentsu, Kanjiro Tanaka, who was assigned by Yoshida to engage in a study about PR, gave a lecture on public relations (Ikari et al., 2015). In his lecture, Tanaka (1949, as cited in Ikari et al., 2015, pp. 86–87) mentioned that the whole process of public relations was as follows: (1) in order for a company to be accepted by the society, corporate activities must align with the public interest, and (2) society needs to be informed of such activities. The proactive introduction of PR by Dentsu, which already had close relationships with many enterprises and government agencies through the advertising business, built the foundation for public relations activities in Japan.

One-stop service by advertising companies

For the PR industry in Japan, what does Dentsu's active involvement with public relations mean? It means that advertising companies like Dentsu came to play a role as a PR agency, rather than specialized PR agencies forming the PR industry independent of the advertising companies. There are three implications of this fact.

The first implication is that there is a tendency for public relations in Japan to be perceived as a part of a marketing function (Ikari et al., 2015; Yamamura et al., 2013). As successor to Kanjiro Tanaka, Hideo Yoshida gave Juichi Odani a special assignment to study public relations theory. He said in 1959, "Marketing is a concept that includes PR, of course. There is PR within the functions of marketing. We need to think so. Advertising also must be within the functions of marketing" (Ikari et al., 2015, p. 80, translated by the author). In 1955, the Japan Productivity Center sent a mission to the US, and they brought the concept of marketing back to Japan (Ikari et al., 2015). According to Shibuya (1991), the dawn of public relations in Japan ended in 1952, because of the poor performance of public relations activities. One of the reasons was that, in the days when the country was short of various supplies, newspapers had a very small number of pages, and there was no space for post-corporate-originated news unless it had a tremendously high news value (Ikari et al., 2015). Even today in Japan, publicity is often mistaken for public relations, and it is positioned by advertising companies as one aspect of the promotion mix. If public relations is a part of marketing and promotion, it does not necessarily form an independent industry. Instead, large advertising companies that engage in marketing and promotion also handle public relations activities as part of the marketing mix for their clients.

The second implication is that in Japan, unlike in the United States and other foreign countries, advertising companies exist as "communication companies" that are not just "advertising companies." Kobayashi (1998) described the development of advertising companies in Japan in four stages: ad space sales representatives, ad space brokerages, comprehensive advertising agencies, and communications companies that include a consulting function. While advertising companies in Western countries act mainly as "advertising agencies," advertising companies in Japan act as "communications companies" that not only execute space brokerage, ad planning, and ad creation, but also provide management counsel to their clients regarding their business and communication strategy. In the United States, in 1993, integrated marketing communication (hereafter IMC) was proposed by Schultz et al. (1993), but in Japan, it has been common to capture advertising broadly right from the very early stage of the development of advertising companies (Kobayashi, 2010). For Japanese advertising companies, IMC was not a new concept (Kobayashi, 1998). In other words, since there had been a common recognition that public relations is one of the advertising companies' activities, the space available for other companies to enter the field as specialized PR agencies was limited. For advertisers, it is easier to build relationships with advertising companies that provide various services altogether.

The third implication is that advertising agencies (in particular, Dentsu), through their ability to identify sponsors, had a strong influence on the program formation at television and radio stations. They were also essential partners for broadcasting stations when implementing events. Public relations doesn't just involve issuing news releases. Holding events is one of the important activities of public relations, and mass media plays a big role as a co-organizer or a supporter of events because they have the ability to publicize events effectively. In particular, because Dentsu was deeply involved in the establishment and operation of radio stations and television stations as described earlier, the company was better able to obtain support from mass media for various events of which it was a part. From the advertisers' perspective, advertising companies, not specialized PR companies, were more favorable partners since they could leverage their relationships with mass media.

Some entrepreneurial booms in the PR industry in Japan

As we have seen, one of the reasons why the PR industry in Japan has been underdeveloped compared with those of other countries is the presence of large advertising companies such as Dentsu. Of course, this doesn't mean that public relations agencies didn't exist in Japan. Some of them specialized in PR activities under advertising companies as subcontractors. Some others engaged in PR activities in niche areas where large advertising companies could not afford to take an interest. These PR agencies have been active since after the end of World War II. According to the Public Relations Society of Japan (PRSJ), it is estimated that there are about 200 PR agencies in Japan (2015). There have been a few entrepreneurial booms in the PR industry in Japan (Ikari et al., 2015). In this section, we will give a brief introduction to them.

Some of the first-generation PR agencies in Japan had strong ties to the US. The first PR agency in Japan, Georgia Day and Associates, was founded in 1949 by Mrs. Day, the information department director of the American Red Cross Far East Headquarters. In 1952, Falcon Advertising and PR started its business. The president of Falcon was an American woman named Rose C. Falkenstein, and the clients of the company were foreign governments and businesses, including the US Department of Commerce, the US Department of Agriculture, the Tourist Bureau of India, Dow Chemical, Goodyear, Scandinavian Airlines, and A&O Orient Line (Morito, 2008). Taro Fukuda, who founded Japan Public Relations, was a second-generation Japanese American born in the United States and had experience working for GHQ as a translator. Yoshitaka Horiuchi, who established Socio Atomic PR in 1962, was born in Hawaii and had a graduate degree from the University of California. Yasuharu Ohara, who founded International Public Relations in 1957, was a person who worked abroad after obtaining an MBA from the University of California. At that time, when Japan was under the control of the US-led Allied forces, people with "English proficiency" were highly regarded, and for the first generation of PR agencies, proximity to the United States, contact with GHQ, and English proficiency were indispensable.

The establishment of the domestic business-oriented first-generation PR agencies started in the late 1950s. The first domestic business-oriented PR agency, the predecessor of Intelligence Idea Center, was founded in 1957. Dentsu PR Center, the predecessor of Dentsu Public Relations, the largest PR agency in Japan today, was founded in 1961 by Hisamitsu Nagata.[2] Nagata introduced concepts from advertising, such as ad value equivalency, to the practice of public relations. In the same year, Hakuhodo, the second largest advertising company in Japan, established a public relations division. One of the last of this generation was Ozma, which was founded in 1963 by Isao Yanagi.

The second-generation PR agencies were established from the mid-1960s to the late-1970s. Whether they were domestic or international, the main activities of the first-generation PR agencies were primarily publicity. In contrast, the second-generation PR agencies developed their capability to conduct investigations on social trends and provided risk management consulting, reflecting issues and problems at that time, such as pollution. In those days, Japanese companies were suffering from a deteriorated relationship with society.

A match-up was formulated around this time that PR agencies cooperate with advertising agencies on specialized problems that could not be solved within advertising companies only. When large advertising companies were assigned a comprehensive communication package, sometimes they were unable to solve certain problems that required special expertise. To solve such issues, tie-ups between advertising companies and PR agencies emerged around this time (Ikari et al., 2015). Companies founded around this time include Kyodo Public Relations (in 1964) and Inoue Public Relations (in 1970). This generation was characterized by a wide variety of their range of operations, from full-service agencies to specialized agencies.

In 1975, the Japan PR Agencies Association was established by domestic-oriented PR agencies as an industry organization. In 1980, it merged with Japan PR Association, which was established in 1964 as an individual membership organization by practitioners of international-oriented PR agencies. The merged entity became the Public Relations Society of Japan (PRSJ), which is still active today.

After the rather quiet period following the so-called oil shock of the late 1970s and early 1980s, the third-generation PR agencies emerged in the late 1980s and early 1990s. Unlike their predecessors, which strove to be comprehensive service providers based on media relations expertise, each of the third-generation PR agencies seemed to promote their unique advantages, such as event promotion, sports management, investor relations, health care, regional promotion, and strategic PR planning, within integrated marketing communications (Morito, 2008).

In the 2000s, reflecting the popularization of the Internet, many PR agencies emerged specializing in web PR, and existing PR agencies were also forced to respond to the move. In addition, the advent of the Internet inevitably blurred the boundary among advertising, public relations, and marketing. As a result, advertising companies began putting more emphasis on activities in and around PR, such as the utilization of social media (as opposed to business models based on media purchase commission) in a way similar to how they incorporated PR during the post-World War II period.

Thus far, we have looked at the development of the PR industry in Japan. Here, we would like to take a look at the size of the current PR industry in Japan, based on the "PR industry survey" conducted by PRSJ (PRSJ, 2015). The estimated turnover of the Japanese PR industry in 2012 was 90.1 billion yen (approximately US$766.8 million at 117.5). This did not include sales of the PR divisions at advertising companies. As mentioned earlier, advertising companies play an important role in public relations activities in Japan. Consequently, the real market size is much larger, although the figure cannot be obtained. The Japanese PR industry is also characterized by the fact that there are many relatively small companies: about 55% of companies have sales of 500 million yen (approximately US$4.25 million at 117.5) or less, and about 90% of companies have less than 100 employees.

Are the requirements of the profession fulfilled?

So far, we have looked at organizational factors that influence the degree of (under-) development of the PR industry in Japan. However, organizational factors alone don't provide enough information to analyze the PR industry. A PR agency is a company that provides intellectual services. Therefore, it is important for PR agencies to regard their employees as valuable individuals, treat them as valuable resources, and to be recognized by society as an industry having excellent human resources. Such a reputation will eventually lead to a healthy development of the industry. In other words, the healthy development of the PR industry depends on whether public relations practitioners in Japan are regarded as professional or not. If public relations practitioners are not regarded as professional, PR doesn't need to exist as an industry, because anyone could do similar work in this field.

According to Cornelissen (2008), the requirements of a profession are (1) the existence of systematic knowledge ("systematic knowledge"), (2) the existence of a code of ethics that leads the practice ("code of ethics"), and (3) the existence of a qualification certification ("certification"). What is the current situation of these three points in Japan?

We will look first at the "code of ethics" and the "certification." As mentioned earlier, PRSJ was established in 1980 and is actively working to improve the status of the PR industry. One of the efforts PRSJ has made is the enactment of the Code of Ethics. In 1983 PRSJ established the first Code of Ethics and revised it in 2016. They provided practitioners with guidance on what is ethical public relations work. In 2007, PRSJ also launched the "PR Planner Qualification Certification System." As of 2016, the number of certified PR planners was more than 2,000. From these facts, we can say that at least two of the three requirements of the profession are satisfied in Japan. PRSJ plays a great role here.

In the United States and other major countries, public relations are systematically taught in journalism schools and communication schools. For example, PRSSA has about 350 chapters throughout the United States. If a university wants to establish a PRSSA chapter, it has to have at least five public relations courses, which is shown in the CPRE guidebook called "Professional Bond." Through this mechanism, throughout the United States, students studying public relations are ready to receive a systematic public relations education.

How about systematic knowledge of PR in Japan? Much of the body of knowledge on public relations is common all over the world, and it has

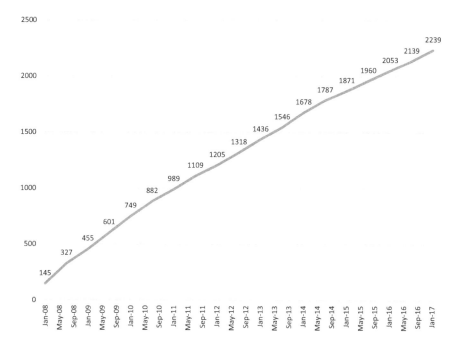

Figure 5.1 The number of certificated PR planners

been introduced to Japan. On top of that, there are country-specific bodies of knowledge, and they have accumulated in Japan, although mainly in the Japanese language. However, accumulating the knowledge physically is not enough. Each individual practitioner has to have such knowledge in him- or herself. To that end, what is necessary is a systematic public relations education.

However, in Japan, the systems of human resource management, in particular recruiting (simultaneous recruiting for new graduates) and the job rotation, are different from those of many other countries, and there is less need for professional education. Consequently, few universities have a systematic public relations program with multiple public relations-related courses (Ibuki, 2016; Miyabe, 2016). Public relations is often taught in schools of management or sociology, and in most cases, there is only one course for public relations in the school, which is an elective. Also, because many companies hire new graduates without pre-determining the jobs they will be assigned,[3] people in the public relations departments of companies, governments, or NPOs do not necessarily have a public relations education from their universities. The situation is also the same for PR agencies. Ibuki (2013) showed that more than 80% of public relations practitioners at PR agencies, who are generally regarded as professionals in other countries, haven't studied public relations at university. Despite such a lack of professional education, half of the survey respondents started working for PR agencies immediately after graduating from university. This means that there are a large number of PR practitioners who began their careers without any professional education. Most PR agencies are small in scale, and they don't hire new graduates. The previously mentioned PR agency employees started working for a limited number of medium- to large-scale PR agencies. Consequently, the general career path for new graduates who want to enter the public relations field has not been established. Those who work for PR agencies are often hired as a mid-career recruitment. Before joining an agency, they were in corporate, working for other agencies, or they were experienced journalists. According to Ibuki (2013), among practitioners working for PR agencies, less than 30% think that structured knowledge and skills learned through lectures are necessary to work for PR agencies. At the same time, close to 70% think that structured knowledge differentiates professionals from others. This implies that structured knowledge is regarded, not as explicit knowledge, but as implicit knowledge. This also is proof that public relations education in Japan is either inadequate or not thorough. Such a situation is not limited to PR. Many corporate employees in accounting sections or legal sections don't necessarily have professional educations or qualifications.

To sum up, in Japan, we can say that public relations has not long been regarded as a true profession. Although PRSJ has been making efforts to improve the situation in recent years, the social perception that public relations is a professional job has not been sufficiently established. This, in addition to the big presence of advertising agencies, is a factor that shows the PR industry is underdeveloped in Japan.

Future development of the PR industry and professions in Japan

In this chapter, we investigated why the PR industry has not matured in Japan despite it being the third largest economy in the world. Based on recent research results, we see two reasons: "the big power of advertising companies" and "the lack of a professionalization trend in society as a whole." In general, there is no one fixed path for industry development. Various factors are intertwined in each country or region, and a historical path dependence occurs. What was shown in this chapter is mostly Japan-specific; however, if we look at each of these factors, they may well be applicable to other countries because public relations activities in Japan were not necessarily inactive.

The situation has been changing in recent years. We are now in the process of digitization and globalization, and there is a big trend of what has been developed by following various paths converging into one (Ohe, 2004). The development of information and communication technology has prompted the professionalization of public relations functions, and the progress of globalization may have led to pressure on businesses to follow the global standard. Changes in the educational and employment environment accompanying the reduction of the population due to an aging society may also be affecting the professionalization of public relations. In response to these changes, the PR industry in Japan helped establish an academic society for public relations and established a qualification certification system. We need to watch where the PR industry in Japan will go next.

Notes

1 Even now, NHK doesn't broadcast commercial advertising. Many countries allow public broadcasting to earn advertising revenue, but in Japan, because of the regulations of the broadcasting laws, advertisement broadcasting cannot be implemented by NHK.
2 Hideo Yoshida, president of Dentsu, died in 1963, but at the time of the establishment of the Dentsu PR Center, he was still the fourth president of Dentsu.
3 In Japan, especially in the case of recruiting new graduates, a company first hires people in the sense that they will be members of the company, and after that, it assigns them to one of the departments (Hamaguchi, 2013). Therefore, the company wants the new graduates to be "white handkerchief," and it brings them up with on-the-job training. In recent years, a change has gradually occurred, but this recruiting system is still the mainstream of recruiting systems for new graduates at Japanese companies. See Appendix 3 for details.

References

AdAge. (2017, May). The agency report. *AdAge*, 20–26.
Chugoku GDP, sekai 2i kakujitsuni, Nihon, 42nen buri tennraku: 10 nen 2 keta seichou [GDP of China will surely go up to the second place in the world, Japan will drop to the third for the first time in 42 years: Two-digit growth in the past 10 years]. (2011, January 20). *Nihon Keizai Shimbun*. Retrieved on April 17, 2016, from www.nikkei.com/article/DGXNASGM1905R_Q1A120C1000000/
Cooper-Chen, A., & Tanaka, M. (2007). Public relations in Japan: The cultural roots of kouhou. *Journal of Public Relations Research*, 20(1), 94–114.
Cornelissen, J. (2008). *Corporate communication: A guide to theory and practice* (2nd edition). London: Sage.
Dentsu, Inc. (1968). *Dentsu 66 nen shi* [66 Years History of Dentsu]. Tokyo: Dentsu PR.
Hamaguchi, K. (2013). *Wakamono to rodo: "Nyusha" no shikumi kara tokihogusu* [Youth and Labor: Unravel the Mechanism of "Entering the Company"]. Tokyo: Chuokoron shinsha.
Ibuki, Y. (2013). PR ejenshi niokeru kouhou senmonshoku no kyaria keisei: teiryou chousa no tanjyun shukei bunseki wo chusin ni [Career development of public relations professionals in the Japanese public relations agencies: On frequency distribution analysis]. *Bulletin of Institute for Comprehensive Research, Kyoto Sangyo University*, 8, 93–101.
Ibuki, Y. (2016, March). When in Japan, do as the Japanese do: Public relations education for undergraduates, job-hunting process, and professionalism in Japan. Paper presented at the *19th annual International Public Relations Research Conference*, Miami, FL.

Ikari, S. (Ed.). (1998). *Kigyo no hatten to kouhou senryaku: 50 nen no ayumi to tenbou* [Development of Corporations and Public Relations Strategy: 50-year History and Foresight]. Tokyo: Nikkei BP Planning.

Ikari, S., Ogawa, M., Kitano, K., Kenmochi, T., Morito, N., & Hamada, I. (2011). *Nihon no kouhou PR no 100 nen* [A hundred years of public relations in Japan]. Tokyo, Japan: Douyukan.

Ikari, S., Ogawa, M., Kitano, K., Kenmochi, T., Morito, N., & Hamada, I. (2015). *Zouhoban Nihon no kouhou PR no 100 nen* [A hundred years of public relations in Japan, augmented edition]. Tokyo, Japan: Douyukan.

Kitano, K. (2008). Koukoku gaisha ni okeru PR kanren bumon no rekishiteki tenkai [Historical development of the departments on public relations in advertising agencies]. In PR History Research Group. (Ed.), *Nihon no kouhou PR shi kenkyu* [Japanese PR History Research] (pp. 37–84). Tokyo: Japan Society for Corporate Communication Studies.

Kobayashi, Y. (1998). *Koukoku bijinesu no kouzou to tenkai: akaunto puranningu kakushin* [Structure and Development of Advertising Industry: Account Planning Revolution]. Tokyo: Nikkei Advertising Research Institute.

Kobayashi, Y. (2010). Koukoku no kongen kinou to yukue wo kangaeru [A Thought on the Basic Function and the Future Direction of Advertising]. In Nikkei Advertising Research Institute (Ed.), *Kiso kara manaberu koukoku no sougou kouza* [Comprehensive Advertising Lectures from Basics]. Tokyo: Nikkei Advertising Research Institute.

Mantetsukai. (2007). *Mantetsu 40 nen shi* [40 Years History of South Manchurian Railroad]. Tokyo: Yoshikawa Kobunkan.

Miyabe, J. (2016, March). Job Rotation and Career Path of PR Managers: HRM and PR in Japanese Companies. Paper presented at the *19th annual International Public Relations Research Conference*, Miami, FL.

Morito, N. (2008). PR gyokai zenhan shi 1948–1979 [First half of the history of PR Industry 1948–1979]. In PR History Research Group (Ed.), *Nihon no kouhou PR shi kenkyu* [Japanese PR History Research] (pp. 204–259), Tokyo: Japan Society for Corporate Communication Studies.

Ohe, T. (2004). Keizai grobaruka to ruuru no touitsu [Globalization of the economy and unification of the rules]. *Chosa to Jyouhou* [Research and Information], 17. Retrieved from www.nochuri.co.jp/report/pdf/r0407top.pdf

PR History Research Group (Ed.). (2008). *Nihon no kouhou PR shi kenkyu* [Japanese PR history research]. Tokyo: Japan Society for Corporate Communication Studies.

Public Relations Society of Japan. (2015, May). *2015 nen PR gyo jittai chousa* [2015 PR industry survey report]. Retrieved from http://prsj.or.jp/wp-content/uploads/2015/05/022ceb90138943a79aafb1fce7ff12ba.pdf

Schultz, D. E., Tannenbaum, S. I., & Lauterborn, R. F. (1993). *Integrated marketing communications: Pulling it together & making it work*. Lincolnwood, IL: McGraw Hill Professional.

Shibuya, S. (1991). *Taishu sosa no keifu* [Genealogy of Mass Manipulation]. Tokyo: Keiso Shobo.

Yamamura, K., Ikari, S., & Kenmochi, T. (2013). Historic evolution of public relations in Japan. *Public Relations Review*, 39(2), 147–155.

6 A tale of two professionalisms

Human resource management (HRM) and the PR function of Japanese companies[1]

Junichiro Miyabe

Introduction

Organization and manager of PR function

In this chapter, we first present an overview of the development of public relations functions in Japanese companies after World War II, focusing on organizational structure and human resources assigned to the function. For Japanese companies, the public relations functions have been practiced for a long time as discussed in Chapters 1, 3, and 4. However, in most cases, it was after the 1970s that in-house PR organizations were organized.[2] Accordingly, persons who are responsible for public relations were assigned as managers in the general practice of HRM[3] at large Japanese companies; PR practitioners are both specialists and generalists at the same time. We will consider this situation from the viewpoint of their professionalism awareness and the issue of acquiring expertise.

Large Japanese companies are generally managed under the HRM system that includes recruiting new graduates, acquiring skills and expertise through the accumulation of experience gained from tasks, and career development within the company. The public relations department is also working under this company-wide HRM practice. How does this affect the activities of the public relations department? Based on the hypothesis that the PR activities of Japanese companies have these characteristics, this chapter attempts to shed light on how Japanese corporate PR personnel are assigned, what their educational background is, and their career formation on the basis of the analysis of the three sets of data and the testimonies of public relations practitioners.

Brief literature review and research questions

Public relations departments in Japan's large companies are positioned in the headquarters with a direct link to top management. On the premise of rational decision making, it can be thought that with regard to the internal organization of a company, the size of the organization in charge and the location within the company hierarchy are determined by judging the importance of the work and the amount of work. And the result of management decision making is revealed in organizational restructuring and/or personnel change, which can be observed from the outside (Miyabe, 2011). In other words, the reasoning behind corporate decision making, that is, corporate understanding of the importance of PR function, is revealed in the management decision to set up and staff a PR department. The result of such a decision can be observed from publicly available data.

Organization structure is not a popular topic in PR/communication scholarship. However, empirical research on organization structure and the related subject of HRM in PR/communication function is one way to understand the detailed working of the function (Moss et al., 2017). This chapter will attempt to show the outcome of this approach through the analysis of Japanese companies.

Most Japanese public relations managers[4] join a company under the employment practice common to Japanese companies, which is to hire new college graduates without prior job assignments or as generalists. According to the discussion on the role of PR practitioners, the division of technician and manager has been identified (Dozier & Broom, 1995). The implication of this discussion is that people who have received a specialized education begin to work as technicians and become managers as they accumulate relevant experience. In other words, it is the formation of a career from technician to manager. The implicit assumption here is that the career of the public relations practitioner is considered within the field of public relations and communication. This means that the type of work one experiences in occupational life (i.e., the range of career) is limited to the PR/communication field. Detailed empirical studies have been conducted in the field of labor economics, where the range of white-collar careers at Japanese, US, British, and German companies are compared, and it has been shown that ones in Japanese companies are relatively wide (Koike & Inoki, 2002). One of the research interests in this chapter is whether similar observations are made in PR/communication management, where certain expertise is assumed to be necessary.

Public relations practitioners and researchers in the West, and especially in the US, consider the practice of public relations as a professional occupation that requires advanced and specialized education and training prior to starting practice. Public relations textbooks begin discussion by pointing out that PR practice is a professional job and devote pages on the discussion of occupational ethics (Cutlip et al., 2006; Newsom et al., 2012). What can be seen from these arguments is the image of public relations practitioner as a professional occupation. Professionalism and professional standards have long been one of the issues of empirical studies (Cameron et al., 1996). Professional education for establishing required expertise is offered at many universities, and the standardization of the educational content is being planned (CEPR Guideline, 2006). However, this is not the case in Japan. So what is the nature of public relations practitioners under Japanese employment practices? If there is a difference, where can we acknowledge it?

As an analytical framework for considering the professionalism of public relations practitioners at Japanese companies, we can turn to the concept of "in-house professionals." In order to continue to provide sophisticated products and services in the increasingly complex and changing market environment, companies need highly specialized personnel. Japanese companies, with limited reliance on the external labor market, necessarily turn to their own internal resources and provide training and support for the acquisition of first-hand experiences through job assignments to potential personnel. The Japan Institute for Labour Policy and Training (2016) calls such competent and specialized employees "in-house professionals," which refers to people with the following characteristics. Human resources recognized as in-house professionals those who (1) demonstrate appropriate conduct as a member of the organization before being professional, (2) commit to both work and organization, with a level of autonomy of work that is higher than that of non-professional employees, (3) are able to play a central role in the decision making of responsible duties regardless of their position in the affiliated companies, and (4) have high-level expertise to be utilized in the affiliated company and the expertise has versatility and marketability. As we will see in detail, Japanese public relations managers are, in many cases, not professionals in the Western sense. The question is, is it possible to understand them as in-house professionals in the way just described?

Based on these research interests, this chapter confirms the existence of public relations departments at Japanese companies with long-term and externally observable data, as well as quantitative and qualitative research on public relations managers. We set the research questions as follows:

RQ 1: How has PR organization at Japanese companies developed and became visible from the outside through externally observable data?

RQ 2: What kind of human resources are allocated to the public relations manager posts at Japanese companies?

RQ 3: Is the career range of Japanese public relations managers wide?

RQ 4: What kind of professional view do Japanese public relations managers have about their positions/work?

RQ 5: Do the professional views of public relations managers at Japanese companies have an influence on public relations activities?

Methodology and data

Methodology

In this research, we will first proceed with a discussion depending only on externally observable and quantitative data, derive tentative conclusions therefrom, and then follow the steps of verifying them by qualitative investigation. In the first stage, from the data published in the annual directory of companies covering 1960–2010, the existence of public relations departments and the demographic characteristics of public relations managers are analyzed. Then, detailed personnel change data published in a business newspaper for 17 years from 2000 to 2016 is statistically analyzed to understand the characteristics of careers of public relations managers at Japanese companies. We will derive tentative conclusions from this quantitative analysis and then qualitatively verify it with a semi-structured interview survey of public relations managers.

Data

For the quantitative analysis of this chapter, we use the data set constructed from the following three publicly available data sources:

- Organizational and demographic data including academic backgrounds on public relations managers from the Annual Directory of Company Officials and Managers (*Kaisya Shokuinnroku*) published by Diamond Inc. The data for 1960, 1970, 1980, 1990, 2000, and 2010[5] are collected.
- *Nikkei Business Daily* (*Nikkei Sangyo Shimbun*) personnel change announcements of public relations and related posts from the Personnel Change and Organization Reform column of *Nikkei Business Daily*. The data collection period is 17 years from January 1, 2000, to December 31, 2016.
- The securities reports (*Yuka Shoken Houkokusyo*) of the top 50 companies with the largest market capitalization.

Historical development of public relations organization at Japanese companies: 1960–2010

We first look at the creation of PR-related[6] organizations within companies. In this analysis, we exclude organizations within PR firms and advertising agencies that provide PR-related services to external clients. The intention here is to verify quantitatively the fact that has previously been discussed only with anecdotal data and personal experience. When recognizing the necessity of management functions, such as public relations, and recognizing that such functions require a certain level of manpower, the company responds with such necessity by creating a dedicated internal organization. Table 6.1 shows the installation status every 10 years from 1960 to 2010 in Japanese listed companies.[7] It is in the 1960s that public relations organizations at listed companies appear as externally observable entities. The number of companies that have established PR-related departments since 1960 has increased remarkably except in 2000.[8] From this table, it is possible to grasp the aspect of the popularization process of PR-related functions and the expansion of their scope of responsibility among Japanese companies.

Table 6.1 Establishment of public relations-related departments

		1960	1970	1980	1990	2000	2010
Number of companies in the directory		750	1,554	1,725	1,988	2,547	3,767
Companies with PR-related internal organizations		30	107	223	403	385	459
Public Relations	Unit within department	18	76	92	122	44	34
	Department	10	31	122	267	342	348
Investor Relations	Including unit within department	0	0	0	0	4	32
CSR	Including unit within department	0	0	8	3	0	55
Listening to customer's voice	Including unit within department	0	0	9	24	3	46
Others (Editorial committee of company history, corporate museum)		3	0	1	18	1	1
Total		31	107	232	434	394	516

Source: Data compiled from the Annual Directory of Company Officials and Managers, Diamond Inc., 1960, 1970, 1980, 1990, 2000, 2010.

The establishment of public relations departments at Japanese companies began in the 1960s and gained momentum in the 1980s. Meanwhile, recognition of public relations functions deepened as a result of changes in the economic environment, including two oil crises, and the corresponding criticism against large companies (Ikari et al., 2015; also Chapter 1).

By looking at the details of the installation with the name of the department as a clue, one can see that until 1990, many public relations functions were placed as a unit within the general affairs department or the president's office, not as independent departments. After 1990, the number of units positioned within other departments rapidly declined. This suggests that, until 1990, PR was not recognized to have enough work volume and/or importance to set up as an independent department-level organization.

As of 2000, department-level organizations are increasing, and the name of the PR-related organizations has begun to diversify. Instead of public relations (*kouhou*), corporate communication (*kouporato komyunike-syon*) is beginning to be used as an organization name. In addition, the establishment of investor relations sections started to be visible from around 2000. Although social contribution is not a new function for the 21st century and a few departments were confirmed in 1980 and 1990 in our data set, the department with the name of CSR could not be confirmed in our analysis in 2000. However, it was confirmed that such departments existed in 55 companies in 2010.

If PR is defined as an interactive communication function between a company and its stakeholders, the existence of a section dedicated to listening is also indispensable. There are customer inquiry units (*okyakusama soudann sitsu*) that receive complaints and requests from customers and other stakeholders. It was confirmed in four companies in 1980 and increased to 17 companies in 1990. And in 2010, there were 46 companies with this type of unit in our data set. The presence of the IR department shows that it is necessary to ensure timely disclosure of information to the financial market and that CSR is indicative of the fact that companies can no longer exist without being good corporate citizens. Public relations' function is evolving from a media relations function to one that is responsible for the existence of the company itself.

The data shows that, although the number of listed companies increased rapidly since 1990 as the expansion of the stock market continued, the establishment of public relations departments in an externally visible way did not match this pace. Although the number of companies that installed public relations departments did increase, the fact that it lags behind the number of newly listed companies implies that many of those companies did not place emphasis on public relations as a function that deserves the establishment of an independent department.

Returning to RQ 1, "How has PR organization at Japanese companies developed and become visible from the outside through externally observable data?" and summarizing the analysis so far, we first confirmed that the establishment of independent public relations organizations in Japanese companies began in the 1960s. In the 1980s and 1990s, there was a growth in the number of companies that established a public relations department. Companies that encountered drastic changes in the economic environment, such as the two oil crises and the collapse of the bubble economy in these two decades, were urged to widely appeal to the public for the legitimacy of their existence. And it was in the 21st century that PR/communication activities expanded to the realm of IR and CSR. In many companies, what was once a sub-function within public relations departments became independent. This signifies that the understanding of the importance of these functions has spread among companies, recognizing that they are so important as to require a departmental-level organization.

Public relations managers of Japanese companies: managers in lifetime employment practice and the range of their careers

We turn our discussion to demographic characteristics and the educational background of Japanese PR managers.

Demographic characteristics of Japanese PR managers: age and educational background

How do employment practices of large Japanese companies, new graduate recruitment, and lifetime employment appear on the profile of public relations managers? Looking at our data in Table 6.2, from 1970 to

Table 6.2 Age profile of PR managers

	Age at entry			% 26 or under at entry	Current age			Length of service		
	n	Average	SD		n	Average	SD	n	Average	SD
1960	47	28.8	8.5	55.3%	47	46.1	4.7	47	17.2	8.0
1970	110	26.2	6.4	69.1%	110	45.6	6.8	110	19.4	7.5
1980	394	25.3	6.2	81.0%	394	47.7	5.6	393	22.4	6.9
1990	793	25.4	6.9	85.9%	810	51.6	5.6	793	26.2	7.7
2000	399	27.5	9.7	78.6%	406	54.5	5.8	392	27.0	10.3
2010	342	30.1	10.9	65.2%	398	55.7	6.9	345	26.0	13.1

Source: Data compiled from the Annual Directory of Company Officials and Managers, Diamond Inc., 1960, 1970, 1980, 1990, 2000, 2010.

2010,[9] the age of joining a company has increased only slightly from 25 years old to 26 years old. However, the age at the time of survey has increased from 45.6 years old in 1970 to 55.7 years old in 2010. And the length of years in service has extended from 20 years to 26 years. Table 6.2 shows the percentage of those who have joined the company at the age of 26 or younger.[10] Since the percentage of 26 years old or younger was over 80% in 1980 and 1990 and 79% in 2000, it can be assumed that the majority of public relations managers in the latter half of the 20th century have joined a company as new graduates and have continued their careers at the same companies. As of 2010, the average age of joining a company is 30 years old, and the percentage of people 26 years old or younger has declined to 65%. From these observations, it is confirmed that the majority of public relations managers have joined a company as new graduates and continued to work at the same company.

Table 6.3 presents our brief analysis of the educational backgrounds of PR managers. Nearly 100% are college graduates; the undergraduate majors are law, economics, and commerce, and there are very few communication majors, if any. In 2010, we observed that 15% of university graduates were science and engineering majors. This signifies a diverse background of Japanese PR managers.

Age at the time of entry of standard workers and public relations managers

The Basic Survey on Wage Structure (the so-called Wage Census), which is one of the Fundamental Statistics according to the Statistics Act, under the jurisdiction of the Ministry of Health, Labor, and Welfare, adopts the concept of "standard workers."[11] Those who find jobs immediately after graduating high school or university and continue to work for the same

Table 6.3 Educational background of PR managers

	n =	Junior high school	High school	Junior college	University	Foreign university	University graduate		Social science	Humanities
							Graduate school	Science & engineering		
1970	150	1.3%	13.3%	12.7%	72.7%	0.0%	0.9%	2.8%	82.6%	10.1%
1990	760	0.4%	7.8%	0.9%	90.7%	0.3%	1.0%	8.5%	76.6%	6.7%
2010	162	0.0%	1.9%	1.2%	95.1%	1.9%	7.6%	14.6%	79.0%	5.7%

Source: Data compiled from the Annual Directory of Company Officials and Managers, Diamond Inc., 1970, 1990, 2010.

companies are recognized as standard workers. In other words, in Japanese society, employment of new graduates and long-term employment (lifetime employment) are considered standard. From this viewpoint, let's look at our 2010 data again. When looking at the data according to the definition of standard workers and considering the possibility of being Ronin, the entry age is concentrated at the ages of 22–26 years old. The practices of recruiting new graduates and long-term employment are recognized as shown in Table 6.4 even in 2010 as well. Fifty-nine percent of general managers and 66% of officers in charge of PR entered the company at age 26 or younger. However, a slightly different aspect was seen in 2010 compared to the situation until 2000. There is an increasing number of cases of joining a company at 27 years old or older.

Term of office and range of career

We will now look at the term of the PR manager position and immediate past and subsequent positions. We have confirmed that the average PR manager has more than 20 years of working experience within the same company. First of all, 66% of public relations managers' terms of office[12] are between one and three years. And there is a tendency for the general managers of public relations departments to have a longer term of office

Table 6.4 Profiles of PR managers and officers 2010

	n =	Entry age[a]				Current age (2010)		Length of service	
		M[b]	SD	Under 26	Over 45	M[c]	SD	M[d]	SD
PR/communication dept. manager	121	31.49	11.63	58.7%	19.0%	54.33	7.90	22.84	12.98
General manager (bucyo) level	26	28.42	9.16	69.2%	11.5%	52.81	6.11	24.38	11.52
Executive officer	27	30.52	10.88	63.0%	18.5%	55.00	5.00	24.48	11.61
Board member	68	33.04	12.46	52.9%	22.1%	54.65	9.26	21.60	13.86
Officer in charge of PR/ communication	216	30.28	11.32	66.2%	16.7%	57.53	5.84	27.26	12.69
Executive officer	24	27.96	9.93	79.2%	12.5%	55.92	6.08	28.00	11.02
Board member	192	30.57	11.45	64.6%	17.2%	57.73	5.78	27.17	12.89

Source: Data compiled from the Annual Directory of Company Officials and Managers, Diamond Inc., 2010.

a Entry age: age when he/she joined the company he/she is working for at the time of the survey.
b $F_{(4,332)} = 1.32$, p = .26, n.s.
c $F_{(4,332)} = 5.31$, p = .00<.01
d $F_{(4,332)} = 2.67$, p = .03<.05

than the executive officers in charge of public relations. The term of office is two years and five months on average for the general managers of public relations departments, while the executive officers in charge of public relations have terms of office of one year and three months. However, it can be confirmed from our data set that there are PR managers who serve as the public relations manager for more than ten years. It should be recognized that there are managers who are building careers specialized in the public relations area. However, there are many cases in which personnel change in less than one year. In extreme cases, the executive officer in charge of PR stays in the position for only one month. From my work experience, two interpretations are possible for such a case. One is a case where an executive officer who is a scarce human resource within a company serves as a public relations officer in an interim assignment, waiting for the next important mission. In this case, the person in charge is considered to be nominal and not substantial. The other interpretation is the judgment of a company that it cannot make the post vacant even for a month. In this case, it suggests that the public relations function is considered important in the company and the executive officer level should actually take control of the function.

Next, from our data set, we are able to trace the career path of 335 PR managers. Our observation shows that PR managers' immediate past and subsequent positions vary widely within the company. Looking at the former position of 105 executive officers in charge of PR, 33 were from the business division and 63 were moved from other headquarters departments. For those 105 executive officers, subsequent posts after the PR position include 34 business divisions and 53 headquarters organizations. There were only

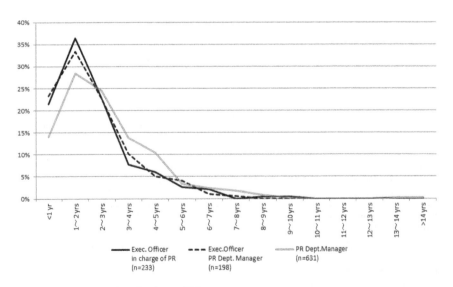

Figure 6.1 Tenure distribution of PR managers

eight managers with public relations posts as the former position and six managers with public relations posts after being a PR manager. Therefore, it can be said that the range of career of the person in charge of the PR/communication field is not confined to this particular field.

Also, regarding the head of the PR department, the aspect of carrier immobilization, or a range of career limited to the PR/communication field, was not noticeable in our data set. We have, in our data set, 113 general managers of public relations-related departments whose immediate past positions were in business departments. Sixty-five out of those 113 returned to business departments, many of them with promotions.

Locus of career formation in board members

In order to confirm the wider range of careers of public relations managers from another viewpoint, we turn to a securities report (*yuka shoken houk-okusyo*, equivalent to Form 10-K) that includes information about board directors regarding their past managerial positions within the company.

Table 6.5 Career path of PR managers

	Immediate past	Subsequent
CEO / Board member / manager of subsidiary	9	18
Head / executive officer / manager of overseas operation	5	4
Executive officers/ auditor / advisor		
Executive officer	8	5
Auditor	0	6
Advisor	0	5
Business section: division head, deputy head, supervisor	21	29
Business section: dept. manager	0	0
Headquarters: planning	7	7
Headquarters: accounting and finance	2	3
Headquarters: personnel, general affairs, quality assurance	16	26
Headquarters: PR and communication	13	13
Business section: division head, deputy head, supervisor	19	21
Business section: dept. manager	59	33
Headquarters: planning	10	21
Headquarters: accounting and finance	5	6
Headquarters: personnel, general affairs, quality assurance	28	28
Headquarters: PR and communication	28	5
Total	230	230

Source: Data set is constructed from personnel change announcements on *Nikkei Business Daily*. Tabulation by the author.

Table 6.6 Career path of executive officers in charge of PR

	Immediate past	Subsequent
CEO / board member of subsidiary	3	3
Head / executive officer of overseas operation	0	2
Executive officer	6	9
Auditor	2	5
Advisor	1	4
Business section: division head, deputy head, supervisor	28	28
Business section: dept. manager	2	1
Headquarters: planning	14	17
Headquarters: accounting and finance	9	1
Headquarters: personnel, general affairs, quality assurance	32	29
Headquarters: PR and communication	8	6
Total	105	105

Source: Data set is constructed from personnel change announcements on *Nikkei Business Daily*. Tabulation by the author.

Table 6.7 Executive directors and officers with public relations experience at the top 50 market capitalization companies

Companies with directors who have PR/communication experience	22
Total number of directors of the top 50 market capitalization companies	596
Among them, directors of internal promotion	394
Directors with PR/communication experience	44
% of directors with PR/communication experience	11.2%
Companies with exec officers who have PR/communication experience	6
Exec officers with PR/communication experience	6
Companies with director/executive officer who has PR/communication experience	26
Director/executive officer with PR/communication experience	50

Source: Data compiled from the securities report for FY2016 of the top 50 companies.

Table 6.7 shows the number of directors and executive officers who had PR-related careers[13] at the top 50 market capitalization companies in FY2016.

As shown in Table 6.7, 22 out of the 50 companies have at least one board member with a PR-related career. Of the 22, there are nine companies with multiple directors with a public relations-related career. The total number of directors at these 50 companies is 596, of which 202 are outside directors. Three hundred and ninety-four directors were internally promoted to the top management position. Forty-four, or 11%, of those directors had held PR-related managerial positions as indicated in their career records. Furthermore, if we extend our list to executive officers, we find four more companies with executives with a PR career. Therefore, 26 companies out of the top 50 have an executive officer or board director with PR experience as a manager. It shows that the careers of former public relations managers are not confined to the public relations/communication field and extend even to the top management level.

Profile of public relations managers

We have looked at the demographic characteristics and career ranges of PR managers at Japanese companies based on publicly available data. Our conclusions in relation to RQ2 and RQ3 are as follows:

- The PR organization of Japanese companies is structured under the framework of the human resource management at Japanese companies that relies on their internal labor market.
- The majority of public relations managers are not employed as public relations professionals or recruited based on prior public relations training or experience.
- Public relations managers are pursuing their careers at companies they joined upon graduation from school. Public relations work is only a step in a diversified career.
- In many cases, public relations managers' careers reach the top management level. However, it is not necessarily as a public relations specialist in the top management team. PR is positioned within the broad range of careers of those successful managers.

Two professionalisms

We have looked at quantitative data on the careers of public relations managers. What became clear here is the real image of the careers of people who started their occupational lives by choosing a specific company to work for rather than getting a job on the basis of a specific profession; their careers span diversified tasks, including a public relations manager's post. Therefore, the career of public relations managers, prior to or after assuming the post, is not confined within the field of public relations and communication but extends to the entire company. Furthermore, as we observed in the previous section, there are cases in which experienced public relations managers climbed the ladder to the position of president/CEO.

In the following section, we analyze the perceptions held by public relations managers and practical activities that are conducted in the public relations department that cannot be grasped from statistical data. Here, we turn to five public relations managers and listen to their stories.

Interviewees

Mr. A: Ten years in the PR department at a service-industry company, five years as a section manager and five years as the general manager of the PR department.

Mr. B: Five years in the PR department as PR section manager at a service-industry company.

Mr. C: Six years as general manager of the PR department.

Mr. D: Over 20 years of PR-related experience at several companies, currently working at a manufacturing company.

Mr. E: Sixteen years in PR and advertising at a manufacturing company.

How do public relations practitioners at Japanese companies come to the posts of PR managers?

Public relations managers who work as regular employees at large Japanese companies encounter public relations during their careers as one of their diversified assignments. The following testimonies suggest that a public relations post is not necessarily one that everyone seeks to hold. It is considered a post that is out of the way of career advancement. Public relations is not fully recognized internally. They started working as managers of PR departments that were not well understood internally.

1   Mr. A: I realized what sort of tasks await me only when I arrived at my new post in the PR Department. I knew that there was a public relations department at the company, but I was not interested in their work. Speaking honestly, I felt it as if it was a sort of demotion, but I thought I should do my best to fulfill my responsibility. Afterword, I realized that I was engaging in a very important work.

2   Mr. C: The transfer to the PR Department was an unexpected announcement. When I was told, I thought . . . why me?

How do public relations managers at Japanese companies gain awareness as a PR professional?

While experiencing various tasks as core employees, they became public relations managers. Although they had a lot of experience within the company and had successful experiences, they had no prior training or knowledge regarding public relations. With what kind of perception did they start working?

1   Mr. B: When I began working as a PR unit manager, I thought that I should aim the level of expertise such that I would be able to go out to the job market as a PR professional. As a result, in the five years before I was transferred back to the business section where I had been, I thought I was able to conduct PR tasks satisfactorily. I think that it is possible to say that I was aiming for professionality in this sense.

2   Mr. D: I consider myself a PR professional. I joined my present company as a specialist of PR and communication. I think that I cannot but consider a career as a PR expert.

3   Mr. C: I was not conscious of PR in particular until I took office as a general manager of PR. About a year after the assumption of the office, there was a moment when I felt that I might have become a PR professional. When I had successfully completed handling a very important and delicate communication issue, my mentor told me that I had graduated his school. As a PR department manager, the most important thing was to establish personal relationships with journalists and people in the media. There are certain issues that only a general manager can handle. At that time, it was crucial to have a strong relationship and mutual trust with people in the media. I came through shambles, so to speak, and, after such an experience, became a professional. All PR managers may have similar experiences. I think that all PR managers are professionals in this sense.

4   Mr. E: I started my career as a factory production planning staff member, and after five years, I was transferred to the planning section of the business division, where I worked for four years. After that, I moved to the advertising department and worked on advertisements and public relations. In 2002, the company established the specialist status as part of the personnel management system. Since I had 12 years of advertisement and PR experience, I decided to apply for the status and was recognized as a specialist. Expectation for specialists is such that we are not allowed to stay at the same level of expertise. You are not recognized as a specialist by colleagues and senior officers unless you are constantly improving your level of expertise. When thinking about how to improve, I completed master's and doctoral programs at a graduate school of business and seriously worked on research presentations at a public relations academic conference. Also, I began to realize that I would not be a specialist if I only had company-specific skills that could only be accepted at this company. I think I am now a professional.

How do public relations managers at Japanese companies capture the essence of public relations work and practice it?

How do public relations managers consider the work of PR? What is the process by which public relations managers establish their own work? In a country where specialized PR education is not established, public relations managers who do not have a standard framework can only grasp the essence of PR from their own experience and from ongoing public relations work. Newly appointed public relations managers discover the essence of public relations with the support from experienced people inside and outside the company.

1   Mr. A: I think there are three skill sets related to PR activities. First, get to know the company well. The second is to understand PR. The third is to know the society. The first one means that one can talk about and

explain the company to people outside of it or to new employees. The second is, for example, that one can talk for an hour about the purpose, role, and significance of PR to their own PR staff and to the members of the senior management. The third, to know the society, one should be able to have a casual discussion with people in the media on current topics for an hour. In order to acquire these skill sets, I think that the abilities to communicate and to think something through are important. Techniques such as writing news releases or setting up press conferences can be learned as necessary.

2   Mr. B: At the initial stage, I attended PRSJ's seminars and workshops. Then I learned the PR skill while working with experienced staff members.

3   Mr. C: The information provided by my predecessor upon the handover was not enough at all to start working as head of the PR department. I thought a lot about how I should perform as a PR manager. I met more than 10 PR managers of various companies to seek advice. I was fortunate to find an experienced PR manager who became my mentor and who gave me invaluable advice. In addition, I established close contact with four or five PR managers of other companies. When I sought advice by email, they always got back to me within 30 minutes. For me, a new PR manager, such a network was of great help. After two or three years, I was able to sit on the other side of the table and provide support to incoming PR managers of other companies.

Position of public relations at Japanese companies

How is the public relations manager positioning public relations work? The next set of testimonies points out that public relations experience is useful for a young prospective executive's career development. These testimonies, as we have seen throughout this chapter, show that the range of the careers of Japanese public relations managers is not confined to the public relations/communication field but extends to a much wider range of fields, including top management. Also, Mr. B's testimony points out that there are different roles depending on the positions within the public relations department.

1   Mr. A: When I became a general manager of PR, what I thought about most was the career path of the staff members. The work of the PR department covers the entire company, and the staff members have opportunities to have daily contact with the members of senior management. The PR unit manager and CSR unit manager are in regular contact with the social and economic environment surrounding the company, and it is a unique position in the corporate headquarters structure. Therefore, these posts provide unique opportunities for the career formation of young managers and staff members.

2   Mr. B: The task at the initial stage after assuming a public relations post is quite different between department general manager and section chief. A general manager should focus on establishing a wide range of human networks as an individual who represents the company. The section chief, on the other hand, is expected to manage day-to-day operations from day one he/she is on the job and is expected to practice public relations in a solid manner.

Professionalism among Japanese PR managers: conclusions for RQ4 and RQ5

Regarding our research questions, the followings are our main conclusions.

RQ4

- Prior formal education in PR is not regarded as essential when assuming a PR post.
- PR is one of the career steps, but the experience of public relations is meaningful in any subsequent career.
- Since PR requires an overall view of the company as a whole, public relations experiences are meaningful in forming careers leading up to top management.
- A PR manager's post is not an isolated entity that is confined within each company. There exist informal networks among public relations managers of various companies that can support newly appointed managers.

RQ5

- PR managers at Japanese companies can think from a company-wide perspective about what is most essential and important for the public relations function.
- The public relations managers in Japanese companies are not appointed as specialists. However, by bringing extensive experience and knowledge, they are able to have the broad perspective necessary for public relations practice.

From these quantitative and qualitative observations, we can conclude that most Japanese public relations managers are not PR professionals in the Western sense. They have not undergone professional education before assuming public relations positions, and their lifelong careers include various responsibilities not limited to the PR/communication field. Then, are they not professionals? In conformity with the concept of the in-house professional as mentioned earlier, it is possible to find in their testimony discourses that meet the conditions. We can see their consciousness as in-house professionals from their testimonies that they aim to achieve a market evaluation of themselves beyond internal evaluation and to acquire expertise not confined within the company's framework. What we see is a business person as a professional utilizing the experience of public relations.

Conclusion: 2017 and beyond

Currently, the labor market in Japan is at a major turning point. Still, large companies' employment practices heavily impact university students and universities alike, and the employer companies also take action on the premise of long-term employment. However, the mid-career job change, which was traditionally exceptional and considered not recommendable, is no longer so. Standard workers who once were the majority of the workforce have started to become less standard. Dependence on the external labor market requires clarification of the job description, which encourages potential employees to establish and clarify their expertise. Amid these changes, people who are involved with public relations practice and view this as their own expertise are beginning to emerge. Mr. D, one of the interview survey participants, is one such pioneer. By increasing the number of people with expertise like his, the technical sophistication of public relations activities in Japan can be expected. But will it be possible to maintain professionals' position of considering public relations activities with the perspective of the company as a whole? In addition, as professionalization potentially narrows down the career path climbing up to the top management level, it may create, on the contrary, a barrier between top management and public relations managers. As the entire Japanese corporate society is in transition, public relations functions are also in the process of transformation, and they are searching for a new model.

Notes

1 This research was supported by the Japan Society for the Promotion of Science (JSPS) KAKENHI Grant Number 25380456 and 16K03803.
2 Here we are considering an in-house organization whose existence can be confirmed from outside the company. Depending on the company, it is generally department-level and upper-level organizations that can confirm its existence from outside the company.
3 Appendix 3 gives a detailed explanation of the HRM practice of Japanese companies.
4 In this chapter, 'public relations manager' refers both to the general manager of the PR department and the executive officer in charge of PR.
5 Unfortunately, publication of this directory was discontinued after the 2011 edition.
6 'PR-related' is considered here to encompass a broad corporate communication function, including investor relations (IR), corporate social responsibility (CSR), customer inquiries (listening to the requests and complaints of customers and conveying them to the relevant departments), in addition to public relations/ corporate communication.

7 Most of the extracted companies are listed on the first section of the Tokyo Stock Exchange.
8 Because it is based on a questionnaire survey by the publisher, there is a possibility of survey omissions due to the refusal to cooperate.
9 The table also includes data for 1960. However, since the entries for the companies correspond to the chaotic period after World War II, with factors such as people returning from military services, it shows a slightly different picture from later years.
10 A high school student who failed the entrance examination at the university of his choice and elected to take the exam a second time the next year is called "Ronin." From the author's practical experience, companies treat those who experienced being "Ronin" for up to two years as equivalent to fresh graduates.
11 The definition given in the 2015 survey is "A standard worker denotes those who are employed by enterprises immediately after graduating school or university and have been working for the same enterprises."
12 The term of office is measured by the number of months between the date of transfer to the PR manager position and the date of transfer to a subsequent position.
13 Data is from the list of the members of the board. The securities report publishes abridged and summarized versions of the career record for each director. Note that this data source does not cover each and every step of the careers, so that there is a possibility that some of the directors may have PR experience in their earlier career stages.

References

Cameron, G. T., Sallot, L. M., & Lariscy, R. A. W. (1996). Developing standards of professional performance in public relations. *Public Relations Review*, 22(1), 43–61.

Commission on Education of Public Relations (2006). *The professional bond: Public relations education in the 21st century*. Retrieved from http://apps.prsa.org/SearchResults/download/6I-2006/0/The_Professional_Bond_Public_Relations_Education_i?

Cutlip, S. M., Center, A. H., & Broom, G. (2006). *Effective public relations* (9th edition). Upper Saddle River, NJ: Pearson Prentice Hall.

Dozier, D. M., & Broom, G. M. (1995). Evolution of the manager role in public relations practice. *Journal of Public Relations Research*, 7(1), 3–26.

Ikari, S., Ogawa, M., Kitano, K., Kenmochi, T., Morito, N., & Hamada, I. (2015). *Zouhoban Nihon no kouhou PR no 100 nen* [A hundred years of public relations in Japan, augmented edition]. Tokyo, Japan: Douyukan.

Japan Institute for Labour Policy and Training (2016). *Kigyou nai purofessyonaru no kyaria keisei* [Career development of in-house professionals]. *Shiryo Sirizu* [Document Series], 178.

Koike, K., & Inoki, T. (Eds.). (2002). *Howaito kara-no jinzai keisei: Nichi, Bei, Ei, Doku no hikaku* [White Collar Human Resource Development: Comparative study of Japan, the US, the UK and Germany]. Tokyo: Toyo Keizai Shinposya

Miyabe, J. (2011, March). An attempt on quantitative profiling of PR practitioners in Japanese companies: Applicability of "revealed preference" approach. In Proceedings of the *14th International Public Relations Research Conference* (pp. 565–574). Retrieved from www.instituteforpr.org//wp-content/uploads/14th-IPRRC-Proceedings.pdf

Moss, D., Likely, F., Sriramesh, K., & Ferrari, A. (2017). Structure of the public relations/communication department: Key findings from a global study. *Public Relations Review*, 43, 80–90.

Newsom, D., Turk, J. V. S., & Kruckeberg D. (2012). *This is PR: The realities of public relations*. Belmont, CA: Wadsworth Pub Co.

7 Impacts of crises on public relations 2007–2017

The "Lehman Shock" and the Great East Japan Earthquake

Naoya Ito

Background

In September 2008, the so-called "worst crisis after World War II" (Cabinet Office, 2009) or "a crisis once in a hundred years" (Cabinet Office, 2011a) occurred. The financial crisis, called in Japan the "Lehman Shock," originated in the United States and spread to the world in the blink of an eye. This financial crisis drastically changed the business environment of Japanese companies. Two years later, on March 11, 2011, the Great East Japan Earthquake (GEJE) occurred, triggering a devastating tsunami in the north-eastern region of the country. As a result, over 15,000 lost their lives, with damage estimated at about 150 billion USD (Cabinet Office, 2012). The impact of the tsunami was aggravated by the nuclear core meltdown and radioactive discharge at Fukushima I Nuclear Power Plant of Tokyo Electric Power Co. (TEPCO). This nuclear disaster was designated a "major accident," or level 7, according to the International Nuclear and Radiological Event Scale.

Within just three years, Japan experienced two noteworthy and historic incidents affecting its economic environment. Suddenly, Japanese companies had to face both an economic and a natural disaster. Suddenly, public relations sections in the corporations were thrown into these crises. During and after these events, what did they change in terms of PR activities? Speaking more generally, what should they do in a period of rapid external environment changes? In this chapter, we focus on the activities of Japanese companies' public relations when facing economic crises and natural disasters. Specifically, we try to describe changes in PR activities induced by these external environmental changes by considering the following two points: (1) quantitative and qualitative changes in activities based on the conceptual model of PR activities and (2) long-term trends behind these transitions. Regarding (1), quantitative changes are observed as those that can be enumerated, such as staff number and budget, whereas qualitative changes are examined by modification of the PR system. These two changes are discussed in a later section. This study is assuming that quantitative and qualitative changes increase during crises that bring large external environmental changes; furthermore, this assumption implies that the change is lessened post-crisis as the external environmental change subsides.

The next section briefly summarizes the two crises, and the third section discusses a conceptual model as a framework to understand changes in PR activities. The fourth section tries to comprehend how the public relations divisions of Japanese companies responded to these two crises. The last section considers the longer-term trends behind these changes and concludes the discussion of this chapter.

Outline of two crises

The Lehman Shock

The *Encyclopedia Britannica's Year in Review* for 2008 starts with the sentence: "In 2008, the world economy faced its most dangerous crisis since the Great Depression of the 1930s" (Havemann, 2008). The crisis started in the US mortgage loan market and quickly spread to the US financial sector and, with unprecedented speed, to the global financial market and the entire global economy (Havemann, 2008).

The Japanese financial industry could survive the impact of the collapse of the US financial market; however, the export industries that support the Japanese economy lost markets in the US and Europe. Likewise, the economies of China and emerging economies were also affected by the global recession, which led to a further sharp contraction of world trade. Japan's exports recorded a –27% year-on-year base in November 2008, the worst result on record (METI, 2009), which continued for four consecutive months from November 2008 to February 2009 (see Figure 7.1).

The starting point of this rapid contraction was linked to the collapse of Lehman Brothers.

Figure 7.2 shows how the Lehman Shock impacted Japan's overall economy by comparing the GDP of Japan, the US, France, and Germany.

According to the Cabinet Office (2011b), Japan experienced the greatest decrease in GDP among these four countries after the Lehman Shock. Compared with Quarter III of 2008, the decreases in GDP in Quarter I of 2009 for the US and France were about 3% and for Germany around 6%, whereas Japan had a decrease in GDP of almost 8%. The reason for this decrease in Japan was due to the high dependency on exports by the Japanese economy. Figures 7.1 and 7.2 indicate the drastic constriction of trust brought about by the Lehman Shock, which halted international trade activities; thus, the Japanese economy experienced the most serious decline of GDP of major advanced countries. With the Lehman Shock, Japanese companies were forced to face rapid external environmental change.

GEJE[1]

At 2:46 p.m. on March 11, 2011, a 9.0 magnitude earthquake struck northeast Japan in the Pacific Ocean, about 80 miles off the coastline and 234 miles from Tokyo. Shortly before 3:00 p.m., the first tsunami hit the

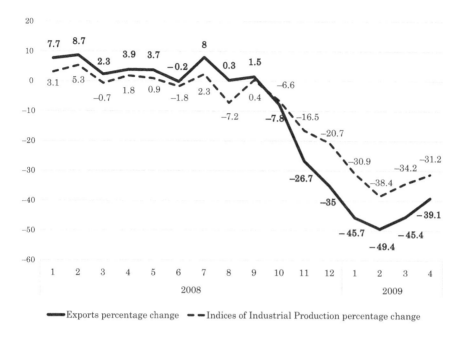

Figure 7.1 Exports percentage change of Japan

Source: Data selected from METI (2009). Translated by the author.

shoreline. Later, a study revealed that the highest point that the tsunami reached was 133 feet above sea level. In total, 216 square miles were washed away by the tsunami. A year later, the Cabinet Office (2012) reported 15,854 people were confirmed dead and 3,726 were missing, and 128,768 houses were totally destroyed, while 245,626 houses were deemed half-destroyed. The number of people in temporary shelters reached 386,739 a week after the quake.

On March 11, of the six nuclear reactors in the Fukushima Daiichi, three were in operation. When the earthquake hit, all three reactors automatically shut down and external power supplies were destroyed. Emergency diesel generators kept the cooling system running. However, an hour later, the first tsunami wave washed away the fuel tank. TEPCO notified the government of the cooling system failure, and the government declared a nuclear emergency situation and issued an evacuation order to residents. The next day, March 12, a hydrogen explosion occurred at the No. 1 reactor, destroying the upper walls of the reactor housing.

On March 14, another hydrogen explosion occurred at the No. 3 reactor. On March 18, TEPCO implemented a scheduled partial blackout for its supply area, including the Greater Tokyo Metropolitan Area, until March 28. On March 19, the government advised residents within a 30-kilometer-radius to evacuate (Cabinet Office, 2012).

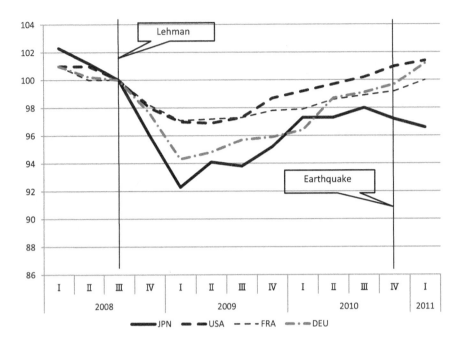

Figure 7.2 Comparison of four countries' GDP shift

Note:

GDP = Real Gross Domestic Product Seasonally Adjusted, 2008 year = 100 points

JPN: Cabinet Office, Government of Japan, GDP Statistics

USA: The United States Department of Commerce, National Economic Accounts

FRA: INSEE, Quarterly National Accounts

Source: Data selected from Cabinet Office (2011b). Translated by the author.

Bangumi Kenkyu Group (2011) (Media Program Research Group) observed that TV broadcasting networks, both NHK and commercial networks, responded to this devastating earthquake immediately and suspended their regular programs to shift to 24-hour continuous special coverage of the situation. NHK aired a continuous special TV program for a week. Commercial TV networks also aired special TV programs with no advertising for three days. Newspapers also did not post any advertisements on their front pages. GEJE prompted all Japanese mass media to create a "media scrum" to report the GEJE.

Aspects of the two crises from a public relations point of view

The economic crisis brought on by the Lehman Shock was the most influential in terms of the subjective economic judgment on business and the worst historically as reflected by the stock price decline of 42.1% at the Tokyo Stock Exchange in 2008 (Nikkei heikin 2011nen, 2011). Paying attention only to the decline of stock prices, the expression to describe this crisis as "the worst incident, once in a hundred years" is literally correct.

A survey conducted by Hokkaido University clarifies the PR activities that the public relations departments of Japanese companies focused on after the disaster (Miyabe et al., 2010; Figure 7.3).

During the first year after the earthquake, corporate public relations departments focused on activities related to PR fundamentals, such as accurate information dissemination, fast and timely execution, and a more finely tuned response. Furthermore, many companies pointed out that they also focused on internal communication. This indicates that Japanese companies were trying to stabilize the situation through internal communication as the changes in external environment and uncertainty toward the future increased. Particularly, the importance of internal communication could be considered an effective PR activity to deal with rapid external environmental change, such as crises, according to the survey results.

Because the GEJE was a natural disaster, PR activities taken in response were different from those of the economic crisis. The PR activity following the GEJE crisis began with safety confirmation for stakeholders. Then, business continuity considerations and responses to domestic and international

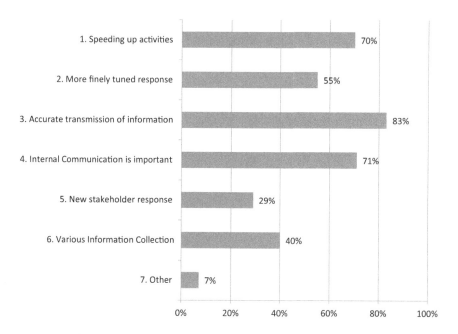

Figure 7.3 Attention to practice after the GEJE

Source: Data selected from Miyabe et al. (2010). Translated by the author.

mass media followed. In addition, unlike in past disasters, Japanese companies actively engaged in CSR activities (Japan Institute for Social and Economic Affairs, 2012a).

According to a survey of consumers' evaluations of the support activities and the PR activities by the companies at the time of the disaster, the first place was awarded to Softbank, with 31.2% of respondents' votes. Softbank announced a proposal to construct a large-scale photovoltaic power plant in the affected area, in addition to the CEO making individual donations. The second place, with 12.3% of the vote, was Yamato Transport for the relief fund associated with its package delivery service and the efforts by the company's delivery drivers to rebuild a logistics network in the affected regions. Third place, with 11.8% of the vote, was UNIQLO for its CEO's private donations and the relief fund driven from their sales (Nikkei BP Consulting, 2011).

Although the CEO of Yamato Transport did not make huge donations, the company came to occupy one of the top three positions. They created funding to support disaster victims and regions by coordinating the interests of diverse stakeholders. This activity signifies the case of PR in conjunction with CSR-based consideration. (Yamamura, 2014).

We now turn to the economic impacts of the two crises on Japanese companies. Figure 7.4 shows two production indices and a short-term diffusion index (DI), which indicates business sentiment or subjective judgment by Japanese companies.

During the first quarter of 2009, after the Lehman Shock, the short-term DI hit the bottom at –58. This was the lowest since the Bank of Japan started this survey. The second worst record so far after World War II was –51 due to the Asian Currency Crisis in 1997. Therefore, based on the short-term DI, the Lehman Shock was the most serious economic crisis since WWII. Comparing the short-term DI at the Lehman Shock and the GEJE, the decline following the GEJE was not as drastic. Although NHK devoted an entire week to special programs and commercial TV networks refrained from broadcasting any advertisement for three days, most companies, except the ones affected by the GEJE directly, were not so adversely impacted.

In addition to the business sentiment index, two production indices, namely the index of industrial production and the index of car production, indicated a sharp decline of production activities after the Lehman Shock. After the GEJE, the industrial production index showed a moderate decline, whereas the index of car production showed a sharp decline comparable with the decline after the Lehman Shock. The sharp decline of production activity in the auto industry was caused by disruption to the supply chain. Manufacturers of certain car parts were located in the north-eastern area of Japan where the earthquake struck. Factories there had no choice but to shut down their operations (Jidosyameka, 2011). The GEJE did not cause similar damage to all industries but had a particularly significant impact on certain industries, such as the automobile industry.

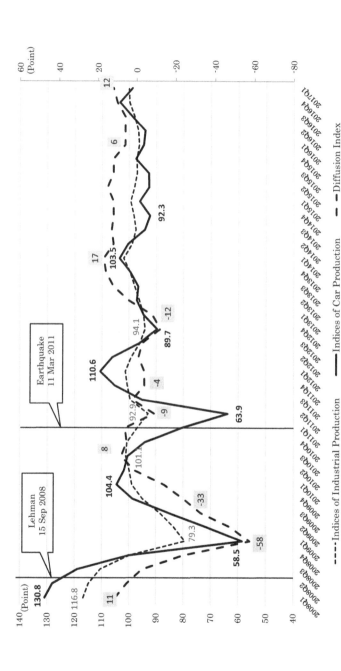

Figure 7.4 Indices of industrial and car production, diffusion index shift

Note:

Left axis: indices of industrial and car production, seasonally adjusted

Right axis: diffusion index (DI), business sentiment index

Source: Indices of industrial and car production: data retrieved from Ministry of Economy, Trade, and Industry. Retrieved from www.stat-search.boj.or.jp/ssi/mtshtml/q.html.

DI: data retrieved from General Explanation of the Short-Term Economic Survey of Enterprises in Japan, The Bank of Japan. D.I./Business conditions index/Large companies/Manufacturing industry/. Retrieved from www.stat-search.boj.or.jp/ssi/mtshtml/q.html

The distinctive feature of the Lehman Shock was the breadth and speed of economic contraction. With the Asian currency crisis of 1997, which was caused by the decline of the Thai baht, it took a few months for the impact to spread to the real economy of Japan, the US, and Europe. However, the Lehman Shock impacted economies all over the world immediately and simultaneously. Figure 7.4 illustrates the devastating impact of the crisis to the Japanese economy.

Although the GEJE left a very large scar on Japanese society, the impact on macroeconomic activity was not as great as that of the Lehman Shock. Japanese companies that were in the process of recovering from the Lehman Shock were forced to shift from responding to a global economic crisis to responding to a large-scale natural disaster. As shown in Figure 7.4, the Japanese economy has been on a gradual expansion trend since 2013.

Understanding changes in public relations activities

Conceptual model

To understand the changes that occurred in the PR activities of Japanese companies when facing these two crises, this study uses a framework based on Cutlip's open PR system model (Cutlip et al., 1978, 2006) as shown in Figure 7.5.

As indicated in Figure 7.5, the PR system is positioned vertically under the management system. Cutlip et al. (2006) introduced three main factors: (1) goal states, (2) structure and process, and (3) variation in the environment. The former two factors are within the PR system, and the third factor is in the external environment. *Goal States* represents the goal of the PR system and has an "anchor-like" characteristic in the system. *Structure and Process* is described as a place where public relations activity is dealt with in the system and *Variation in the Environment* is outside of the PR system as defined by Cutlip et al. (2006). Change in the external environment is adopted as input to the PR system. Cutlip et al. (2006) explained that the maintenance goal of the "open system" is homeostasis, which means a static and fixed state; however, an opposite idea, "morphogenesis," has a dynamic feature that makes changes to the goal and the system itself.

When adopting the idea of an open PR system by Cutlip et al. (2006), this study focuses on the concept of "positive and negative feedback." As quoted in Cutlip et al. (2006), Littlejohn (2002) defined negative feedback as feedback that reduces gaps and corrects deviations of the system. Littlejohn (2002) claimed that negative feedback can reinforce and maintain the stability of the system. However, positive feedback increases gaps and amplifies deviations of the system; in addition, it can promote and enhance changes in the system. By adopting the concept of positive and negative feedback, this study is able to measure positive and negative feedback to understand the effective changes of PR (Ito, 2011).

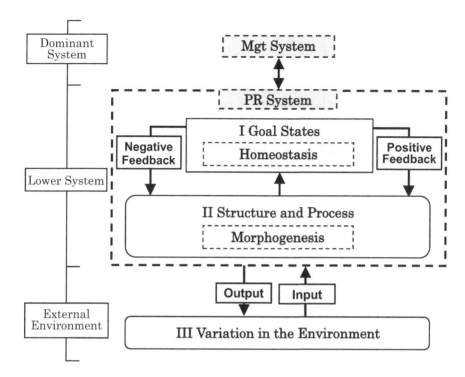

Figure 7.5 Open PR system model

Source: Concept model drawn by the author; it is a revised version of the model from Ito (2011).

Definition of "change" and data

Regarding quantitative change, PR staff number, PR department budget, and PR work volume are three variables to be asked about on the questionnaire. Qualitative change, however, is not observable because of the change inside the system. Normally, questions of composition concept designed in advance should be used to measure qualitative change; however, this study uses relevant questions from surveys conducted by JISEA and Hokkaido University. For changes in the PR system in the economic crisis, this study uses response data from the question asking about the adoption of new PR activities, whereas for the natural disaster crisis, we use response data from the question asking about modification of PR management. Using these questions makes it impossible to check the reliability of Cronbach's alpha for the composition concept; however, these questions are used to substitute for questions on PR system change. Analyzing the quantitative and qualitative changes in PR activities will give us an explanation as to how the open PR system model worked to accomplish self-adjustment toward the external environmental changes that Japanese companies experienced.

According to Littlejohn (2002), in an open system model, external environmental change that meets a certain threshold induces a transition of feedback in the system from negative to positive. This transition in feedback accounts for self-adjustment of the PR system. This study assumes that these two crises, the Lehman Shock and the GEJE, exerted enough impact to cause a feedback transition because many Japanese companies had never experienced such economic and social turmoil and uncertainty in the post-WWII era. Although the impact of these two crises differ depending on industry, this study focuses on the impact on all industries. In the next section, when we calculate the difference between the ratio of companies that changed and the ratio of companies that did not change as indices, we abstract differences by industry and see the whole picture.

The analyzed data were obtained from the following three sets of questionnaire surveys on corporate public relations activities. The first set of data is the survey conducted by the Japan Institute for Social and Economic Affairs (JISEA), "Attitude Survey on PR Work of the Company," every three years since 1980. The survey questionnaires are addressed to member companies of the Japan Business Federation and JISEA.[2] This study uses relevant data from the 7th survey to the 12th survey (JISEA, 2000; JISEA, 2003; JISEA, 2006; JISEA, 2009; JISEA, 2012b; JISEA, 2015). In relation to the two crises, the 10th and 11th surveys are important. As shown in Table 7.1, the 10th survey was conducted in November–December 2008 (during the crisis) and the 11th in November–December 2011 (after the crisis).

The second set of data is provided by the survey conducted by Hokkaido University in 2009 (Miyabe et al., 2010), one year after the Lehman Shock. Questionnaires of the survey are addressed to the CCO and PR director of companies listed on the First Section of the Tokyo Stock Exchange. The third set of data is obtained from JISEA's special survey on corporate PR responses to the GEJE and conducted in 2012, one year after the earthquake. The questionnaires are addressed to the main corporations of JISEA's survey so that the number of surveyed companies is limited.

Changes in public relations practice

Quantitative change

In this section, we start with the analysis of quantitative change utilizing the previously mentioned data set to review changes in the PR practices of Japanese companies in the past decade – the time when Japan experienced these two crises.

Our analysis focuses on the response data for three questions from the JISEA surveys that asked about the fluctuation of staff numbers, budget, and the amount of work. Survey respondents selected whether it increased, remained the same, or decreased. The index takes the difference between the increased and decreased rates, a data contraction concept similar to

Table 7.1 Summary of surveys

Survey name	Survey date	Survey method	Company number	Sample (response rate)	Reference
7th survey	Jun 1999– Aug 1999	mail surveys to CCO	1077	451 (41.9%)	JISEA (2000)
8th survey	Dec 2002– Feb 2003	mail surveys to CCO	879	484 (55.1%)	JISEA (2003)
9th survey	Nov 2005– Jan 2006	mail surveys to CCO	881	418 (47.4%)	JISEA (2006)
10th survey	Nov 2008– Dec 2008	mail surveys to CCO	884	412 (46.6%)	JISEA (2009)
11th survey	Nov 2011– Dec 2011	mail surveys to CCO	533	234 (43.9%)	JISEA (2012b)
12th survey	Oct 2014– Nov 2014	mail surveys to CCO	534	231 (43.3%)	JISEA (2015)
Lehman Shock survey by Hokkaido University	Sep 2009– Oct 2009	mail surveys to CCO and Director	545	161 (29.5%)	Miyabe et al. (2010)
Earthquake survey by JISEA	Feb 2012– March 2012	mail and fax surveys to CCO	152	71 (46.7%)	JISEA (2012a)

Source: By author

Note: The 7th survey was addressed to CEOs as well.

the business sentiment DI. The rate refers to the ratio of companies that answered that a corresponding factor had increased. Figure 7.6 illustrates the changes in the staff numbers, budgets, and amount of work of PR sections in Japanese companies after 2000. After 2006, the staff number index shows an increasing trend, with more than 10 points until 2012. The average number of staff is on an increasing trend until 2009 (no data for 2012 and 2015). The staff number index for the post-economic crisis period in 2009 is 12.4 points, and for the post-natural disaster crisis in 2012, it is 10.2 points. For 2015, the staff number index exhibits 7.8 points. These results indicate that the number of companies with staff number increases exceeded those with staff number decreases by more than 10 points starting in 2006 and continued during the two crises. However, this trend continues to 2015, which is different from the assumption of this study.

We now turn to the budget of the PR departments. Figure 7.6 shows the budget index to be negative in all the observed years except 2006. Compared with 2000 and 2003, indices for 2009 and 2012 minus values are small. For 2009 and 2012, the fact that the surveys are conducted one year after the crises may affect the results. The budget for the year after the crises returned to normal, so it seems that it decreased from the year of crisis.

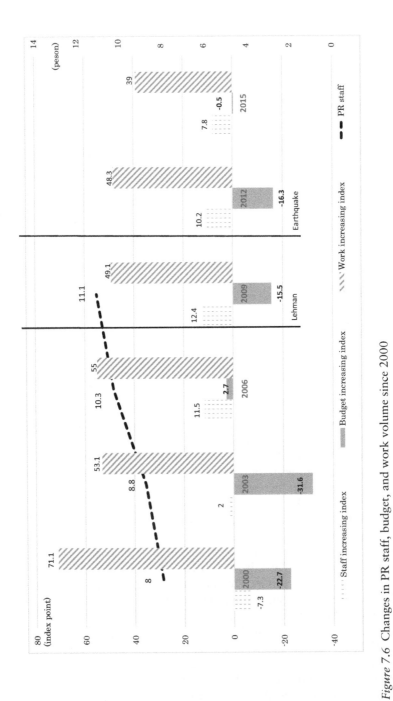

Figure 7.6 Changes in PR staff, budget, and work volume since 2000

Note

Left axis: PR staff index, budget index, and work volume index

Right axis: PR staff number

Source: Data compiled from JISEA (2000, 2003, 2006, 2009, 2012b, 2015).

The work volume index exhibits positive values in all the observed years. The indices were 71.1 points for 2000 and over 50 points for 2003 and 2006. One year after the crises, indices for 2009 and 2012 also show positive values, indicating that PR departments faced increasing work volumes. This study assumed that the quantitative change would be lessened in the post-crisis times with subsiding external environmental change. However, work volume seems to be increasing according to the index. Although the hypothesis, which is the starting point of consideration in this chapter, was rejected, the discussion in this chapter also reveals an increase in external environmental change that is revitalizing corporate public relations in the post-crisis period. This increase in external environmental change is taken up once again in the discussion part of this chapter.

According to our indices, changes in public relations practices over the past 10 years, including the two crises, are summarized as follows. Despite an increasing trend of work volume and corresponding increase in staff numbers, work was carried out while budgetary measures were not taken. Even in relation to the two crises, this overall trend has not changed; thus, our initial working hypothesis was not supported.

Rejection of this hypothesis verifies that the external environmental change in corporate public relations has increased continuously over the past 10 years. Were Japanese companies trying to cope with such external environmental changes with the same PR system as before the crisis? Or did the two crises trigger the change in the pre-crisis public relations system? To answer this question, in the next section, we will look at the qualitative change in corporate public relations.

Qualitative change

This section considers qualitative changes in the PR system induced by the two crises. For the Lehman Shock, we rely on data from the survey by Hokkaido University (Miyabe et al., 2010). For the GEJE, we rely on data from an *ad hoc* survey by JISEA (JISEA, 2012a).

The questionnaire survey by Hokkaido University included a question asking about changes in PR practices in the period of one year after the Lehman Shock. Respondents were asked whether the company changed its public relations response from what it was in the year after the Lehman Shock. If respondents indicated that they responded differently, then they were asked about scenes that took different measures and asked whether different measures were *ad hoc* measures or became part of public relations activities. A response is considered to indicate positive feedback if the respondent answered that the company had adapted some practices that were different or new from the previous or ordinary practice. A company that has adapted or is planning to adapt *ad hoc* practices into the list of PR practices is considered to have positive feedback that leads to modification of PR practices. However, a response is considered to indicate negative feedback if the respondent answered that the company did not adapt any *ad hoc* or new practice during a year after the Lehman Shock. The survey data shows that 32.9% of responses were positive feedback while 43% were negative. Thus, the qualitative change index for the Lehman Shock is –10.1.

The questionnaire survey conducted by JISEA (JISEA, 2012a) asked questions about the revision of risk management (RM) and business continuity plan (BCP) manuals. A response of action taken to revise or consider revising their manuals indicates that the company responded positively to the crisis, whereas the company that did not take any action is considered to have negative feedback. For the RM manual revision, 52.2% of respondents showed positive feedback and 46.5% negative feedback. For the BCP manual, 53.6% showed positive feedback and 46.5% negative. Thus, the qualitative change indices for the GEJE are 5.7 for the Lehman Shock and 6.1 for the GEJE (Table 7.2).

These two surveys targeted a similar group of respondents; however, the sample selection methods were not exactly the same. As a result, the samples overlap but are not identical. Therefore, we refrain from discussion based on a direct comparison of the results of these two surveys; instead, we consider whether positive or negative feedback dominates in each sample. The Lehman Shock shows that negative feedback is larger than positive feedback; thus, it was a crisis of the negative feedback dominant type for the entire Japanese company. The GEJE shows that the positive feedback was larger than the negative feedback; thus, it was a crisis of the positive feedback dominant type. Looking at the type and impact of the crisis, the Lehman Shock was an economic crisis that affected the entire Japanese economy and that recorded the worst DI. However, direct damage by the GEJE concentrated on the north-eastern part of Japan; except for some companies, it has not seriously damaged the western part of Japan. In addition, the drop in DI is small compared to that accompanying the Lehman Shock. Considering the scale of the impact on the economy and business activity by the crisis, the Lehman Shock should produce a positive feedback dominant type and the GEJE should produce a negative feedback dominant type. However, the observed survey data indicated the opposite result. Considering why the actual observation data is reversed, we look at the difference in nature between an economic crisis and a natural disaster. As seen in Figure 7.3, the response of Japanese companies' PR departments to the

Table 7.2 Qualitative changes in PR practices

Crisis	Positive feedback	Negative feedback	Index
Lehman Shock	32.9%	43.0%	–10.1p
GEJE RM	52.2%	46.5%	5.7p
GEJE BCP	53.6%	46.5%	6.1p

Source: By author.

economic crisis consisted of the accurate transmission of information (83%), internal communication (71%), and speeding-up (70%). These tasks are part of daily public relations work; however, qualitative improvement was required under the economic crisis. Meanwhile, the crisis response of public relations required for natural disasters is an extraordinary activity. These extraordinary public relations activities are generally described in the RM and BCP manuals, and the changes of the public relations system appear as a revision of the manuals. In conclusion, positive feedback at the time of the economic crisis is relatively difficult, as it requires the qualitative improvement of day-to-day public relations activities. In contrast, positive feedback at the time of natural disasters appears in the form of revisions to RM and BCP manuals and is comparatively easy to execute once decisions are made. As a result, positive feedback from natural disasters is easier to realize than positive feedback from economic crises, and the result seems to have come out in the survey. Natural disasters are easier to understand in the sense of a "crisis" than economic crises, and positive feedback is likely to occur.

Discussion: future tasks for Japanese companies' PR

As discussed in the previous section, the perceived impact on Japanese companies, indicated by the short-term DI, caused by the Lehman Shock (−58) was much larger than that of the GEJE (−9). Companies that suffered direct damages had to deal with the issue of business continuity; however, excluding some of the companies, such as motor vehicle manufacturers, the GEJE did not impinge on Japanese companies outside of the affected areas. In other words, the GEJE did not have a serious influence. Thus, there is a difference between an economic crisis that impacts every Japanese company and a natural disaster that affects some industries and companies.

Regarding quantitative change, the PR staff number increase index became positive after 2003; in addition, the PR work volume index has been continuously high (positive) since 2000. This indicates that the PR work volume of Japanese companies has been increasing since 2000 and the corresponding adjustment by increasing staff numbers is still not enough.

Furthermore, the tendency of increase in work volume and PR staff indices continues in the post-crisis periods although Japan faced gradual economic recovery. This indicates that the increase of work volume and PR staff was not relevant to any particular crisis but to other factors.

On the qualitative change, survey data referred to in the previous section indicated that almost half of the companies responding to the survey practiced negative feedback to maintain the PR system during the two crises. There is no difference in the magnitude of negative feedback between the two crises. An analysis of positive feedback and short-term DI has brought different results. The Lehman Shock affected Japanese companies more than the GEJE did according to short-term DI analysis; however, the GEJE influenced them more than the Lehman Shock in positive feedback. Regarding the reason for the difference between the two crises, considering the differences of the natures of economic crises and natural disasters would be the best approach. The economic impact on companies was more serious in the economic crisis, whereas the impact on media and the PR system was more serious in the natural disaster.

This study adopted the hypothesis of an open PR system model, where qualitative and quantitative changes of PR are decreased when the external environmental change subsides. However, this hypothesis was rejected by the positive numbers of PR staff and PR work volume indices from the latest data of JISEA (2015). Furthermore, changes in the external environment have continued to increase and companies' public relations work continues to increase.

According to the comparison of results from the latest JISEA survey (2015) and JISEA (2012b), the number of companies responding positively to the question asking about the PR section's concern in day-to-day operations has increased; furthermore, the ratio of answers that selected the item "range of PR practice is too broad" has the highest rate of increase at 9.7 points (17.1–26.8%). Besides, the second highest increase in the rate of answer is in the item "PR section does not have enough staff," which gained 7.4 points from the 2012 survey to the 2015one (32.9–40.3%).

Then, what is the reason that the PR section has a wide range of practices? Based on the comparison of JISEA survey results and considering the contents of PR practices, dealing with SNS has increased 11.5 points (18.8–30.3%). Second, managing CSR activities has increased 6 points (30.8–36.8%). Hence, it can be assumed that the two practices relating to SNS and CSR contribute to PR sections' wide range of work after crises. The importance of long-established relationships with news media and of internal communication has not been changed as in the past; however, managing SNS and CSR requires speed and attentive consideration to deal with stakeholders, including those who are new to Japanese companies. Thus, timely and appropriate communication and choosing suitable channels are going to be important.

Although Japanese companies have strived to gain a sound relationship with their stakeholders, there are several points that need attention. All stakeholders have reduced trust in various organizations, including companies, through the two crises. According to the data from the Edelman Trust Barometer, the Japanese have become "the least trusting people" since 2015 (Edelman, 2015). Under the circumstance of all stakeholders losing their trust in society, Japanese companies themselves are not excluded from this situation. Although Japanese companies, as the main actors in society, impressed consumers by dedicating themselves to CSR activities after the GEJE, they lost people's trust on a large scale partially because of serial corporate scandals.

To resolve this deplorable situation, the Japanese government has been earnestly trying to recalibrate the scenario. The Japan Revitalization Strategy, released in June 2013, focuses on developing the innate characteristics of corporations by taking a second look at corporate governance to survive and win global business (PM of Japan and his Cabinet, 2013). Furthermore, on May 1, 2015, business laws were revised to fortify corporate governance. In addition, the Tokyo Stock Exchange corporate governance code was established in June 2015. Hence, 2015 is known as "the first year of corporate governance" (Gabanansu kaikaku, 2 nenme no kadai ha ESG, 2015), as many policies were enacted in that year. As was mentioned previously, Japanese companies' PR departments need to introduce proper information speedily and through convenient channels that are suitable to all stakeholders, particularly in a period when stakeholders, including Japanese companies, lose their trust. In the era when trust in Japanese companies is declining, the PR function of a company is forced to expand to meet such a challenging task.

In the last decade, Japanese companies have experienced their two severest crises. With the open PR system model, the relationship between external environmental change and the PR system was considered in this chapter. The open PR system revises itself to fit the situation during crises arising from external environmental change; moreover, it is supposed to shift from change to stability when the crises end. Unlike the hypothesis of the adjustment of an open PR system model, the results of surveys reveal that the change in PR system has been ongoing continuously after the two crises. As with the two crises, changes in the PR system are needed even after the crisis. In addition to increase of speed and the meticulous attention of Japanese companies' PR sections, they are required to continue contrivances with flexible ideas and advanced ethics. In conclusion, the PR sections of Japanese companies need to continue to change themselves for the foreseeable future.

Notes

1 The summary description of the GEJE and Fukushima Daiichi nuclear accident here is based on Yamamura et al. (2012).
2 The Japan Business Federation (JBF) is a comprehensive economic organization with a membership comprising 1,350 representative companies of Japan, 109 nationwide industrial associations, and 47 regional economic organizations (as of April 1, 2017). The JISEA works as a PR department of JBF. However, the membership companies of both organizations are somewhat different. Retrieved from www.keidanren.or.jp/en/profile/pro001.html

References

Bangumi Kenkyu Group [Media Program Research Group]. (2011, May 2–7). [What did TV communicate when the GEJE occurred?]. *Broadcasting Research and Survey*, Research Institute of NHK Broadcasting Culture, 2–7.

Cabinet Office. (2009). *Nenji keizai zaisei hokoku H21* [Annual Report on the Japanese Economy and Public Finance 2009]. Retrieved on November 8, 2017, from http://www5.cao.go.jp/j-j/wp/wp-je09/09b01010.html

Cabinet Office. (2011a). *Nihon keizai 2011–2012* [Japanese Economy 2011–2012]. Retrieved on November 8, 2017, from http://www5.cao.go.jp/keizai3/2011/1221nk/n11_3 /n11_3_0.html

Cabinet Office. (2011b). *Nenji keizai zaisei hokoku H23* [Annual Report on the Japanese Economy and Public Finance 2011July]. Retrieved on November 8, 2017, from http://www5.cao.go.jp/j-j/wp/wp-je11/h01_01.html

Cabinet Office. (2012). *Bosai hakusho H24* [White Paper on Disaster Management 2012]. Retrieved on November 8, 2017, from www.bousai.go.jp/kaigirep/hakusho/h24/bousai2012/html/honbun/4b_8s_14_00.htm

Cutlip, S. M., Center, A. H., & Broom, G. M. (1978). *Effective public relations* (1st edition). Englewood Cliffs, NJ: Pearson Prentice Hall.

Cutlip, S. M., Center, A. H., & Broom, G. M. (2006). *Effective public relations* (9th edition). Upper Saddle River, NJ: Pearson Prentice Hall.

Edelman. (2015). *Edelman trust barometer global results 2015*. Retrieved on November 8, 2017, from www.edelman.com/insights/intellectual-property/2015-edelman-trust-barometer/global-results/

Gabanansu kaikaku, 2 nenme no kadai ha ESG [Governance Reformation, the second-year task is ESG]. (2015, September 21). *Nihon Keizai Shimbun*. Retrieved on November 8, 2017, www.nikkei.com/article/DGXMZO91895430Y5A910C1I00000/

Havemann, J. (2008). The financial crisis of 2008. *The Encyclopedia Britannica*. Retrieved on November 8, 2017, from www.britannica.com/topic/Financial-Crisis-of-2008-The-1484264

Ito, N. (2011). Lehman shock impact on Japanese companies and changes of corporate communication: How to measure qualitative change in PR system of companies, *14th annual International Public Relations Research Conference Proceedings* (pp. 322–338). Retrieved from www.instituteforpr.org/wp-content/uploads/14th-IPRRC-Proceedings.pdf

Japan Institute for Social and Economic Affairs. (2000). *Dai 7kai kigyou no kouhou katsudou ni kansuru ishiki jittai chousa* [The Seventh Survey Report on the Attitude and Status of Corporate Public Relations Activities]. Tokyo: Japan Institute for Social and Economic Affairs.

Japan Institute for Social and Economic Affairs. (2003). *Dai 8kai kigyou no kouhou katsudou ni kansuru ishiki jittai chousa* [The Eighth Survey Report on the Attitude and Status of Corporate Public Relations Activities]. Tokyo: Japan Institute for Social and Economic Affairs.

Japan Institute for Social and Economic Affairs. (2006). *Dai 9kai kigyou no kouhou katsudou ni kansuru ishiki jittai chousa* [The Ninth Survey Report on the Attitude and Status of Corporate Public Relations Activities]. Tokyo: Japan Institute for Social and Economic Affairs.

Japan Institute for Social and Economic Affairs. (2009). *Dai 10kai kigyou no kouhou katsudou ni kansuru ishiki jittai chousa* [The 10th Survey Report on the Attitude and Status of Corporate Public Relations Activities]. Tokyo: Japan Institute for Social and Economic Affairs.

Japan Institute for Social and Economic Affairs. (2012a). *Higashinihon daishinsai ni miru kigyou no kikikanri to koho chosa* [Survey on Risk Management and PR in the Great East Japan Earthquake]. Tokyo: Japan Institute for Social and Economic Affairs.

Japan Institute for Social and Economic Affairs. (2012b). *Dai 11kai kigyou no kouhou katsudou ni kansuru ishiki jittai chousa* [The 11th Survey Report on the Attitude and Status of Corporate Public Relations Activities]. Tokyo: Japan Institute for Social and Economic Affairs.

Japan Institute for Social and Economic Affairs. (2015). *Dai 12kai kigyou no kouhou katsudou ni kansuru ishiki jittai chousa* [The 12th Survey Report on the Attitude and Status of Corporate Public Relations Activities]. Tokyo: Japan Institute for Social and Economic Affairs.

Jidosyameka ga chokumenshita sapuraichen no wana [Automobile Maker facing Supply chain Trap]. (2011, May 17). *Toyo Keizai*. Retrieved on November 8, 2017, from http://toyokeizai.net/articles/-/6960

Littlejohn, S. W. (2002). *Theories of human communication* (7th edition). Belmont, CA: Wadsworth /Thompson Learning.

Ministry of Economy, Trade and Industry. (2009). Tsusho hakusyo H21 [White Paper on International Economy and Trade]. Retrieved on November 8, 2017, from www.meti.go.jp/report/tsuhaku2009/2009honbun/html/i2120000.html

Miyabe, J., Ito, N., Watanabe, K., Yukawa, K., Kitami, K., & Firkola, P. (2010). Hokkaido Daigaku kigyou komyunike-syonn cyousa 2009 [Hokkaido University Corporate Communication Survey 2009]. *The Journal of International Media, Communication, and Tourism Studies*, 11, 61–121.

Nikkei BP Consulting. (2011). *Kigyomei soki chosa* [Corporate name recall survey] Retrieved on November 8, 2017, from http://consult.nikkeibp.co.jp/consult/news/2011/0902bj/

Nikkei heikin 2011nen wa 17% yasu liman irai no gerakuritsu [Nikkei Stock Average, 17% down in 2011, down ratio since the Lehman Shock]. (2011, December 30). *Nihon Keizai Shimbun*. Retrieved on November 8, 2017, from www.nikkei.com/article/DGXNASFL3007P_Q1A231C1000000/

PM of Japan and His Cabinet. (2013). *Nihon saiko senryaku-Japan is back* [Japan Revitalization Strategy-JAPAN is BACK]. Retrieved on November 8, 2017, from www.kantei.go.jp/jp/singi/ keizaisaisei/kettei.html

Yamamura K. (2014). Yamato employees lead response to earthquake relief efforts. In Turk, J. V., Valin, J., & Paluszek, J. (Eds.), *Public Relations Case Studies from Around the World* (pp. 259–280). New York, NY: Peter Lang Publishing.

Yamamura, K., Miyabe, J., Ito, N., & Wada, M. (2012). Quake Hits PR: The Impact of 3.11 Earthquake on Public Relations in Japan, *15th International Public Relations Research Conference Proceedings* (pp. 823–831). Retrieved from www.instituteforpr.org/wp-content/uploads/15th-IPRRC-Proceedings.pdf

8 The current situation of corporate public relations in Japan

An attempt to assess comprehensive public relations activities from eight aspects

Koichi Kitami

Introduction

Corporate public relations activities have continued to become more and more advanced and complex. While public relations activities at Japanese companies have for a long time focused mainly on building relationships with mass media, the scope has expanded to a wider range of activities.

In order for a company to determine which area of public relations to enhance, it is necessary to have a deep understanding of each of the various public relations activities in a systematic and practical way. Although experience and intuition are important in the actual practice of public relations, understanding public relations activities requires something more than just experience and intuition. In addition, companies need to enhance public relations capabilities that are required to achieve company specific business goals.

The discussion in this chapter is based on the results of a survey conducted in 2016 of the heads of public relations at Japanese companies. Through the analysis of the survey results, we will try to identify the current situation of public relations activities at Japanese companies and the issues to do with public relations activities that these companies face.

Literature review

It is not easy to define the scope of public relations activities. There have been various discussions on this. Hutton (1999), for example, defined public relations as "managing strategic relationships." He listed the following as the main functions of public relations: research, image making, counseling, management, early warning, interpreting, communicating, and negotiating.

Indeed, public relations is about managing strategic relationships. However, in practice, public relations professionals in Japan do not seem to be clear about what to manage, eventually focusing mainly on the management of communication with the media. The practice of effective public relations requires implementation of activities of a much wider scope than simply managing media relations.

There are various arguments as to what range of activities should be included in public relations. Various studies have been conducted to find out the actual situation of public relations activities. In Japan, for example, Miyabe et al. (2010) and the Japan Institute for Social and Economic Affairs (2015) have conducted surveys to find out the scope of corporate public relations activities. These surveys reveal the scope of public relations activities at Japanese companies. Although these surveys provide an outline of corporate public relations activities in Japan, they do not offer an industry-to-industry comparison, nor do they provide information to allow a company to assess its own public relations activities.

There are similar studies overseas, such as the GAP study by the University of Southern California Annenberg School for Communication and Journalism and the European Communication Monitor by EUPRERA and EACD. These studies are surveys focusing on the practitioners of communication. The studies, as part of the inquiry, ask about the conditions necessary for public relations professionals (European Communication Monitor 2014; Lurati & Mariconda, 2014). These previous studies provide a macroscopic view of public relations activities conducted by companies. However, they do not provide information as to where each company stands in comparison with other companies. The current study, in contrast, provides an indication as to where a particular survey respondent stands, as an average figure can be provided.

Various models have also been proposed to analyze corporate PR activities. One such model to analyze public relations activities is the PII model. This model proposes indicators in three stages of public relations activities to evaluate the public relations effect at each of the stages. The three stages are preparation, implementation, and impact (Cutlip et al., 1985). MacNamara (2006) has further developed this PII model and created the pyramid model of public relations research. In the pyramid model, PR activities are categorized into three stages of inputs, outputs, and outcomes. Inputs is about research for target audiences, medium choice, and message content. Outputs is about how messages are sent out, carried in the media, and received by the target audiences. Outcomes is about the extent to which public relations activities achieved their objectives. Both models aim to evaluate public relations activities and their effect, but modifications are required to gain an understanding of the everyday activities of public relations professionals.

In this study, we analyzed the public relations activities at Japanese corporations by classifying their activities into eight aspects that were built upon the pyramid model, adding insights that the authors gained as practitioners in the field.

Analysis model in this study

The Corporate Communication Strategic Studies Institute of Dentsu Public Relations Inc. (Dentsu PR) developed an analytical model, with its focus on identifying the status of corporate public relations activities. At the time the survey was conducted, the author was a member of the Corporate Communication Strategic Studies Institute and played a pivotal role in creating the model and conducting the study. In this model, 80 items related to corporate public relations activities were identified and classified into eight aspects, namely, collecting information, analyzing information, building strategy, creating information, transmitting information, building engagement, risk management, and public relations organization (refer to Appendix: 80 activity items). Collecting information and analyzing information correspond to the preparation in the PII model. Building strategy and creating information correspond to the implementation. Transmitting information and building engagement correspond to impact. Risk management and PR organization do not correspond to any of the PII model aspects, but risk management is the most crucial aspect of PR activities as it can determine the fate of a company and relies heavily on collaboration with other departments. PR organization is also a fundamental aspect of PR activities in Japan, as use of outside PR firms in the broad spectrum is not a common practice, if not non-existent, and PR departments of some of the listed companies can be quite large, resulting in the importance of PR organization.

These eight aspects are indispensable for companies to build better relationships with various stakeholders in society. Figure 8.1 shows how these eight aspects relate to each other.

Before transmitting information, it is necessary to collect and analyze information relevant to the issue in question, to know how society sees the company, and to understand what the society expects from the company and of the company. Such information is essential in crafting messages strategically, and unless the messages are crafted strategically, they don't resonate with the target audience.

Collecting information refers to the activities related to collecting and gaining understanding of the relevant information regarding the company, industry and competition, stakeholders, and society at large. In recent years in Japan, the roles expected of public relations departments are not confined to transmitting information on goods and services but have expanded to managing the reputation of the company among shareholders, business partners, employees, customers, and other relevant parties. Along with these changes, the medium of importance has also expanded from traditional media, such as television, newspapers, and magazines, to include online media and social networking sites as the reputation of and trust in companies among a wider spectrum of stakeholders have become important. It has also become important to gather information on regulatory bodies and competitors.

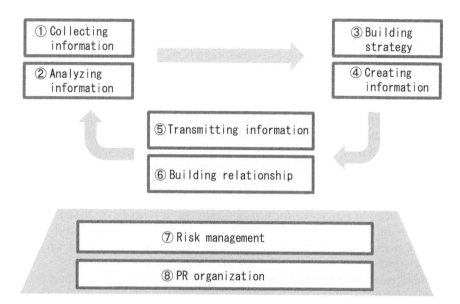

Figure 8.1 Eight aspects of public relations activities

Source: The concept of eight aspects is by the Corporate Communication Strategic Studies Institute. Organization based on PII frames is by the author.

Analyzing information is an activity related to gaining insight and understanding the context surrounding the company regarding the issues the company is facing covertly or overtly. By analyzing the collected information, the company can anticipate societal movements in the future and changes in the competitive environment. By anticipating the future when crafting messages, they can be better received, as they are more likely to be in line with the social trends, resulting in a more compelling story. To this end, it is necessary to constantly observe media trends, influences, and social media, not only in the domestic environment, but also overseas. Through such efforts, it becomes possible to understand the environment surrounding the company that helps people better understand issues that affect management decisions and public relations activities. It is also important to obtain feedback to assess effectiveness of public relations efforts.

Building strategy is an activity related to the establishment of public relations strategies that reflect the management objectives. Public relations activities cannot show their effects overnight. It is necessary that long-term public relations strategies are linked to the corporate vision and management strategy. It is necessary to identify the target audience, as each public requires a different communications strategy. To that end, it is important to grasp the strengths and weaknesses of the company using management tools such as the SWOT analysis.

Creating information is an activity to develop messages and visuals tailored to target audiences, with the understanding of the characteristics of the selected media, to gain the recognition, understanding, and empathy of the stakeholders. What is important here is the understanding of society and the insight gained through the analysis of the information obtained. Creating information is strengthened by aligning messages with societal needs and creating stories that follow the company's public relations strategy. If information originating from the business section is transmitted as it is, without regard to societal context, it will not resonate with the target audience and may end up giving a negative impression of the company.

Transmitting information is an activity to disseminate information utilizing various media, such as traditional mass media, owned media, social networks, and so on. In transmitting information, what is important is the communication activity by the top management. It is necessary to pay attention not only to the interaction with media, such as interviews and press conferences, but also to public speaking opportunities targeting various stakeholders.

Building engagement is an activity to develop mutual understanding with important stakeholders and constantly enhance the relationship with these stakeholders, building trust in the organization. For public relations professionals in Japan, one of the most important tasks is to build close relationships with media reporters. By engaging with reporters on a daily basis and strengthening their relationships with them, public relations professionals can gain insight as to how reporters think and act. In Japan, where public relations education is weak and most of the public relations professionals are not equipped with such an education, engaging with reporters is very important. However, the reporters are not the only stakeholders public relations professionals build relationships with. With the advent of globalization, diversification of communication media, and growth in the use of social network sites, it has become important now to build relationships with various stakeholders. Consequently, it has become necessary to work closely with other corporate departments, such as IR, human resources, marketing, and customer relations. In today's business environment, companies should try to build relationships with every kind of stakeholder, as none is less important than any other.

Risk management is an organizational activity to maintain and improve the skills to predict, prevent, and manage risks surrounding the company and to contain the damages arising from emergency situations. Compared to the past, there has been a dramatic increase in the business continuity plan (BCP) partly due to the experience Japan has had from earthquakes and increased exposure to global economic turmoil (Small and Medium Enterprise Agency, 2016).

Many large companies have set up departments responsible for handling BCP, but public relations departments seem to lack knowledge and expertise in BCP. However, in times of crisis, it is public relations departments that need to speak on behalf of the company. Therefore, it is important for public relations departments to actively participate in crisis management activities and establish their position within the company as having relevant expertise.

PR organization is an activity related to the decision-making mechanism and to system development to integrate management activities and public relations activities. In order for public relations functions to fulfill their role of supporting management, they need to have solid and strong organization. What is important is to have a close relationship with top management. In emergencies, public relations personnel act as spokespersons for management on behalf of them. In order to build a relationship that enables public relations personnel to talk with top management on a daily basis, the ideal situation is to have the public relations department report directly to the top management. Links between management strategy and public relations strategy can be established if a person in charge of public relations is a member of the dominant coalition.

Using the eight aspects mentioned earlier, the Corporate Communications Strategic Institute of Dentsu PR Inc. conducted a survey on public relations activities at Japanese companies in 2014 and 2016. In 2016, when the survey was planned and conducted, the author was a member of the Corporate Communications Strategic Institute of Dentsu PR and played the leading role in this survey project. The discussion in this paper is based on the 2016 survey.

The research subjects were heads of public relations departments at companies listed on major stock exchanges in Japan, excluding advertising and PR firms. The companies listed on multiple stock exchanges received only one copy of the survey questionnaire. The outline of the survey research is as follows:

Survey on Public Relations Activities at Japanese Companies

- Respondents: Heads of public relations departments/sections at companies listed on the Tokyo Stock Exchange, Mothers, JASDAQ, the Sapporo Securities Exchange, the Nagoya Stock Exchange, and the Fukuoka Stock Exchange (3,664 companies). Advertising and public relations companies were excluded.
- Survey type: Mail survey
  *note: Dentsu PR's clients received the surveys in envelopes that were handed out by Dentsu PR employees
- Response rate: 14.5% (533 valid responses out of 3,664 surveys mailed)
- Period: February to April, 2016

For industry classification, Kaisha Shiki-ho's[1] 16 categories were adopted for this study.

Each company's public relations activities in each of the eight aspects, "Collecting information," "Analyzing information," "Building strategy," "Creating information," "Transmitting information," "Building engagement,"

"Risk management," and "PR organization" were scored. Through these eight aspects, it was possible to analyze the resources needed for PR activities. In addition, we have conducted an industry comparison and highlighted the strengths and weaknesses of the PR activities at Japanese companies.

Ten activity items were selected for each of the eight aspects of public relations. A total of 80 activity items were determined. The respondents were asked whether they engaged in each of the 80 activity items or not. In total, there were 80 questions.

The activity items were assessed by a panel of experts. The panel consisted of 12 members in total, with four scholars, four journalists, and four practitioners. Among the 10 items within each of the eight aspects, each panel member cast three votes for items that he or she thought were important. Each of the 36 votes (three votes by each of the 12 panel members) by the panel members was given a value of 1. Each item was given a base point score of 6.4. In total, with the base score and the voted score, a company had a chance to gain a maximum score of 100 for each aspect, if the company conducted all of the 10 activity items within the aspect. In addition to these 80 questions asking if the PR departments conducted particular PR activities, the survey asked who the key stakeholders are and what the key PR activities were as perceived by them.

Results

Overall results

The survey on the public relations activities at Japanese companies resulted in the following score (see Table 8.1). For all the eight aspects, the average score was 32.6 out of 100 points.

Table 8.1 Aspect score average and total score average

Aspects category	Average score
Collecting information	43.4
Analyzing information	27.7
Building strategy	26.0
Creating information	26.0
Transmitting information	52.7
Building engagement	23.3
Risk management	27.6
PR organization	34.4
Average score	32.6

Source: Data selected from the Survey on Public Relations Activities at Japanese Companies, the Corporate Communication Strategic Studies Institute. Translated by the author.

Among the eight aspects, "Transmitting information" stands out with a score of 52.7, followed by "Collecting information" (43.4). These two fundamental aspects of public relations are the most practiced PR activities in Japan. The lowest score aspect was "Building engagement" (23.3), followed by "Building strategy" and "Creating information." These seem to be the public relations activities where Japanese companies fall short.

Among the eight aspects, "Building engagement" was the aspect with the lowest score. Traditionally in Japan, key tasks of public relations departments have been to produce PR magazines and company newsletters and to handle media relations. However, as various pressure groups have become more active and the importance of public affairs has increased, stakeholders for public relations in Japan have diversified. The idea of engagement has come to Japan only recently, and it hasn't gained a position as a common public relations activity.

"Building strategy" is an aspect that is still not widely practiced. However, when asked what they would like to strengthen in the future, out of the 80 question items, "formulation of a long-term PR strategy," one of the items in the "building strategy" aspect, was the most frequent answer with 49.9% of the respondents checking this item. Compared to advertising activities, it takes a longer period of time for PR activities to show their effect. Therefore, it is important to have a long-term public relations strategy.

Public relations activities by industry at Japanese companies

The results were analyzed by industry. Table 8.2 shows the aspect scores for each industry, sorted by the average score. The industry with the highest average score was the electricity and gas industry, followed by the transportation and warehouse industry, the food industry, and the financial, securities, and insurance industry.

PR activities and stakeholders

Key stakeholders as perceived by PR professionals

"Stakeholders" refers to those who have stakes in an organization. It has been considered in Japan that key stakeholders for public relations departments are "customers," "shareholders/investors," and "media." However, the survey results (Figure 8.2) revealed that "suppliers" (68.9) were the third most important stakeholder following "customers" (90.8%) and "shareholders/investors" (89.9%), surpassing "media" (67.9%).

Another important finding is that "employees and their families" (67.7%) were ranked at the same level as "media" (67.9%). The implication of this is that the range of stakeholders has grown much wider than "customers," "shareholders/investors," and "media," which have been regarded in the past as the main target of public relations activities.

Table 8.2 Score by industry

		n	Average score	Collecting information	Analyzing information	Building strategy	Creating information	Transmitting information	Building engagement	Risk management	PR organization
2016	All average	533	32.6	43.4	27.7	26.0	26.0	52.7	23.3	27.6	34.4
No.1	Electricity · Gas	9	47.0	66.5	37.4	39.1	31.8	62.2	40.7	51.0	47.2
No.2	Transportation Warehouse	16	41.2	51.5	32.4	30.8	29.9	62.5	29.9	46.0	46.3
No.3	Foodstuffs	27	39.0	49.1	32.0	24.4	34.8	66.8	29.6	39.3	35.7
No.4	Finance · Securities · Insurance	30	39.0	54.9	29.2	29.2	29.5	55.4	30.7	41.1	41.9
No.5	Telecommunications	60	35.4	45.4	34.6	30.5	28.8	60.0	22.7	23.7	37.4
No.6	Other products (glass, stone, rubber, etc.)	15	35.3	37.9	30.4	29.2	29.6	55.9	27.7	32.6	39.0
No.7	Textiles, Chemistry, Medicine	52	34.4	42.0	25.5	27.6	24.2	56.0	29.2	33.1	37.5
No.8	Machine	28	33.8	42.8	31.1	28.5	31.7	49.4	21.5	26.3	39.1
No.9	Electrical equipment	48	32.6	39.9	28.8	26.5	25.6	54.8	19.2	28.6	37.2
No.10	Transportation equipment · Precision equipment	26	30.7	44.1	25.9	23.8	21.6	47.5	24.3	27.1	31.5
No.11	Other	19	30.6	45.1	26.2	25.0	28.1	50.9	21.3	17.0	31.0
No.12	Service industry	69	30.4	41.9	26.6	24.9	27.2	51.4	19.8	21.9	29.4
No.13	Wholesale · Retail	74	28.2	41.0	23.4	22.5	21.8	46.1	20.6	21.1	28.7
No.14	Construction	26	27.4	39.1	26.3	17.9	18.8	43.8	17.9	26.2	29.3
No.15	Steel · Nonferrous metal	21	25.9	33.9	18.5	23.0	18.5	43.7	22.0	20.4	27.0
No.16	Real estate	13	24.9	35.9	20.8	23.3	19.3	35.9	14.6	19.4	29.8

Source: Data selected from the Survey on Public Relations Activities at Japanese Companies, the Corporate Communication Strategic Studies Institute. Translated by the author.

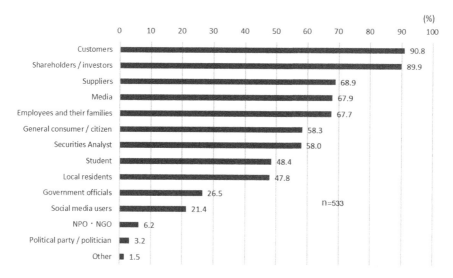

Figure 8.2 Key stakeholders as perceived by PR professionals

Source: Corporate Communication Strategic Studies Institute. Translated by the author.

This coincides with the Japanese government's drive to promote "work-style reform" and indicates that public relations departments have come to view employees as one of the key stakeholders. The time when the public relations departments only had to deal with the media is now over.

Key PR activities

Figure 8.3 shows the key activities conducted by PR professionals. "Top message, corporate vision" was the most frequent response; 80.9% of the respondents chose it. This was followed by "product/service PR" (67.7%) and "internal activation" (58.3%). The emphasis placed on "internal activation" is consistent with the finding that "employees and their families" were the fourth most important stakeholder. In Japan, internal communication has long been seen as the territory of the human resources department; however, these findings indicate that internal communication has become an important part of public relations activities. The most important PR activity, "Top message, Corporate vision," also has a strong implication as an internal message, whether it is communicated internally or through external media.

Discussion

In this chapter, we have tried to glimpse the current situation of public relations activities of listed companies in Japan from eight aspects. "Gathering

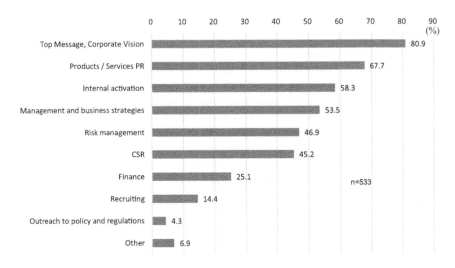

Figure 8.3 Key PR activities

Source: Data selected from the Survey on Public Relations Activities at Japanese Companies, the Corporate Communication Strategic Studies Institute. Translated by the author.

information" and "Transmitting information" were the highest among the eight aspects (Table 8.1).

However, the score for "building strategy" was lower than the average score of all eight aspects. This implies that Japanese companies need to conduct public relations activities more strategically. While the communication media employed by public relations have expanded to include the Internet and social networking sites, it has been suggested that this strategy is not well incorporated there. As a practitioner-turned-academic, I have to admit that PR activities in Japan are still focused mainly on responding to media inquiries. There is a need for "building strategy" to go beyond simply crafting messages and scenarios.

To improve the ability of public relations departments to build strategy, it is important for them to gather information from both inside and outside the company. Gathering information allows a company to gain insight into issues surrounding the company. It is the responsibility of a public relations department to analyze the information collected and share it systematically within the company. Based on this information and the insight gained through the analysis of such information, public relations departments need to grasp their strengths and weaknesses and formulate a public relations strategy that best suits the organization and its environment. The strategy defines what messages are sent to whom.

The results of the survey show that the electricity and gas industry had the highest score in the highest number of aspects. Second was the transportation and warehouse industry. Interestingly, these were the industries with the highest level of governmental regulation.

In all 16 industries, risk management had the highest score among the eight aspects. However, in 2016 in Japan, various issues arose. In the energy industry, retail sales of gas and electricity were deregulated. In the food industry, there were multiple instances of food contamination. In the financial industry, there was leakage of personal information. In industries that are prone to high-risk incidents, they tend to show high scores for risk management.

Many industries are embracing new PR opportunities. Aviation and railway companies in the transportation industry are experiencing high levels of media exposure thanks to the rapid increase in the number of foreign tourists. Electronic commerce has brought new business opportunities for the warehouse and logistics industries. In contrast, the electrical equipment industry, which was once Japan's hallmark, ranks ninth among the 16 industries. It is an irony that public relations activity is not active in the industry where it is most needed.

Also, looking at important stakeholders for public relations departments, it's not just media anymore. A broader range of stakeholders, such as "business partners" and "employees," are regarded as important. In fact, "customers," "shareholders/investors," and "suppliers" are ranked above "media." This shows that public relations departments in Japan are no longer dealing only with media.

What is significant about this research is the importance attributed to "employees," as "internal activation" was also among the top three PR activities. In recent years, we have witnessed changes in the business environment, such as repeated corporate scandals, frequent mergers and acquisitions, calls for a more diverse work environment, and the popularity of social networking sites that have forced many companies to change the way they cope with the environment.

Internal communication can increase employee motivation, leading to the creation of a participatory business culture. A participatory business culture will create a space for constructive discussions and positive employee proposals, thus yielding improved performances. Therefore, as organizations work together to tackle business activities, there is an increasing momentum to actively engage in internal communication. From experiences as a practitioner, I have found that internal communication is not just the role of simply propagating the intent of a company (management team) to stakeholders through in-house newsletters and the like. Internal communication has begun to be recognized as having the function of raising the awareness of the employees and promoting changes to an active attitude.

Media relations have played a major role in public relations activities at Japanese companies. However, as a wider variety of publics have become important today, it is necessary for companies to conduct public relations as it was intended, to build mutually beneficial relationships with various publics. However, in reality, with limited human resources and limited budgets, it is difficult to deal with all themes and all stakeholders. It is important for corporate PR departments to ask what their "PR goals" are. To that end, it is necessary to create strategies and determine priorities based on the strategies. Corporate PR departments must always keep the PR strategy in mind while engaging in public relations activities.

The research in the past has identified public relations in Japan as a publicity model (e.g., Sriramesh et al., 1999). However, the findings of this study revealed PR practices beyond mere public information and media relations. The revelation of the importance placed on internal communications and various stakeholders is a contribution the current study has made to PR academia. Another contribution is that the study allows for an industry-to-industry comparison. There is room for further study expanding the current study to non-listed companies and for making a comparison between globalized companies and ones with domestic operations only and between B-to-B (business to business) business companies and B-to-C (business to consumer) business companies.

Note

1 *Kaisha Shiki-ho* is an investor handbook that lists all the listed companies with information such as balance sheets, profit and loss statements, stock ownership, and analyses of future outlooks. *Kaisha Shiki-ho* has been published every quarter since 1936, and its classifications are popular among corporations.

References

Cutlip, S. M., Center, A. H., & Broom, G. M. (1985). *Effective public relations*. Upper Saddle River, NJ: Pearson Prentice Hall.

European Communication Monitor. (2014). *European communication monitor 2014: Excellence in strategic communication - Key issues, leadership, gender and mobile media: Results of a survey in 42 countries*. Retrieved from www.zerfass.de/ecm/ECM-2014-Results-ChartVersion.pdf

Hutton, J. G. (1999). The definition, dimensions, and domain of public relations. *Public Relations Review*, 25(2), 199–214.

Japan Institute for Social and Economic Affairs. (2015). *Dai 12 kai kigyou no kouhou katsudou ni kansuru ishiki jittai chousa* [The 12th Survey Report on the Attitude and Status of Corporate Public Relations Activities]. Tokyo: Japan Institute for Social and Economic Affairs.

Lurati, F., & Mariconda, S. (2014). *Swiss corporate communication and public relations practice monitor: 2013 report*. Retrieved from www.prsuisse.ch/sites/all/files/swiss_observatory_2013_e_-long.pdf

MacNamara, J. R. (2006). *PR metrics: Research for planning and evaluation of PR and corporate communication*. Retrieved from http://195.130.87.21:8080/dspace/bitstream/123456789/231/1/Macnamara-PR%20metrics.pdf

Miyabe, J., Ito, N., Watanabe, K., Yukawa, K., Kitami, K., & Firkola, P. (2010). Hokkaido Daigaku kigyou komyunike-syonn cyousa 2009 [Hokkaido University

Corporate Communication Survey 2009]. *The Journal of International Media, Communication, and Tourism Studies*, 11, 61–121.

Small and Medium Enterprise Agency. (2016). *Chusho kigyo hakusho* [White Paper on Small and Medium Enterprises in Japan]. Retrieved from www.chusho.meti. go.jp/pamflet/hakusyo/H28/h28/html/b2_4_2_2.html

Sriramesh, K., Kim, Y., & Takasaki, M. (1999). Public relations in three Asian cultures: An analysis. *Journal of Public Relations Research*, 11(4), 271–292.

Appendix
80 activity items

1 Collecting information

The company continually monitors the coverage of newspapers and magazines about the company.

The company regularly checks trends in the industry and among competitors.

The company continuously keeps track of regulatory and administrative trends that affect the company.

The company continually monitors television coverage of the company.

The company continually monitors the company on social media and the web.

The company keeps track of the latest trends in the media (change in reporters' responsibilities, new media outlets, and so on).

The company keeps track of reporters' thoughts and opinions through its own personal contacts.

The company regularly collects customer and the general public's attitude toward and evaluation of the company.

The company collects relevant overseas information to help public relations activities.

The company collects information from influencers (such as experts and NPOs) through its own personal network.

2 Analyzing information

The company analyzes the effect of owned media such as HP sites.

The company quantifies and analyzes the exposure of each news release.

The company regularly analyzes its industry and competitors.

The company measures its coverage in newspapers and on TV.

The company analyzes and clarifies the PR issues of the company and records them in writing.

The company analyzes mentions and the reputation of the company and the industry on social media.

The company makes predictions of major future events and social trends.

The company analyzes the company rankings announced by the media, think tanks, and so on.

The company conducts qualitative assessments of its print and broadcast coverage.

The company grasps and analyzes actions of and remarks by influencers (experts, NPOs, and so on).

3 Building strategy

Public relations strategy is linked to management strategy.

The company develops a public relations strategy with awareness of the company's strengths and weaknesses.

The company sets focus media and develops individual strategies tailored for such media.

The company secures a public relations budget suited for its PR strategy.

The company has a mid- to long-term public relations strategy.

The company has its own target figures (such as page views and number of likes) for the company's website and social media.

The company shares its public relations strategy with its group companies.

The company sets targets regarding the amount and content of coverage for the company and its products.

The company analyzes the competitors' PR strategies and takes necessary actions.

For each stakeholder, the company has desired evaluations to be obtained and set strategies.

4 Creating information

The company has public relations materials (data, facts, and so on) in line with its PR strategy.

The company has press materials on companies, products, and services.

The company has the message and story in line with its public relations strategy.

The company has public relations tools that utilize visuals and graphics.

The company has internal and external structures that professionally create messages for top executives.

The company carries out its business activities and CSR activities, which emphasize public relations perspectives.

The company creates publicity materials and information that matches the characteristics of digital tools.

The company utilizes viral movies and videos for public relations activities.

The company regularly conducts media training for top executives to enhance their presentation skills and expressiveness.

The company cooperates with NPOs and research organizations to create public relations materials and information.

5 Transmitting information

The company posts news releases on the company website.

The company has its own print media (corporate brochures, PR magazines, and so on).

The company regularly sends out news releases.

The company transmits information tailored to each important stakeholder (ex. IR material, company newsletter, and so on).

The company website is regularly updated, at least twice a month.

Top executives are interviewed by the media on a regular basis.

The company transmits information using social media.

The company has its own web media (product sites, web communities, mobile applications).

The company uses wire services to send out news releases.

The company collaborates with NPOs and research organizations to transmit information.

6 Building engagement

The public relations division, together with the IR department, conducts investor relations.

Top executives have regular opportunities to meet employees in person.

The public relations division shares information with the customer consultation room and carries out appropriate relationship-building activities.

The president regularly has opportunities to talk with the media.

The public relations department regularly holds a roundtable discussion with press club members.

The company regularly offers opportunities to customers and local residents to interact in person with them.

The company operates community sites and interacts with product customers.

The head of the public relations department has regular opportunities to meet with influencers in person (such as experts and NPOs).

The public relations department has a website, such as an online press room, dedicated to media.

The head of the public relations department has regular opportunities to meet with government personnel and politicians in person.

7 Crisis management

The company has an internal contact network to be mobilized in case of emergency.

The company educates employees and part-time workers about ethics and crisis consciousness.

The company has a crisis management manual that specifically describes actions for public relations.

The company studies risk incidents that occurred in the industry and among competitors.

The company regularly holds crisis management committee meetings in which the public relations department participates.

The public relations department participates in the development and operation of a business continuity plan (BCP).

The company has a social media operations guideline and risk response manual.

The company regularly carries out emergency simulation training (including for departments other than public relations).

The company regularly conducts simulated press conferences.

The public relations division regularly reports on management risk estimates to executive officers.

8   PR organization

The company has a division specializing in public relations.

The president and the public relations department have the opportunity to exchange information.

The public relations department cooperates with the advertising department.

The company has an executive director in charge of public relations.

The company has a database and intranet on public relations.

Each division in the company understands the work of the public relations department.

The company has outside directors and advisory boards, including experts from outside of the company.

The public relations department has a mechanism to periodically exchange information with each division in the company as well as overseas subsidiaries.

The public relations department regularly exchanges information with public relations departments of its group companies.

The current top executive has experience working in the public relations department.

Concluding remarks
How general are we?

*Tomoki Kunieda, Koichi Yamamura,
and Junichiro Miyabe*

This book presented historical research and discussions on different aspects of public relations in Japan. It addressed a significant gap in the English public relations literature by providing multi-layered accounts on how public relations developed in Japan. Rather than providing a generalized history, this book presented various studies and discussions on specific fields or aspects of public relations in Japan. As concluding remarks, we, the editors, will review each chapter to discuss an overarching concept. First, we will go over what has and what has not been covered in this book, followed by the editors' answers to the three questions presented in the introductory chapter. We will conclude by discussing the concept of *generalist PR* to understand public relations in Japan.

Brief summary

Through this book, we have covered the following subjects. Chapter 1 provided an overview of the history of public relations in Japan. The postwar history of public relations implied that there was a cyclical change in the way public relations was practiced, shifting between a manipulative practice and dialogical practice. Chapter 2 examined the four routes in which public relations was introduced from the United States after World War II. It is worth noting that one of the major drivers of the introduction of public relations was the securities industry trying to promote it so that companies listed in the security exchange could better promote their own stock.

Chapter 3 gave an account of public relations by the capital city of Tokyo since the Meiji Restoration in 1868. The local government's history revealed how and why public relations departments were established and developed. Chapter 4 looked at the history of in-house magazines published as early as the 1890s to unveil the gradual development of internal communication. From its early stages, in-house magazines were published for various managerial purposes, especially for labor management.

Chapter 5 looked at the historical development of advertising and public relations agencies, revealing the fact that many practitioners working in agencies did not receive formal education specializing in PR. Chapter 6 analyzed the backgrounds and careers of past PR managers in Japanese companies, confirming that the careers of the Japanese PR managers are not limited to the public relations and communication areas.

Chapter 7 discussed the Japanese companies' efforts to transform their public relations activities to cope with changing external environments in two crises of the last decade. Chapter 8 grasped the state of the current public relations activities of Japanese companies. While it was confirmed that it spread to diverse activities from conventional media relation-centered activities, there was still a need to engage with management more strategically.

As each chapter focused on specific issues or particular times depending on the authors' research interests, it is important to acknowledge that certain issues and approaches that are necessary to understand the history of public relations in Japan were not included or discussed in this book. Some of them are as follows.

First, although many Japanese organizations appear in this book, a detailed study of individual cases was not included. Except for Chapter 3, which focused on the government of Tokyo, the chapters looked at history shared among different organizations within their respective areas. As each organization practices public relations differently, examination of individual PR activities may reveal interesting aspects of history that might otherwise disappear in the process of generalization. Such PR cases may also be discussed within the context of an organization's management history to provide a deeper understanding.

Next, in relation to the lifetime employment practice, the scope of discussion has not been extended to the activities of mid- to lower-level PR practitioners working in corporate public relations departments. In Chapter 5, the author referred to practitioners who work for PR agencies, but the discussion did not go into detailed analysis of the scope of work and their career paths. It can easily be speculated that many practitioners in Japan are subject to job rotation beyond communication-related departments, but the detailed analyses of their daily activities and careers are not included in this book.

This book does not contain detailed discussions of the media organizations even though Japan has a large media industry. Japan has some of the largest newspapers and broadcasting organizations in the world, and the presence of *kisha clubs*, or press clubs, has been pointed out as a unique, long-standing feature of Japanese media relations (Freeman, 2000; Kelly et al., 2002). In fact, media relations are recognized by Japanese PR practitioners as the most important activity (Japan Institute for Social and Economic Affairs, 2013). Understanding Japanese media and its history will certainly provide deeper understanding of the country's public relations practices and industry.

Since the 1990s, when PR practices became specialized, investor relations (IR) has gained importance among corporate public relations as a field of PR that requires professionalization and specific technicalities. In addition, from the perspective of building, maintaining and strengthening relationships with stakeholders, corporate social responsibility (CSR) activities have come into view. Although there are many studies in Japan concerning these fields, discussions on these activities are not included in this book.

The rapid spread of the Internet since the 1990s and the rise of social media greatly changed the public relations and corporate communication environment. Although there is an increasing number of research, studies and discussions in Japan with regard to the influence and effect of the new media on public relations, this subject is not included in this book.

It is also important to consider the issue of wartime propaganda when discussing the history of public relations, as the relationship between the two has been debated for a long time. In fact, there is a rich accumulation of propaganda-related research in Japan from before and after WWII. However, wartime propaganda and its relation to postwar public relations has not been discussed in this book. Some of the activities in the pre-war period were closely related to the development of public relations after WWII (Kushner, 2006; Tamai, 2017).

In terms of two-way communication, the aspect of listening is an interesting historical issue too. As mentioned in Chapter 3's case study of Tokyo, the Japanese administrative agencies, especially local governments, often use the expression *kouchou*, or public hearing, as the name for a specific type of PR department. Some local governments, like the City Government of Sapporo, have established departments with names that can be translated as the Section to Listen to the Citizens. In private companies, customer inquiry units have been set up as specialized sections to deal with claims and complaints. In recent years, there have been attempts to utilize feedback from customers acquired through this channel for product or service development. It certainly is an important aspect of public relations, but it is not discussed in this book.

Three questions from the introductory chapter

As mentioned in the introductory chapter, the purpose of this book is to clarify the characteristics of Japanese public relations through discussions of the three historical questions. This section provides answers to the questions posed by the editors based on the discussions in previous chapters, followed by the summary of their understanding of a major feature of public relations in Japan.

Question 1: how did Japanese public relations develop?

As mentioned in Chapters 3 and 4, activities that directly led to today's public relations (prototypes of modern public relations) existed in the 1870s after the Meiji Restoration. In other words, public relations in Japan have a history of 150 years. If we consider the publicity of administrative information as quasi PR activity, we can go back over one thousand years. Also, public relations related to commercial activities can be traced back to the Edo Period (1603–1868).

Regarding the history of public relations before and during World War II, which has been neglected in past research, it was shown that some of the PR activities that the government and companies conduct today were already implemented in this period and some were quite strategic (Chapter 4). In the history of propaganda not mentioned in this book, some of the activities in the early days were closely related to the development of public relations after World War II (Kushner, 2006; Tamai, 2017).

Meanwhile, after World War II, the interest in and efforts to implement public relations spread through the campaign by the US-led occupation forces. With the change in the political, economic, social, and business environments surrounding companies and public organizations, the domain and content of public relations activities expanded and deepened. In such postwar history of the development of public relations, the mechanism of the generalist PR, in which people who had not necessarily joined the organization as PR professionals were responsible for PR, was established. As a result, the size of the PR industry in Japan is relatively small compared to the size of the economy; however, in-house public relations activities in organizations developed and continue to be implemented actively.

Question 2: what were the political, social, and economic conditions that supported or inhibited its development?

Watson (2015, p. 6) defined the springboards of PR development as "factors such as economic, political and social conditions, events and personalities that enabled PR to advance into a distinct field" and restraints of the development as "cultural, economic, political and social aspects that delayed the emergence of PR as a ful-fledged practice." A typical springboard of PR development in a country is nation building, democratization, liberalization of the economy, and globalization of corporate practices. In Japan's case, as has been described in Chapter 2, the democratization after WWII provided the basis for postwar PR development.

Although it can be considered as an issue of path dependency,[1] the condition that regulates socio-economic activities, especially the conditions derived from the lifetime employment practice has been a major constraint on the development of public relations. This condition prescribes the position of public relations within the organization, the background of practitioners, and their careers. Thus, this institutional setting inhibited the birth and social recognition of public relations professionals or specialists.

Meanwhile, the environmental change in the two periods of drastic economic change, namely, the rapid industrialization after the Meiji Restoration and the period of recovery from the devastation of World War II followed by rapid economic growth, revealed various social problems as growth distortion factors. This, in turn, spurred the communication activities of organizations and resulted in the evolution of the public relations activities of Japanese organizations.

We may be able to interpret these observations in the context of generalist PR. The periods before and during World War II were the eras when the basis of generalist PR as a management practice was formed. Then, the post-World War II period until the 1980s was the time when US public relations was introduced, and the establishment of generalist PR practice was completed as a management practice. If we extend this discussion to the period after the 1990s, the stagnation of the economy and the increased degree of uncertainty, especially the economic environment since the 2000s, might be considered as the third period of drastic change for the Japanese socio-economic system. This third period may be coined as the era of the arrival of the specialist/generalist mix. Globalization that started in the 1990s began exerting a noticeable effect on human resources management in the 2000s. Specifically, among large Japanese corporations, Nissan, which accepted foreign capital participation, and Nippon Sheet Glass and Takeda Pharmaceutical, which accepted non-Japanese top management, signify full-scale globalization. We are likely to see a drastic change in the way public relations is conducted in Japan.

Question 3: why didn't Japan develop a large public relations industry despite its rapid economic development?

The discussion in Chapter 5 cites two reasons for the underdevelopment of the PR industry: the existence of a large advertising company incorporating PR-related services into the business and the lack of professionalization in society as a whole. The provision of the one-stop service from ad planning, design, and media purchase to public relations by major advertising companies including Dentsu, restrained the growth of PR industry as a professional service provider. Investor relations support services, as a derivative of the initial public offering (IPO) business by securities companies, is also a kind of one-stop service that inhibited the growth of specialized PR service. It can be pointed out that PR-related professional services are often provided by parties outside of the PR industry. However, this alone is insufficient to explain the fact that demand for specialized PR services in Japan is small.

The synthesis of the discussions in each chapter provides the following view on outsourcing in Japanese companies that may have heavily affected the size and the growth of the PR industry in the country. Under the structure and business practices of Japanese companies, it is difficult to outsource public relations activities as the consensus-building process and context are considered important. The company-specific know-how accumulated in the company through the execution of public relations work under the lifetime employment practice also may be considered as a factor that makes it difficult to seek external sources as PR-related service providers. Unlike advertisements, which usually allow sufficient lead time to plan, produce, and implement them, prompt action is required for public relations activities, particularly at the time of crisis. It was difficult for the public relations department to utilize external services under such organizational conditions.

Features of public relations in Japan: editors' view on generalist PR

Japan's public relations did not start with the introduction of American PR

As is clear from the preceding discussion, public relations activities existed in Japan long before the active introduction of American PR after World War II. Although not mentioned in this book, it is possible to further retrospectively identify PR-like activities from existing research by Japanese economic and business history scholars. However, this does not mean that the introduction of the concept and practice of public relations from the United States in the postwar period was meaningless. It is possible to see the impact of the introduction of PR in the postwar period in the development and expansion of PR activity and the processes widely acknowledged in Japan and incorporated into Japanese management behavior.

The background of the public relations practitioner is different from the American model

PR tactics and tools were introduced from the United States. Japan has incorporated many of them, and they were developed as present-day practices. Therefore, public relations activities themselves or the tools to be used seem to be equivalent to public relations activities in the West. However, there is a characteristic different from what we see in the institutionalized Western PR. It is the profile of PR practitioners. The background, the manner of carrying out the task, and the careers of the people in charge of the activity in the organization are distinctively different. Japanese public relations managers do not join the companies as public relations specialists; they join human resources with potential to be future management executives. They accumulate rich experiences in various functions in the company through a series of job rotations beyond communication functions. Thus, they acquire rich in-house knowledge and have successful experiences of contributing to corporate goals and objectives. Moreover, they have internal human networks built throughout their careers, so they can move quickly in emergency situations. Also, as evidenced by the fact that we can find numerous CEOs of Japanese listed companies with PR experience, PR practitioners' careers are not limited within the scope of the public relations and communication fields. We called such arrangement a "generalist PR."

Generalist PR and specialist PR

From the comparison between generalist and specialist, each has advantages and disadvantages. Public relations in Japan are not necessarily inferior or lagging behind. Japanese-style public relations managers are familiar with internal situations, have multi-layer internal networks, understand corporate management goals, and tend to have stronger motivation to contribute to corporate outcomes. However, their technical skills are inferior, and there is a tendency toward PR activities that depend on context rather than logic. For this reason, despite the strength of being familiar with the situation of the company and having the advantage of well-established internal networks, it is difficult to have a rational viewpoint as a boundary spanner, and in the event of considerable fluctuations in the business environment or in the response to crisis, sometimes it becomes a weakness. Meanwhile, in the specialist type, interest tends to be focused more on the sophistication and refinement of the technical aspects of public relations activities, finding the meaning of their existence in communication activities, and their focus tends to be away from the achievement of organization goals.

Future prospects

The history of Japan has, in a way, always revolved around its relationship with foreign countries, which is sometimes tense and violent, as its core. The modernization of Japan, though it may not be the main factor, developed with problems surrounding relations with foreign countries. Each chapter of this book discusses the influence from overseas on public relations in various forms. Up until the 1970s, internationalization was mainly the activity of exporting goods produced in Japan overseas and importing the necessary raw materials, and "special, privileged people," such as artists, scholars, and business people, have been active overseas for a while acquiring new knowledge and technology and bringing them back to Japan. It can be said that it was to selectively interpret and digest foreign knowledge, technology, and institutional settings and transform them into Japanese knowledge and technology. However, in the globalization that became evident since the 1990s, every aspect of Japanese corporate activities has been exposed to overseas influences, and the people who compose the company are rapidly becoming multinational and multicultural. Also, in public administration, the need to consider non-Japanese residents as service recipients has become critical. There are opportunities and threats to the existing institutions, which will encourage changes in various aspects of society. In conformity with the subject of this book, there is a sign of a change in the generalist-centered public relations of Japan. A significant change is bound to be brought about in the way public relations will be practiced and managed in Japan in the future.

Based on such a historical perspective, how do we expect the generalist PR to transform? Generalists are not amateurs. Leaders who survive and develop organizations in a turbulent and unpredictable world need equal qualities for all activities of the organization and are required to guide them appropriately. It is not a specialist in a specific field, but the qualities of generalists are required. However, in a complex world where progress comes at unprecedented speed, professionals with a solid knowledge base and high ethical standards are necessary. In the future, we will be sure to see a new model of public relations being created, arising from the conflict between and integration of generalists and specialists.

The editors hope that studies on the generalist PR model will further originate from Japan, where such practices actually exist as the dominant model and are not necessarily viewed with negativity, building upon the findings of this book as a starting point. Ultimately, the uniqueness and universality of the generalist PR practice should be further clarified through international comparative studies.

Note

1 Path dependency: The concept, developed in evolutionary economics, is that economic and social institutions, once established, restrain and regulate further development.

References

Freeman, L. A. (2000). *Closing the shop: Information cartels and Japan's mass media*. Princeton, NJ: Princeton University Press.

Japan Institute for Social and Economic Affairs. (2013). *Shuyo kigyo no kouhou soshiki to jinzai 2013 nen ban* [PR organization and human resource in leading companies 2013]. Tokyo: Japan Institute for Social and Economic Affairs.

Kelly, W., Masumoto, T., & Gibson, D. (2002). Kisha kurabu and koho: Japanese media relations and public relations. *Public Relations Review*, 28(3), 265–281.

Kushner, B. (2006). *The thought war: Japanese imperial propaganda*. Honolulu, HI: University of Hawaii Press.

Tamai, K. (Ed.). (2017). *Shasin Shuhou to sono jidai* [Photo Weekly and Its Era]. Tokyo: Keio University Press.

Watson, T. (2015). What in the world is public relations? In Watson, T. (Ed.), *Perspectives on public relations historiography and historical theorization* (pp. 4–19). Basingstoke, Hampshire: Palgrave Macmillan.

Appendix 1
Glossary of key terms

Dentsu Inc.   Dentsu is the largest advertising agency in Japan and the fifth largest global agency company in 2016, according to the advertising and marketing news media AdAge. The company was founded in 1901 as an ad agency with a wire service company as its affiliate and divested the wire service in 1936. Dentsu's business is unique in that it handles almost all aspects of advertising agency work, from marketing, creative planning, design, and production to media planning and media purchase. It is sometimes criticized for its strong influence over media, as it guarantees the entire ad placement for many of the popular TV programs. Dentsu has a PR agency called Dentsu PR as its subsidiary, but it also has a PR business department within itself to offer comprehensive service, including PR, to its clients.

GHQ (General Headquarters), Supreme Commander for the Allied Powers   When Japan surrendered to the Allied forces in 1945 after being defeated in World War II, US-led forces occupied Japan. The governing body was the Supreme Commander for the Allied Powers, commonly called the GHQ or Shinchugun (Occupation Army). While GHQ indirectly controlled Japan through its national and local government, in reality, GHQ's orders, or even suggestions, were deemed as ultimate commands. GHQ maintained control of Japan until 1952 when the Peace Treaty with Japan, signed in 1951, became effective.

Japan Association of Corporate Executives, JACE (Keizai Doyu Kai)   The JACE was established in 1946 by top and senior executives of major corporations as individuals. JACE engaged in discussions on various domestic and international economic issues and issued policy proposals on various matters.

Japan Business Federation, JBF (Nihon Keizai Dantai Rengokai)   The Japan Business Federation, commonly called Keidanren, is a comprehensive economic organization with a membership comprised of 1,350 leading companies, 109 nationwide industrial associations, and 47 regional economic organizations (as of April 1, 2017). As the organization representing Japan's business circle, JBF engages in dialogues with the government, labor unions, citizens, foreign governments, economic organizations, and international organizations on various issues. It was established in 2002, when the Japan Federation of Economic Organization (JFEO) and Japan Federation of Employers' Association (JFEA) merged to form the Japan Business Federation as a new comprehensive economic organization.

Japan Federation of Employers' Association, JFEA (Nihon Keieisha Dantai Renmei)   In April 1948, the JFEA, a nationwide association of top executives commonly called Nikkeiren, was launched with the objective of establishing an appropriate relationship between labor and management. While JFEO handled economic issues in general, JFEA engaged in information gathering and PR activities on labor issues to maintain coordination among managements of major corporations.

Japan Institute for Economic and Social Affairs, JIESA (Keizai Koho Center)   JIESA was founded in November 1978 when companies were struggling to communicate with the society about the value of their existence. JIESA aims to facilitate the relationship between society and the business community by communicating the ideas and actions of the business community to society, listening to the voices of the public, and facilitating international dialogue. JIESA has been conducting a triennial survey of corporate PR activities since 1980 and the Corporate PR Forum, seminars targeting PR practitioners of the member corporations, since 1981. JIESA is a subsidiary organization of the Japan Business Federation, and the chairman of JBF concurrently serves as the chairman of JIESA.

Japan Public Relations Association, JPRA (Nihon Kouhou Kyokai)   In 1954, the Kouhou Kenkyu Kai (PR Study Group) and Zenkoku Kouhou Kenkyu Kai (National PR Study Group) were established. In 1963, Kouhou Kenkyu Kai became Nihon Kouhou Kyokai (JPRA) and in the following year absorbed Zenkoku Kouhou Kenkyu kai. The JPRA aims to support national and local governments' PR activities by providing consulting services, publishing a monthly magazine, and holding seminars for government PR officers.

Japan Society for Corporate Communication Studies, JSCCS (Nihon Kouhou Gakkai)   The JSCCS was founded in 1995 to promote academic and practical research on the management of public relations and communication activities. JSCCS holds annual research conferences, symposia, and open seminars for practitioners and academics. JSCCS also has various study groups with focuses on different fields of public relations. As of September 2017, it has 631 individual members and 48 organizational members.

Kisha Club (Press Club) Kisha club is an unincorporated organization attached to major subject organizations of press coverage. It is not a professional membership association, such as the Japan National Press Club or Foreign Correspondents' Club of Japan. Each of the national government ministries, prefectural governments, major cities, and major political parties has its own Kisha Club. Many large companies and industry organizations have Kisha Clubs too. Kisha Clubs are closed to non-members, and it is often difficult for foreign press and independent journalists to obtain membership. Many Kisha Clubs are provided by the subject organization with a room for their members to use as a satellite office near the press conference site. By contacting appropriate Kisha Clubs, PR practitioners can reach journalists who cover specific fields. Kisha Club members often enjoy close relationships with the organization's PR arms. They are often criticized for being closed in nature and susceptible to manipulation in return for access to exclusive information.

kouhou (public relations) The Japanese translation for public relations is *kouhou*, written in Chinese characters or kanji as 広報. The word is composed of two kanji, one for "wide" and another for "report/inform." In fact, in a narrow sense, kouhou means, as its kanji imply, to widely notify through a one-way communication. However, it is also commonly used in a broad sense, referring to the two-way communication between an organization and its public. The practice of gathering and listening to the public's voices is often called *kouchou* 広聴, composed of kanji for "wide" and "listen." A typical usage of the narrow sense may be found in some local governments who call their PR departments *kouhou kouchou bu* 広報広聴部, which can be translated literally as department that widely notifies and gathers people's voices.

In addition, there are other Japanese words with the same pronunciation, kouhou, with slightly different meanings. One such variation, kouhou 公報, has the Chinese character for "public" or "government" and another for "report/inform," which is often used to address official announcements by the government. Another set of variations are 廣報 and 弘報, both of which use the old kanji for "wide" and are used to mean to widely notify.

While the first kouhou, 広報, has been in use since after the WWII, the ones with the old kanji for "wide" have been used from much earlier. The first appearance of the latter, 廣報, on record was on May 9, 1872, in a Japanese daily newspaper *Yokohama Mainichi Shimbun* (Kitano, 2009). It was marked as an identification symbol on the railroad timetable and fare chart of the train service between Yokohama and Shinagawa. The word was used to show that the post was an advertisement. The other word, 弘報, appeared in the name of the first advertising company in Japan, 弘報堂 (Kouhou Do). When the South Manchurian Railroad Company set up its PR department in 1923, its name was 弘報処 (Kouhou Dokoro). The department engaged in activities similar to what we deem as public relations today. After WWII, 弘報 was sometimes used in the names for PR departments, but today, 広報 is generally used in the names for such departments.

The fact that there are four different kanji for kouhou with similar but different meanings, most of which commonly refer to one-way communication, has certainly contributed to the general misunderstanding of public relations among the Japanese as being one-way communication instead of two-way communication.

Mass media in Japan There are two characteristics of mass media that are somewhat unique to Japan. One is the relatively strong presence of traditional media, and the other is the syndication among newspapers, central TV networks, and local TV stations. Each of the 47 prefectures has one or two major local newspapers, often with the largest circulation in each market. Five newspapers are published nationwide, with an average daily circulation during the first half of 2017 at 8.8 million for *Yomiuri Shimbun*, 6.3 million for *Asahi Shimbun*, 3 million for *Mainichi Shimbun*, 2.7 million for *Nikkei Shimbun*, and 1.6 million for *Sankei Shimbun*. Each of the national newspapers has a TV network either as a subsidiary or parent company, with the exception of *Mainichi Shimbun*, which released shares of the TV network TBS Holdings in the 1970s when the newspaper went through restructuring. TV network stations and newspapers have financial stakes in many local TV stations. Most of the TV content is produced by the key network station or a few sub-key stations within the network and many popular programs are broadcast nationwide, including centrally contracted advertisements.

Surveys show a high rate of trust in media among the Japanese. A Gallup survey in 2015 showed that in the US, those who trusted mass media were at 40% and 32% in 2016. A similar survey conducted in Japan in 2016 by Nomura Research Institute (NRI) showed that 63.5% trusted newspapers and 62% trusted the NHK. In a survey conducted by the Japan Press Research Institute in 2016 asking Japanese people to rate mass media as to how much they trusted it, from the scale of 0 (not trusting at all) to 100 points (fully trusting), newspapers scored 68.6 and NHK TV scored 69.8 points. Although declining recently, Japanese mass media still enjoys a high level of trust among the people.

NHK (Japan Broadcasting Corporation)   NHK is a public broadcaster chartered by the Broadcasting Act of 1950. The act stipulates that anyone who installs a TV receiver must pay a subscription fee, and NHK is prohibited from carrying advertisements. Its predecessor began radio broadcasting in 1925. NHK has 54 stations nationwide and 30 overseas branches for news gathering. While it is independent of the government and manages its operation solely on the income from the subscription fees, certain managerial matters, such as the budget and top management appointments, are subject to approval by the National Diet. Although NHK is often credited for its quality programs, there have often been criticisms for its close ties with politics and lack of editorial independence.

Public Relations Society of Japan, PRSJ (Nihon PR Kyokai)   The PRSJ was established in 1964 and merged with the PR Industry Association (established in 1974) in 1980. PRSJ obtained the "public interest incorporated association" status in 1988. Besides holding seminars and events for PR practitioners, PRSJ organizes the "PR Planner Qualification Examination" and issues PR Planner Certification since 2007.

Appendix 2
Chronology of PR in Japan 1861–2017

Year	PR/Communication	Media and journalism	Socio-economic trends	
			National	International
1861		Publication of the *Nagasaki Shipping List and Advertiser*, Japan's first modern newspaper in English, begins.		Lincoln takes office as US president; the American Civil War.
1862		Bansho Shirabesho (Foreign Book Research Office) begins translating the *Javasche Courant*, a Dutch colony publication in Batavia (currently Jakarta, Indonesia) into Japanese and publishes it as *Kanpan Batabiya Shimbun*. This is the first regularly published Japanese language newspaper.		
1867				World Exposition at Paris, Japan's first participation in expo.
1868		*Chugai Shimbun, Kouko Shimbun*, and *Moshio Gusa* begin publication.	Restoration of Imperial Rule; Meiji Restoration is initiated. The name of the era Meiji is adopted.	
1871		*Yokohama Mainichi Shimbun*, the first daily newspaper, begins publication.	Publication Law is enacted. The Iwakura Mission, team of high-ranking government officials for preliminary negotiation toward revision of unequal treaties, is dispatched.	

Year				
1872	Expression of *"Kouhou"* appears on *Yokohama Mainichi Shimbun* for the first time.	*Tokyo Nichinichi Shimbun* begins publication.	The team visit the US and European countries and return to Japan on September 13, 1873, with the first-hand knowledge of Western countries.	
1874		*Yomiuri Shimbun* begins publication.		
1875			Libel Law of 1875 and Press Ordinance of 1875 are issued.	
1876		*Chyugai Bukka Shinpo* (renamed to *Chyugai Shougyou Shinpo* in 1889) begins publication. The newspaper becomes, in 1946, *Nihon Keizai Shimbun* (Nikkei, or literal translation, Japan Economic Daily).		Graham Bell invents a practical telephone.
1877	*Houtan Zasshi*, the first PR magazine, is launched.		The first Industrialization Exposition of Japan.	
1879		*Asahi Shimbun* begins publication in Osaka (also launched in Tokyo in 1888).		
1882		*Jiji Shinpo* (newspaper) begins publication.		
1886	*Kouhoudou*, the oldest ad agency in Japan, established.			

(Continued)

Appendix 2 (Continued)

Year	PR/Communication	Media and journalism	Socio-economic trends	
			National	International
1892		*Mancyouhou* (newspaper) begins publication.		
1894			Sino-Japanese War of 1894–1895 begins.	
1895	*Koukoku Hakuhoudou* established.			
1897	*Gakutoh*, the oldest active PR magazine launched by *Maruzen*, foreign book distributor and publisher. *Honbu jyunmpo* launched by *Mitsui Bank*.			
1901	*Nihon Koukoku Co. Ltd., Denpo Tsushinsya* established. Denpo Tsushinsya later becomes Dentsu.			
1902	*Shahou* launched by *Nihon Seimei*.			
1904	*Kanebo no Kiteki*, in-house magazine launched by *Kanegafuchi Bouseki*.		Russo-Japanese War (1904–05) begins.	

Year		
1905		Treaty of Portsmouth ends the Russo-Japanese War. Widespread discontent among the populace results in riots in major cities in Japan.
1906		South Manchuria Railroad (*Mantetsu*) incorporated.
1914	"Let's go to the Imperial Theater today, tomorrow to Mitsukoshi" – tagline for the Mitsukoshi Department Store.	The First World War begins.
1917		Establishment of the Committee on Public Information, or Creel Committee. October Revolution in Russia.
1918	Japanese Army dispatched to Vladivostok, organizes public affairs unit.	
1923	Mantetsu organizes Public Relations unit.	
1925	Radio broadcasting begins in Tokyo and Osaka.	
1926	NHK (*Nihon Housou Kyoukai*, Japan Broadcasting Corporation, government-supported public broadcasting network) is officially founded.	
1929		US stock market crashes, the Great Depression begins.
1930		Showa Depression (1930–1935) begins.

(*Continued*)

Appendix 2 (Continued)

Year	PR/Communication	Media and journalism	Socio-economic trends	
			National	*International*
1932	Information Committee is jointly set up by the Ministry of Foreign Affairs and the Ministry of Army.		Declaration of the founding of the state of Manchukuo. May 15 Incident: Prime Minister Inukai assassinated during a coup attempt by young naval officers.	
1933			Japan withdraws from the League of Nations to express its opposition to the report of the Lytton Commission, which criticizes Japan as an aggressor in Manchuria.	New Deal Policy of President Roosevelt; Adolf Hitler becomes prime minister of Germany.
1936	Manchuria Public Relations Association founded. Organization's aim is to control media activities. Broadcasting Department of Manchuria Telephone and Telegraph Co. begins broadcasting advertisements.	Domei Press Agency established.	February 26 Incident: 1,400 troops participate in an unsuccessful coup d'etat.	
1937	Information Division of the Cabinet Office founded.		Marco Polo Bridge Incident: Sino-Japanese War of 1937–1945 commences.	

Year			
1938	Public Affairs Office founded at Manchukuo Administration Agency.		
1939		Passage of the National Mobilization Law. National Service Draft Ordinance issued to ensure an adequate supply of labor in strategic industries.	The Second World War begins.
1940	Information Agency established.		
1941	Media Technology Study Team established by advertising and related professionals. Integration of newspapers into one in each prefecture (the situation continues to present day).	December 8: Pacific War commences.	
1945	Kyodo Press Agency and Jiji Press Agency established.	Japan accepts the terms of the Potsdam Declaration. Emperor Showa announces the end of hostilities in a national broadcast. General Headquarters of the Supreme Commander for the Allied Power (GHQ/SCAP) issues directives aimed at the democratization of Japan. GHQ issues directive aimed at breakup of industrial and financial combine (Zaibatsu dissolution). Public Opinion Research Section founded at the Information Agency.	The United Nations founded.

(Continued)

Appendix 2 (Continued)

Year	PR/Communication	Media and journalism	Socio-economic trends	
			National	International
1946		Nihon Shimbun Kyokai, The Japan Newspaper Publishers and Editors Association, established.	Emperor Showa renounces his divinity in New Year's address to the Japanese people. He begins a series of goodwill tours of the country. Occupation purge of prewar and wartime Japanese leaders. Keizai Doyukai (Japan Association of Corporate Executives) founded. Foundation of Keidanren (Federation of Economic Organizations). Japanese Confederation of Labor Unions, Japanese Congress of Industrial Organizations formed. Constitution of Japan promulgated; it goes into effect in 1947.	
1947	GHQ suggests setting up Public Relations Office at prefectural government.		GHQ bans General Strike of 1947. The first general election of prefectural governor is held. Enactment of Labor Standard Law and Anti-monopoly Law. Nikkeiren (Japan Federation of Employers' Association, JFEA) founded.	Pakistan and India become sovereign nations.
1948				Republic of Korea established in the southern part of the Korean Peninsula and the Democratic People's Republic of Korea in the north.

Year				
1949	Public Relations and Information Service Association founded. Civil Information and Educational Section of GHQ holds a series of workshops on PR. Georgia Day and Associates, the first PR agency, established. Dentsu sets up Committee on PR and PR Department.	National Public Opinion Research Institute founded.	Comprehensive anti-inflation measure (so-called Dodge Line policy) introduced; a fixed exchange rate of Yen 360 to US $1 established.	North Atlantic Treaty Organization (NATO) founded. People's Republic of China established.
1950	Publication of promotional magazine of Japan Securities Investment Association, *Public Relation*, begins.		Formation of Sohyo (General Council of Trade Unions of Japan).	Korean War (1950–53) begins.
1951	The first course on PR starts at Sophia University in Tokyo.	Commercial radio broadcasting begins.	JFEA's Management Study Team visits the US; the team brings back concepts of HR and PR. San Francisco Peace Treaty and the US-Japan Security Treaty signed.	
1952	JFEA launches PR Study Group. Falcon Advertising and PR founded.		San Francisco Peace Treaty goes into effect. Japan regains sovereignty. Japan's IMF accession application is approved.	European Coal and Steel Community
1953	JFEA starts PR Study Group. Japan Airlines organizes public relations office.	Television broadcasting begins.	First case of pollution-related Minamata disease reported.	

(Continued)

Appendix 2 (Continued)

Year	PR/Communication	Media and journalism	Socio-economic trends	
			National	*International*
1954	Public Relations Study Group founded. National Study Group of PR founded. Japan PR Kondankai (Japan Roundtable of PR) starts.		Japan joins GATT.	Mutual defense organization of the Soviet Union and its satellites states established under the Warsaw Pact.
1955	Tokyo Gas Co. sets up Public Relations section.		Japan Productivity Center founded, dispatched Top Management Study Team to the USA. Special trains for junior high school graduates to migrate from rural areas to industrial centers to fulfill massive demand for labor begin operation.	
1956	Keizai Doyukai (Japan Association of Corporate Executives) publishes report on corporate social responsibility. Matsushita Electric Industrial Co., Ltd. (later renamed as Panasonic Corporation) establishes PR Division.	*Shukan Sincyo*, weekly magazine, begins publication.	Official recognition of Minamata Disease. The 1956 White Paper on the Economy declares an "end to the post war era." Japan joins the United Nations.	

1957	Proactive PR activity at the time of Prime Minister Kishi's state visit to the US. The first national competition for in-house magazines. Intelligence Idea Center founded.	First female weekly magazine *Shūkan Josei* (Weekly Women) launched.	Japan Marketing Association founded. TVs, washing machines, and refrigerators are considered by consumers as three must-purchase consumer durables, thus opening the era of mass-consumption.	Soviet Union successfully launches satellite Sputnik No. 1.
1958	In-house magazine boom. Japan PR founded. Hill and Knowlton Japan founded.		Japan External Trade Organization (JETRO), an organization to promote export, is established. *Introduction to Management* by Fujiyoshi Sakamoto becomes a best-seller. Management science boom.	
1959		Weekly magazines, including manga (comic) weekly, begin publication.	Royal wedding of Crown Prince Akihito, live coverage of wedding parade ignites purchasing of TVs. Car ownership begins to spread. "Consumption is virtue."	
1960	PR Unit of Prime Minister's Office established, take over PR work of Cabinet Secretary Office. Cosmo PR and PR Japan founded.	Color television broadcasting starts.	Massive demonstration against signing US-Japan Security Treaty. Trade and foreign exchange liberalization plan. Economic Plan to Double Income.	Organization of Petroleum Exporting Countries (OPEC) founded.

(Continued)

Appendix 2 (Continued)

Year	PR/Communication	Media and journalism	Socio-economic trends		International
			National		
1961	Press Service Center and Dentsu PR Center founded.		SONY issues the first American Depositary Receipt (ADR) at NY Stock Exchange. Japan Consumers' Association funded.		Organization for Economic Cooperation and Development (OECD) organized.
1962	JFEA sets up In-House Magazine Center.	TV broadcasting receiving contract exceeds 140,000.	Proclamation of Act against Unjustifiable Premiums and Misleading Representations. Sale of thalidomide in Japan halted.		US President Kennedy announces four rights of consumers.
1963	Japan Public Relations Association is founded based on Public Relations Study Group. Ozma PR founded.				
1964	Dentsu and Hakuhoudou, the two largest advertising companies in the country, set up PR service departments. Kyodo PR founded. Japan PR Society founded. Japan Public Relations Association merges National Study Group of PR. PR magazine *Energy* is		Japan joins OECD. Liberalization of travel abroad. Consumer Science Center founded. Tokaido Shinkansen (bullet train) begins operation. Tokyo Olympics.		

Year		
1965	Sun Creative Publicity founded.	Special loan by Bank of Japan to near bankrupt Yamaichi Securities. Second Minamata disease discovered in Niigata Prefecture.	Cultural Revolution in China begins.
1966		The Fair Trade Commission recommends six household appliance companies to terminate television price cartel. New set of must-purchase consumer durables, color TV set, air conditioner, and car, are widely accepted as 3C by consumers.	
1967	Sakura Maru, a trade exhibition ship, cruising the world to promote Japan and its products.	First stage of liberalization of direct investment from abroad. Basic Pollution Control Law. Yokkaichi pollution asthma lawsuit begins.	European Communities (ECSC, EEC, and Euratom) founded. ASEAN founded.
1968		Automobile ownership exceeds 10 million units. Japan's first high-rise office building completed. Basic Law for Consumer Protection enacted. Air Pollution Control Law and Noise Regulation Law. Japan's GNP becomes second largest in the world.	

(Continued)

Appendix 2 (Continued)

Year	PR/Communication	Media and journalism	Socio-economic trends	
			National	International
1969			Campus unrest. Second stage of liberalization of direct investment from abroad implemented. Tomei Expressway fully opened connecting Tokyo and Nagoya. Ministry of Health and Welfare announce White Paper on Pollution. Kumamoto Minamata disease patient files damages lawsuit against a chemical company, Chisso. Defect automobile problem. Food poisoning becomes a social issue.	Lunar landing of US spacecraft *Apollo 11*.
1970	PRAP Japan, Inc.		World Exposition in Osaka. Textile trade negotiation between Japan and the US failed. Central Anti-Pollution Office founded. Photochemical smog reported in Tokyo. SONY listed at NY Stock Exchange. National Consumer Affairs Center of Japan founded. National Consumers Meeting announces resolution on boycotting color TV. Rise of consumerism.	US Senate approved Anti-Pollution Act (Muskey Law).

1971	NHK Television begins full-time color broadcasting.	US consumer movement leader Ralph Nadar visits Japan. Environment Agency founded. "Limit to the Growth" published by Rome Club. Revaluation of yen to Yen 308 to US $1.	US President Nixon ends convertibility of US dollar to gold.
1972		Publication of the first White Paper on Environment. Minister of International Trade and Industry Kakuei Tanaka announces his policy idea of "Japan archipelago remodeling plan" while running for prime ministership. This ignites boom in real-estate investment.	US President Nixon visits China.
1973	Keizai Doyukai (Japan Association of Corporate Executives) publishes report "Toward Mutual Trust between Society and Corporation." Cabinet Public Relations Office is founded at Cabinet Secretariat. Burson-Marsteller starts operation in Japan.	Yen moves to floating exchange rate scheme. Natural Resources and Energy Agency founded. Law to regulate buy up and hoarding. A run on Toyokawa Credit Union caused by a groundless rumor. Mass hoarding of toilet paper, detergent, and other consumer goods.	Peace agreement in Vietnam. President Nixon declared the end of the Vietnam war. The fourth Middle-East War begins. Oil crisis
1974		The first convenience store opens its doors in Tokyo.	Watergate incident, President Nixon resigns.

(Continued)

Appendix 2 (Continued)

Year	PR/Communication	Media and journalism	Socio-economic trends	
			National	*International*
1975	PR Work Japan Society founded.		Environment Agency announces Showa 51 emission control regulation. Consumer protection ordinance established by local and prefectural governments.	The first G7 Summit.
1976	Keidanren publishes report on PR activities of corporation and industry associations. Tokyo Stock Exchange announces proposal for corporate PR activities.		Lockheed Scandal: ex-prime minister Kakuei Tanaka charged with taking bribes from Lockheed Aircraft Corporation.	
1977			Voluntary export control of color TV is agreed between Japan and the US. Rapid increase of export.	Trade deficit of the US against Japan reaches 5.3 billon dollars.
1978	*Keizai Koubou Center* (KKC, Japan Institute for Social and Economic Affairs) founded. International Public Relations Association holds directors' meeting and Seminar on International PR in		Japan-China Peace and Friendship Treaty signed and ratified. Governor of Kanagawa Prefecture announces the coming of the age of local regions. Conflict over semiconductor trade between Japan and the US.	

1979	The second oil crisis. Oil majors notify increase of oil price to Japanese refineries. G7 Summit in Tokyo.	Nuclear power plant accident at Three Mile Island, Pennsylvania, US.
1980	Corporate identity boom. Public Relations Society of Japan (PRSJ) is chartered by merging Japan PR Society and PR Work Japan Society. JISEA (Keizai Kouhou Center) conducts the first survey on perception of corporate public relations activities.	Honda announces construction of auto plant in Ohio. Trade talk between Japan and the US. Japan's auto production becomes the largest in the world.
1981		Japan-US auto talk. Voluntary export restraint is agreed. Japan and the US agree to lower the tariff on semiconductor at equal percentage. Second Provisional Commission for Administrative Reform proposes privatization of Japan's three major public corporations. Sinkansen network expanded to Northern Japan.	President Reagan assumes office.
1982		

(Continued)

Appendix 2 (Continued)

Year	PR/Communication	Media and journalism	Socio-economic trends	
			National	*International*
1983			Japan's first communication satellite successfully launched. Kanagawa Prefecture enacts information disclosure regulations. Government bond outstanding exceeds 100 trillion yen.	
1984			US-Japan trade negotiation on beef and oranges.	
1985	JISEA (Keizai Kouhou Center) starts corporate PR award.		Market-oriented sector-specific trade negotiation between Japan and the US begin. Nippon Telephone and Telegram and Japan Monopoly Corporation are privatized and NTT and JT founded as private entities. Equal Employment Opportunity Law for Men and Women. Plaza Accord and rapid upward revaluation of Yen.	
1986	Cabinet Public Relations Officer post created.		Uruguay Round started. Recession caused by upward revaluation of yen.	Chernobyl nuclear accident in the Soviet Union.
1987			Rapid inflation. Japan National Railway privatized and divided into 6 regional companies.	Black Monday; stock price crash at NY Stock Exchange.

Year			
1988		Toshiba Machinery violates Coordinating Committee for Multilateral Export Controls (CoCom) regulation. *Rengo* (Japanese Trade Union Confederation) formed. SONY acquires CBS Records. Introduction of the 3% consumption tax.	US Senate passed the Comprehensive Trade Bill (Super 301).
1989		Emperor Showa deceased. End of Showa Era. SONY acquires Columbia Pictures. Japan-US Structural Impediment Initiative. Mitsubisi Jisho acquires Rockefeller Center, Tokyo Stock Exchange recorded the highest price of 38,915 Yen. Stock price collapses. Matsushita Electric acquires MCA. Collapse of the bubble economy.	Collapse of the Berlin Wall. Tiananmen Square Incident.
1990	*Kigyo Mesenat Kyougikai* (Association for Corporate Support of the Arts) founded. Keidanren 1% Club founded.		Reunification of Germany.
1991	Keidanren announces Global Environment Charter. Keidanren announces Corporate Behavior Charter. Keidanren organizes a forum on reconsideration of corporate responses.	Compensation for losses for selected clients by major securities companies revealed.	Persian Gulf War, Collapse of Soviet Union.

(Continued)

Appendix 2 (Continued)

Year	PR/Communication	Media and journalism	Socio-economic trends National	International
1992			Securities and Exchange Surveillance Commission established. Nonperforming loans reach 7,992.7 billion yen at 21 major banks.	Rio de Janeiro Earth Summit.
1993	Vector Inc. founded.		Liberal Democratic Party lost its majority in the diet.	European Union inaugurated.
1994	Internet PR begins.		Product Liability Law.	NAFTA takes effect.
1995	Japan Society for Corporate Communication Studies founded.		The Fortune Global 500 lists 141 firms from Japan, more than any other country. Hanshin-Awaji Earthquake (Kobe-Osaka area).	World Trade Organization (WTO) established to replace GATT.
1996			Legalization of holding company.	
1997			Enforcement of Act on the Promotion of Sorted Collection and Recycling of Containers and Packaging. Yamaichi Securities and Hokkaido Takusyoku Bank go bankrupt. Kyoto Conference on Global Warming (COP3) held in Kyoto.	
1998			Financial Supervisory Agency established. Injection of public funds of 1,815.6 billion yen to 21 major banks.	

Year	PR industry	Society / economy	Media	World
1999	IPRA holds International PR Symposium in Tokyo.	Tokyo Stock Exchange launches "Mothers" stock market for venture companies.		EU currency unification.
2000	Graduate School of Media and Communication, Hokkaido University.	Major revision of Commercial Code. Daily products of Snow Brand Milk Industry cause food poisoning to over 10,000 people.		
2001				Sept. 11 terrorists attack on World Trade Center, New York.
2002		The balance of nonperforming loans of major 13 banks at the end of March record approximately 26.8 trillion yen.		
2003		Nikkei stock average price record lowest after the collapse of the bubble economy. Proclamation of Personal Information Protection Law.	Start of terrestrial digital broadcasting.	
2005	PRAP Japan, Inc. becomes listed at JASDAQ through initial public offering. Kyodo PR becomes listed at JASDAQ through initial public offering. *PRIR*, industry journal, begins publication.	Major revision of Companies Act. Privatization of National Postal Service.		

(Continued)

Appendix 2 (Continued)

Year	PR/Communication	Media and journalism	Socio-economic trends	
			National	International
2007	PRSJ launches PR Planner accreditation scheme.			Sub-prime loan problem in the US.
2008				Collapse of Lehman Brothers.
2009			Liberal Democratic Party defeated in the House of Representatives election.	
2010			Japan Airlines applies for the corporate reorganization law. US Toyota recalls 2.3 million units with accelerator problems. President Akio Toyoda attends the US House hearing.	China's GDP surpasses Japan's; China becomes second largest economy in the world.
2011			Great East Japan Earthquake. Nuclear power plant accident at Fukushima No.1 Plant of TEPCO.	
2012	Vector Inc. becomes listed at Mothers market of Tokyo Stock Exchange through initial public offering.		The Liberal Democratic Party wins the general election of the House of Representatives.	
2013				Japanese plant engineers at a natural gas facility in Algeria held hostage by terrorists.

Year			
2014		Consumption tax is raised from 5% to 8%.	Series of street demonstrations, Umbrella Movement, in Hong Kong.
2015	*The Yomiuri Shimbun* publishes its 50,000th issue. Nikkei, Inc. acquires Financial Times Group. The largest acquisition of foreign media by Japanese media group.	Twelve countries, including Japan and the US, reach agreement on TPP, Trans-Pacific Partnership. Nikkei average stock price recovers 20,000 yen for the first time in 15 years.	
2016		Bank of Japan introduces negative interest rate. Household appliance manufacturer Sharp under management restructuring decides to receive support of Hon Hai Precision Industry of Taiwan.	A shooting incident by a group of Islamic extremists in Dhaka, the capital of Bangladesh, killed seven Japanese ODA specialists.
2017	The Graduate School of Information and Communication founded.		President Trump assumes office.

This chronology was prepared with reference to the following materials.

Ikari, S., Ogawa, M., Kitano, K., Kenmochi, T., Morito, N., & Hamada, I. (2011). *Nihon no kouhou PR no 100 nen* [A hundred years of public relations in Japan]. Tokyo, Japan: Douyukan.
Iwanami Shoten. (2001). *Kindai Nihon Sougou Nenpyou 4th Edition (1853–2000)* [Comprehensive Chronology of Modern Japan, 4th edition, 1853–2000]. Tokyo: Iwanami Shoten, Publishers.
Miwa, R., & Hara, A. (2007). *Kin-Gendi Nihon Keizaisi Youran* [Handbook of Economic History of Modern Japan]. Tokyo: University of Tokyo Press.
For the translation to English we referred to the following Internet sites and material.
National Diet Library: www.ndl.go.jp/modern/e/utility/chronology.html
Historiographical Institute, University of Tokyo: www.hi.u-tokyo.ac.jp/index.html
Kodansya International. (1999). *Chronology of Japanese History.* Kodansya International.

Appendix 3
Note on Japanese employment practices

Junichiro Miyabe

Introduction

This appendix focuses on the human resource management practices common to large Japanese companies, hoping to help readers better understand the discussion in this book. The description in this appendix applies not only to Japanese companies but also to government organizations. The employment practices that we will explain here are not specific to the public relations department. The entire organization is working under such practices. Like other departments within Japanese organizations, the public relations department is composed mainly of employees who joined the company under these practices.

The features that are generally recognized as Japanese-style management models (not necessarily through academic discussions) are lifetime employment, seniority-based wages, and an enterprise labor union. These characteristics are considered to be major factors that helped realize the rapid economic growth during the period from late 1950s to the early 1970s. Many of the practices formed during this period remained in Japanese corporate society even in the 2010s, affecting various aspects of corporate behavior. Among these characteristics, we will focus on lifetime employment. Our description is based on research accumulated in the fields of labor economics, human resource management theory, and career studies.

It is important to note that the employment practices that we are trying to explain here do not necessarily apply to the majority of Japanese workers. According to the estimation by Ono (2010), the number of employed workers that these practices apply to directly is only about 20% of the entire labor force. Nor does it mean that these practices cannot be observed at all in other countries. As we will see later, many aspects of these practices can be observed in several Western countries as well. Nevertheless, they are shown here as "Japanese-style" because they form the general framework of the Japanese labor market and still constitute the single most important route from school to workplace for high school and college graduates. Despite various criticisms and problems, which include interference with the academic calendar, these practices continue to exist because of the following factors: Almost all large major companies follow these labor practices; new graduates, who compose the main segment of job seekers, under these practices have a strong tendency to prefer to work at large companies, and these practices influence the overall behavior of new graduates; as a result, SMEs that do not comply with such labor practices are also affected when trying to recruit younger employees.

If we were to describe the essence of the Japanese-style employment practice from a human resource management perspective, it is not to hire people with skills and knowledge required by the work; it is to assign a job after hiring a person (Hamaguchi, 2013).

Japanese-style employment practice: how it works

Kato (2002) extracted characteristics of the human resource management practices of Japanese companies through comparison between Japan and the US by implementing surveys of corporate managers in the two countries. He summarized the results as follows: (1) Promotion speed: The number of years of service before promotion to present position (in the case of a human resources manager) is 10 years on average in the United States and 26 years on average in Japan. Similar trends can be seen with other managers' positions. (2) Other company experience (whether one has experience as a full-time regular employee at another company before joining the current company): In Japan, 94% of human resources managers and 92% of section chiefs did not have experience working for another company as a full-time regular employee. Meanwhile, in the US companies, the figures are 15% for the personnel department manager and 27% for the section chief. This also applies to other managers' positions. (3) Range of career: Looking at career formation beyond specific functions, in the case of Japanese personnel department managers, 57% have had sales and marketing experience, whereas only 26% of human resources managers in the United States have had experience outside of HRM. However, this difference varies depending on the function.

Now we will look at human resource management practices at Japanese companies focusing on aspects such as the mass recruitment of new graduates, job rotation, personnel change, training and human resource development, and career development within the company. The description here is based on the practices at large listed companies in Japan.

For new graduates, the entrance to the company is a once-in-a-lifetime event

On April 1 of every year, the first day of the fiscal year in Japan, ceremonies to welcome newcomers are held not only at companies but also at various Japanese organizations including government organizations. In the example for 2017, Toyota Motor Co., Ltd., held an entrance ceremony[1] at their headquarters, where 2,151 new employees (the total number of new recruits was 2,633) attended on April 3, the first working day of the new fiscal year. Of these, 1,780 people were blue collar and 803 were white collar. According to the company's announcement, the white-collar employees included 174 administrative workers and 629 engineering workers. For new graduates who graduated from college in March, attending the entrance ceremony on the first business day of April signifies the start of his or her long employment life as a regular employee at a large company. For new graduates, the opportunity to get a position as a regular employee at a large company happens once at the time of graduation; as one labor economist proclaimed, opportunity is just once (Genda, 1997).

Meanwhile for companies, new graduate recruitment is the main, if not the only, opportunity to hire competitive human resources who will contribute to corporate activities for a long time and who will become executives in the future.

The Keidanren (Japan Federation of Economic Organizations), which has most of the big companies in Japan as its members, has set guidelines on recruiting new graduates every year and set the schedule for recruitment activities in order to reduce excessive competition and minimize the negative impact on the educational calendar. The guideline set a schedule such as the following.

March 1 of the year before the employment begins: Start disseminating corporate information to prospective students, including in-person corporate briefing sessions and other PR activities.

June 1: Start selection activities, such as interviewing students. Companies start issuing informal job offers.

October 1: Formal acceptance letter issued by the companies.

March: Graduation.

First business day of April: Entrance ceremony.

The personnel department leads the recruiting and hiring practices in the company. When hiring new graduates, managers of various departments play important roles in the selection process, but the final decision is made by the personnel department. Also, the personnel department will decide which department the newcomer will be allocated to. In other words, what kind of work a newcomer starts his or her occupational life with depends on the decision made by the personnel department.

Employment contracts exchanged between companies and new graduates do not have a termination date. This indicates that both employees and employers recognize long-term commitment as an implicit consent. It is assumed that the employment will continue for a long time, specifically until the day of the mandatory retirement.

This transition from school to workplace applies not only to college graduates but also to high school and vocational school graduates. Yoshimoto (1998) conducted an international comparison of the transition process from school to workplace using statistical data from the 1996 OECD

Employment Outlook, looking at the unemployment rate one year after leaving school and the average number of occupational experiences after the youth left school. Japan is lower than Europe and the United States, and it shows that this system functioned efficiently at least until the 1990s.

Accumulation of experience within a company: job rotation and range of career

As seen in the example of Toyota, the white-collar employees are classified into two categories: engineering and administrative. Those assigned to engineering jobs engage in production and R&D and are assigned to departments, such as product development, production technology development, and intellectual property rights, among other technical areas; those assigned to administrative work engage in other functions, such as sales and marketing, planning, finance, and other non-engineering functions. These categories, administrative and engineering, correspond roughly to the degrees in science and engineering and degrees in social sciences and humanities. Since companies do not consider the majors of newly entered college graduates as key determinants of their job assignment (Yashiro, 1999, p. 30), it is necessary to find out which jobs out of the various operations in the company are best for them after they enter the company. In order to judge their aptitude, the method that Japanese companies collectively developed is the job-rotation system, where young employees are placed in various departments. It can also be noted that much of the white-collar expertise is company-specific and is established exclusively within each company. Therefore, accumulating diversified experiences within the company is a way to improve white-collar productivity (Yashiro, 1999, p. 30).

In an extensive literature review, Yashiro (1999) referred to Shirai (1992) on the function of job rotation as (1) relocation based on business necessities – changes in labor demand caused by the expansion and reduction of business, (2) educational transfer – to have extensive experience of various functions according to the personnel plan, (3) relocation as employment adjustment measures – reduction of excessive personnel from a shrinking business achieved not by dismissal, and (4) relocation accompanying demotion and disciplinary action.

In relation to (2), particularly important for new recruits is the function of finding aptitude. The recruitment strategy of large Japanese companies, as mentioned, is centered on the mass recruiting of new graduates who do not have work experience. Therefore, the placement of new employees in individual duties is decided within the enterprise after the hiring decision is made. In doing so, companies try to find aptitude by rotation.

In relation to promotions, job rotation has a function to allow employees to acquire the coordination and integration skills necessary for managerial positions (Ouchi & Jaeger, 1978). Having a human network in other departments leads to the acquisition of relevant information, which is desirable for carrying out the work in charge. Experiencing other departments by rotation contributes significantly to the formation of human networks.

From this description, it can be inferred that white-collar employees at a large Japanese company have a wide range of business experiences in their occupational lives. Ouchi and Jaeger (1978) discussed the fact that at Japanese firms cross-functional job rotation is frequently performed, whereas in the case of the United States, employees' careers often remain in specific departments. Koike and Inoki (2002) made this point clear by empirical research. In particular, Morishima (2002) compares the range of careers of managers between Japan and the United States. What has been observed is (1) from observation of three functions, namely, personnel, accounting, and sales, human resource development is carried out by experiencing various areas of work within the function. Here, the difference between functions is larger than the difference between Japan and the US. Forty-nine percent of the human resource managers in Japan have sales experience, while only 8% of the human resources managers in the US have experienced it. On the other hand, 50% of the sales managers in the US have experienced public relations and advertising, while 14.6% of sales managers in Japan have such experience. From this, we cannot draw a conclusion that Japan is generalist-oriented and America is specialist-oriented. (2) The difference between Japan and the United States is that nearly half of Japanese managers engaged in functions other than their current position immediately before becoming section chiefs or department managers. In addition, in Japan, there are many cases where the function a person is currently engaging in as manager is not necessarily the job function that the manager has the longest experience within the company. From these observations, Morishima concluded that the experience of multiple functions is considered to be a way to nurture the manager of the future. In Japanese companies, since selection to the upper management team is carried out relatively late in one's career, it is too late to widen the range of careers when someone becomes a candidate for senior management. Therefore, opportunities are systematically given early in the person's career through job rotation. In the case of the United States, there is no need to widen the range of careers because selection toward upper management is made relatively early.

Human resource development as an investment

As Japanese companies presume lifelong employment, the risk that return on investment for human resources cannot be realized is relatively small. Therefore, investment in human resources has been quite active. At Japanese companies, various types of training are carried out in the form of OffJT (off-the-job training), which starts at the freshman training period immediately after employees join the company. This is where basic rules and appropriate behavior on the job, including understanding of the company's mission and vision, are taught. Opportunities for acquiring various skills and knowledge within the company are provided, and manager training is conducted as essential training for each step of the vertical movement as they climb up the corporate ladder. Many companies have an organization called the Human Resources Development Department or Training Department, and often they maintain OffJT facilities.[2]

New employees, fresh out of school, join a company without having any knowledge about or experience in specific business. The department that accepts such newcomers needs to encourage the accumulation of experience through day-to-day work and provide guidance about how to contribute to departmental goals, specifically profit targets. This is on-the-job training or OJT, and it is considered an important task of the manager, especially the department head. It is an important job of the manager to nurture not only newcomers but everyone in the organization he or she is responsible for.

Competition leading to top management: promotion structure of the white collar, competition in the internal labor market

Japanese companies do not treat young employees who join the company in the same year selectively in terms of promotion and wage raises until a certain tenure year. But this does not mean that promotion selection is not done. The results of each year's evaluations are accumulated, and after a certain period after joining the company, promotion gaps will occur among those with the same year of entry (Yashiro, 1999, p. 42). Also, managers face intense competition toward a limited number of management positions as they climb the corporate ladder.

Why such practices were established?

Chuma (1987) explained why and how Japanese employment practices, characterized by lifetime employment, a seniority wage, a company union, and a compulsory retirement system, were established during the rapid development of large-scale modern industries in the 1920s. Chuma also clarified from the comparison with the United States that at the beginning of these employment practices, it was not necessarily Japan's specific practice. The following account is based on Chuma (1987).

> It has been clarified from many empirical studies that the four points that characterize Japanese employment practices were established and became prominent mostly from the 1920s to the 1930s (pp. 307–309). This was the depression period after the First World War and subsequently the Great Depression period. But, at the same time, it was the period of rapid expansion of domestic and foreign markets induced by the development of transportation and telecommunication networks as well as the large-scale modernization of various factories due to the electric power revolution. In Japan, in addition to these factors, the conditions of the mass introduction of advanced industrial technology

from Europe and the United States also overlapped, and the heavy and chemical industries developed dramatically (p. 309). The introduction of the latest technologies, including large-scale production systems and the introduction of electric power, has resulted in a rapid expansion of demand for a large number of technicians and engineers who manage them and ensure stable operations. At this time, the external labor market was not functioning sufficiently, thus inevitably each company had to train factory workers and engineers in-house and aim to make them work for a long time, if not a life-time. This is a similar situation to the one in the United States, and, since 1905 a number of corporation schools were founded at many American companies.

(p. 315)

Furthermore, it was difficult to raise the retention rate of technicians who were trained in-house, and it was a serious problem for companies at the time. For this reason, various retention measures for experienced workers were introduced. A seniority wage system was established from raising wages according to the degree of skill. Various paternalistic measures to enhance workers' loyalty, affection, and satisfaction were introduced. In addition, in large-scale and complicated enterprise organizations, labor management by the shop masters on the factory floor became inefficient; the personnel department that directly managed recruiting, dismissal, training, and promotion appeared mainly in large enterprises. Also, in the 1920s, many companies introduced company unions or works councils. The enterprise-specific labor organization, which is regarded as one of the Japanese-style employment practices, was introduced to Japanese factories in the 1920s, following the example of factories in the United States.

There was no noticeable difference in the employment practices of Japan and the US from the 1920s until the beginning of the 1930s. It was considered a desirable corporate strategy for companies in the United States to avoid dismissal as much as possible during recession by relocation within the company. However, as the Great Depression progressed, the factory operation rate of major companies dropped to 20% or less (Chuma, 1987, p. 317); companies were no longer able to maintain the level of employment. And when large companies such as US Steel and General Electric decided on large-scale worker reductions, other companies followed suit at once. The employment practices that had been dominant until then were based on an implicit promise of long-term employment on the part of the company and, in turn, trust by labor. However, the large and extensive personnel reductions lost this trust at one stroke (Chuma, 1987). Furthermore, the 1937 Federal Supreme Court decision that the Wagner Act of 1935[3] was constitutional led to the rapid disappearance of company unions and paternalistic measures among American companies.

Meanwhile, the impact of the recession was similarly severe in Japan, but the transition to the wartime economy, which became more prominent in the mid-1930s, relaxed the impact of the recession. At the same time, the inefficiency of production due to the company-to-company movement of skilled labor led to the encouragement of workers to remain at the same company for a long time. As a result, the employment practices survived as a whole. From the reconstruction period after the Second World War to the period of rapid economic growth, the employment practices became more sophisticated and consequently were strongly established as "Japanese-style" employment practices.

Professionals in the company

Increasing the number of people with specialized knowledge and skills is a vital task of the management that affects the performance of companies facing complicated market and business environments. In response to this challenge, how do Japanese companies with a strong reliance on the internal labor market respond? The presence of professionals in companies is discussed here based on the research report of the Japan Institute for Labor Policy and Training (JILPT 2016).

First, the definition of traditional "professional," such as medical doctors and lawyers, assumes (1) highly organized expertise and specialized skills that can be acquired through long-term education and training, (2) autonomy of profession, (3) high professional norms and ethics as members of a professional group (JILPT, 2016). "Due to the large scale and complicated management tasks, it has become impossible to respond to technologies that have been learned through previous apprenticeship training, and the necessity of extremely specialized higher education has increased" (p. 11), thus a new type of professionals who work within the company have emerged. The JILPT report calls such human resources "in-house professionals." In the context of the Japanese companies, sometimes the term "specialist" or "expert" may be used as a synonym for "professional." According to JILPT (2016), from the review of literature, employees who have been engaged in a specific task for a long time at a company and have accumulated experience and knowledge about the work are deemed specialists or experts. The distinction between specialist and in-house professional is versatility of expertise beyond a specific company. If expertise is applicable beyond a specific company, then employees who acquire such expertise are in-house professionals. Specialists and experts are those who base their expertise on company-specific capabilities.

JILPT (2016) analyzed the characteristics of in-house professionals through an interview survey of intellectual property rights and legal affairs staff. The following is a summary of the conclusion of JILPT (2016, pp. 83–87).

1   The essence of in-house professionals

    a   Always be conscious of being a member of the organization.
       In order to demonstrate ability as a professional effectively within the company, he or she needs to respond to the corporate culture.

When providing professional advice and alternatives for management decisions, he or she should look beyond corporate profit and consideration for social ethics and values beyond the boundaries of the company.

b The difference from general white-collar employees and in-house professionals is centered on professionalism based on the expertise that enables responding to diverse and complex situations and the existence of certain consistent judgment axes when facing new incidents. They also have an understanding of various business subjects and personnel in the organization based on their diverse work experience.

2 Foundation of in-house professionals

a The activities as an indispensable member of an organization become appropriate by mastering basic business skills, while professional activities are impossible without mastery of expert knowledge. For in-house professionals, information gathering, adjustment, and negotiation skills, both inside and outside the company, and acquisition of core expertise are essential foundations.

b In the background of basic business skills and mastery of expert knowledge, one of the major factors for forming and expanding skill and knowledge is consciousness and an attitude to continue self-improvement efforts.

3 Career of an in-house professional

a The career of an in-house professional progresses stepwise, starting typically at preparation stage, up to independence, and then to professional.

In the case of an employee who doesn't get an assignment within the field where he or she aspires to be a professional upon entering the company, whether or not he or she can be an in-house professional depends on his or her potential concern and interest in that particular field. It is important that he or she acquires certain knowledge and practical understanding of the specialized field before he or she starts working in the field.

b In the stepwise transition to professional, it is important to integrate diverse work experiences and knowledge and establish firm relationships with management.

c Job rotation has a certain impact on fostering in-house professionals. The influence of the seniors and managers in departments is enormous, and the supervisors who understand the essence of professionalism can act effectively, while supervisors who do not understand the essence of professionalism may act as suppressors. Job rotation is a way to train in-house professionals at the company; however, it works negatively if it is not based on the expertise necessary for in-house professionals.

d   In order to be an in-house professional, the subjective choice of career is indispensable. Many large companies have adopted a personnel system that is advantageous for long-term service as a part of Japanese employment practice. And there is a strong incentive to stay in the company until retirement age even if the professional ability cannot be utilized.

Changes in Japanese-style employment practices

Is Japanese-style employment practice changing? Since the 1990s, the so-called lost decades of the stagnant Japanese economy, this has been a topic that attracted social and journalistic attention. The fact that a number of university graduates failed to get jobs as standard workers where they can expect lifelong employment and were forced to take unstable temporary jobs was reported somewhat sensationally. Economists pointed out that changing companies in the middle of a career is now not a rare case, which they claim is an indication of the change in the lifelong employment practice. Based on the tone of the economic media, we may take a critical position that the rigid and inefficient system of lifelong employment cannot respond to changes in the current economic environment and that the labor market should change to a more flexible external labor market mechanism. However, there are also views to evaluate the stability and resilience of this mechanism (Kato & Kambayashi, 2016; Miyakawa, 2015).

According to the analysis using the microdata on the long-term trend of job tenure, the length of service at a current company for regular workers, it became clear that job tenure became shorter at the end of the high economic growth period of 1973 (Kawaguchi & Ueno, 2013). In the period of high economic growth, Kawaguchi and Ueno (2013) argued, the profitability of all assets was sufficiently high, and it was possible to train company-specific human assets over time, but when the economic growth rate slowed down, this condition no longer held and resulted in the shortening of job tenure. It was not caused by the lost decade of the 1990s. From this, they predicted that long-term employment will continue to change.

Meanwhile, Ono (2010) argues that Japanese companies are trying to overcome the changes in the global economy by suppressing new recruitment and increasing non-core workers, but they continue to respect the implicit contract of lifetime employment and are still trying to protect core employees. Thus, he concludes, "lifetime employment is far from dead for those who are in the core" (p. 23).

Notes

1   From Toyota's April 3, 2017, news release. Although it is noted that mid-career recruitment and foreign employees are included in the number of people, the overwhelming majority are new graduates.

2 The description here is based on the author's experience as a recruitment and human resources development officer at a Japanese company.

3 Wagner Act: The National Labor Relations Act of 1935—employer interference with the company union or welfare system / facility in such a way that the management side has some influence on the formation of the intention of the workers was regarded as an unfair labor practice.

References

Chuma, H. (1987). Nihonteki koyou kankou no keizai gourisei saikentou: 1920 nendai no nichibei hikaku [Reexamination of economic rationality of "Japanese-style" employment practice: Comparison between Japan and the US in the 1920s]. *Keizai Kenkyuu*, 38(4), 307–320.

Genda, Y. (1997). Chansu ha ichido – Sedai to chinginkakusa [Chance is once – Generation and wage disparity]. *Nihon Roudou Kenyu Zasshi*, 39(10), 2–12.

Hamaguchi, K. (2013). *Wakamono to roudou – Nyuusya no sikumi kara tokihogusu* [Youth and Labor – Clarified from the System of Joining the Company]. Tokyo: Chuo Koron Shinsya.

Japan Institute for Labour Policy and Training. (2016). Kigyou nai purofessyonaru no kyaria keisei [Career development of in-house professionals]. *Shiryo Sirizu* [Document Series], 178.

Kato, T. (2002). Dai kigyou ni okeru kyaria keisei no nichibei hikaku [Japan-US comparison of career development in large companies]. In Koike, K., & Inoki, T. (Eds.), *Howaito kara-no jinzai keisei: Nichi, Bei, Ei, Doku no hikaku* [White-collar Human Resource Development: Comparative study of Japan, the US, the UK and Germany] (Chapter 12). Tokyo: Toyo Keizai Shinposya.

Kato, T., & Kambayashi, R. (2016). 1980 Nendai ikou no cyouki koyou kankou no doukou [Trends in Long-term Employment since 1980s in Japan]. *Keizai Kenkyuu*, 67(4), 307–325.

Kawaguchi, D., & Ueno, Y. (2013). Declining long-term employment in Japan. *Journal of the Japanese and International Economies*, 28 (June 2013), 19–36.

Koike, K., & Inoki, T. (Eds.). (2002). *Howaito kara-no jinzai keisei: Nichi, Bei, Ei, Doku no hikaku* [White Collar Human Resource Development: Comparative Study of Japan, the US, the UK and Germany]. Tokyo: Toyo Keizai Shinposya.

Miyakawa, E. (2015). Shinsotsu ikkatsu saiyou no keizai riron – Kaiteiban [A Model of Labor Market for lifetime Employment: Revised Version]. *Kokumin Keizai Zasshi*, 212(3), 63–82.

Morishima, M. (2002). Nichibei Kanrisyoku no kyaria no haba hikaku [Japan-US comparison of managers' range of careers]. In Koike, K., & Inoki, T. (Eds.), *Howaito kara-no jinzai keisei: Nichi, Bei, Ei, Doku no hikaku* [White Collar Human Resource Development: Comparative study of Japan, the US, the UK and Germany] (Chapter 11). Tokyo: Toyo Keizai Shinposya.

Ono, H. (2010). Lifetime employment in Japan: Concepts and measurements. *Journal of the Japanese and International Economies*, 24(1), 1–27.

Ouchi, W. G., & Jaeger, A. M. (1978). Type z organization: Stability in the midst of mobility. *Academy of Management Review*, 3(2), 305–314.

Shirai, T. (1992). *Gendai Nihon no roumu kannri* [Labor Management in Modern Japan]. Tokyo: Toyo Keizai Shinposya.

Yashiro, M. (1999). *Dai kigyou howaito kara – no kyaria* [Career of White-Collar Employees at Large Companies]. Tokyo: The Japan Institute for Labour Policy and Training.

Yoshimoto, K. (1998). Gakkou kara syokugyou heno ikou – Ikou sisutemu no kouritsusei to kaikaku no houkou [International comparison of transition from school to work – Efficiency of transition system and direction of reform]. *Nihon Roudou Kenkyu Zasshi*, 40(7), 41–51.

Index

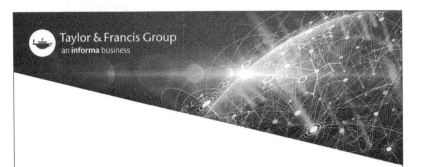

For Product Safety Concerns and Information please contact our EU representative GPSR@taylorandfrancis.com Taylor & Francis Verlag GmbH, Kaufingerstraße 24, 80331 München, Germany

Printed and bound by CPI Group (UK) Ltd, Croydon, CR0 4YY

01/05/2025

01858424-0001